PROCLAMATION COMMENTARIES

Revised and Enlarged Edition

The General Letters

Hebrews, James, 1-2 Peter, Jude, 1-2-3 John

Gerhard Krodel, Editor

FORTRESS PRESS   **MINNEAPOLIS**

THE GENERAL LETTERS
Hebrews, James, 1–2 Peter, Jude, 1–2–3 John
Revised and Enlarged Edition

Library of Congress Cataloging-in-Publication Data

The general letters : Hebrews, James, 1–2 Peter, Jude, 1–2–3 John /
    Gerhard Krodel, editor — Rev. and enl. ed.
      p. cm. — (Proclamation commentaries)
    Includes bibliographical references and index.
    ISBN 0-8006-2895-0 (alk. paper)
    1. Bible. N.T. Hebrews—Criticism, interpretation, etc.
    2. Bible. N.T. Catholic Epistles—Criticism, interpretation, etc.
    I. Krodel, Gerhard, 1926– . II. Series: Proclamation commentaries
    (Rev. and enl. ed.)
    BS2775.2.H4 1995
    227'.906—dc20   95-3489
                                            CIP

Manufactured in the U.S.A.   AF 1-2895

99   98   97   96   95   1   2   3   4   5   6   7   8   9

THE GENERAL LETTERS

Proclamation Commentaries

CONTENTS

EDITOR'S FOREWORD

In his *Ecclesiastical History* (2.23.25) Eusebius referred to "seven Catholic" (that is, general) letters (James, 1 and 2 Peter, Jude, 1, 2, and 3 John) that had been "used publicly in most churches" in the fourth century. Hebrews was not one of them. It made its way into the church's canon under the name of Paul, even though Paul's name is not mentioned in it and Pauline authorship was generally rejected by the Western church until the middle of the fourth century. Hebrews is included in this volume because it fits better among the General Letters than among the Deutero-Paulines. The designation "Catholic," or General, Epistle was apparently first applied to 1 John (Eusebius *Ecclesiastical History* 7.24.7) and subsequently extended to the whole group. It meant to convey the idea that these "letters" were intended for a general readership. This is obviously not the case for some of them; for example, 3 John is addressed to an individual, 2 John and 1 Peter to specific communities.

The General Letters and Hebrews are documents of the struggles of different churches at the end of the first century and the beginning of the second. Their authors made use of diverse traditions that reflect the catholicity of the emerging church. The interpreters of these writings also belong to different Christian traditions, but through their common endeavor to understand and interpret these diverse witnesses of the NT they express one aspect of the unity and catholicity of the church in which the NT has a normative function. It is our hope that the General Letters interpreted in the following chapters may shed light upon contemporary problems, such as spiritual lethargy in our churches (Hebrews), riches and poverty (James), the place of the people of God in the world (Hebrews, 1 Peter, and James), the withdrawal into individualistic piety (all of them speak to this issue), the dangers of syncretism and antinomianism (Jude and the Johannine Epistles), and the rejection of an eschatological future (2 Peter). These writings contain untapped resources that can help us gain new perspectives and renew commitments to Jesus Christ and the proclamation of salvation through him in a world where sin, suffering, despair, and death are rampant.

Hebrews presents itself as a "word of exhortation" (13:22) in which chris-tological exposition is intertwined with ethical admonition. Reginald Fuller (Professor Emeritus of New Testament, Virginia Theological Seminary) shows that Hebrews is an extended midrash on Psalm 110 to which the author appended chapter 13. Its Christology undergirds the exhortations addressed to believers who have grown weary on their earthly journey during the interim between Christ's first and second coming. It also un-derscores the solemn warning against apostasy (6:4-8; 10:26-31; 12:16-17). Christ's identity with human beings in terms of experiencing temp-tation, suffering, and death (4:15; 5:7-8) is matched by his divinity, which Hebrews demonstrates by means of the Melchizedek typology. The "order of Melchizedek" is superior to the order of Abraham, the Levitical priest-hood, and the law, and as the high priest Christ sacrificed himself once and for all times (7:27; 9:26) on earth, "endured the cross, disregarding its shame" (12:2). Exalted to God's right hand the eternal high priest makes intercession for all who draw near to God through him (7:25; 9:24).

While Hebrews reads like a sermon (or a series of sermons) and ends like a letter, James begins like a letter but does not conclude like one. "Its structure is a puzzle," writes Frances Taylor Gench, Associate Professor of Biblical Studies, Gettysburg Lutheran Seminary. Traditional admonitions that are loosely joined together and short essays on particular themes make up this general circular letter, which has the form of parenetic instruction and is addressed to the twelve tribes in the Diaspora. James is a document of Hellenistic Jewish Christianity from a time when observances of ritual laws and of circumcision have become irrelevant (in contrast to Acts 21:18-25). The perfect law of liberty (1:25) consists of wisdom traditions that are also present in some "Q sayings" of Jesus and in the moral instructions of 1 Peter. While James is short on Christology (1:1; 2:7; 5:7), Gench shows that it is decidedly theocentric. It is God who "in fulfillment of his own purpose . . . gave us birth by the word of truth, so that we would become a kind of first fruits of his creatures" (1:18). The exhortations of James indicate how Christian life ought to be lived here and now under God, the giver of true wisdom in distinction from false wisdom (3:13-18). The issue of faith and works in James is actually an issue of two kinds of faith: of dead faith that does not deserve to be called faith and of true faith, which according to Paul is also "active in love" (Gal. 5:6). Thus James is not a critique of Paul but of a sloganeering, lackadaisical Paulinism that repeats formulas, ignoring the ethical consequence of Christology ("that we may walk in newness of life," Rom. 6:4). Nevertheless, Paul would never have argued about justification as James did in 2:14-26.

Like James, 1 Peter (interpreted by Gerhard Krodel) is a circular letter addressed to "the exiles of the Dispersion" in Asia Minor. The Christians of Asia Minor are challenged to be God's eschatological alternative to the society around them. Their mission is to proclaim by word and action "the mighty acts of him who called you out of darkness into his marvelous light" (2:9). As God's alternative they must avoid cultural assimilation and draw boundaries between their former behavior and their present surroundings on one hand and their new status in Christ on the other. Simultaneously they must live within the structures of society by doing that which is good, including bearing unjust suffering, as they follow Christ's example. With 4:12 an apocalyptic perspective is introduced as the messianic woes of the end time are experienced by the communities. They are God's final testing and the beginning of his judgment, which commences with the household of God (4:17). The expectation of Christ's parousia in glory calls for joyfulness in the midst of persecution. At the same time watchfulness and resistance are commanded, because "like a roaring lion your adversary the devil prowls around, looking for someone to devour" (5:8). The purpose of 1 Peter is twofold: the exhortation of Christians under duress and the witness to the true grace of God (5:12), which brought about their rebirth (1:3) and made them God's own people (2:9).

The Second Letter of Peter is interpreted by Frederick W. Danker, Christ Seminary-Seminex Professor Emeritus of New Testament. His insights into the Hellenistic benefactor-recipient pattern shed new light on this writing, especially on its first chapter and the use of the transfiguration tradition. At the transfiguration "God, the Supreme Benefactor, confirmed that the prophetic Scriptures found fulfillment in God's climactic action" (Danker) through Christ, the Great Benefactor. The fact that Christ's power and presence have been observed in advance (1:16) guarantees that "the day of the Lord" will come (3:10). Just as at the transfiguration the "voice was conveyed" *(pherō)* to Jesus by the Majestic Glory, just so "no prophecy was ever conveyed *[pherō]* by human will." On the contrary, "men and women spoke the word [received] from God as they were being conveyed *[pherō]* by the Holy Spirit" (1:17, 21). The same divine voice that spoke at the transfiguration of Jesus found expression in the prophetic and apostolic writings and guarantees the climactic revelation of the end. Two Peter was written to reinforce and defend the expectation of the parousia in the face of false teachers and scoffers (2:1; 3:3), some of whom "twist" the content of Paul's letters (3:16). In his polemics against their libertinism the author of 2 Peter made liberal use of the letter of Jude but tried to avoid Jude's references to OT pseudepigrapha. He expanded Jude by introducing examples of righteousness in the midst of moral depravity (2:5,

7-9). The twofold intention of the letter becomes apparent: (1) maintaining the future apocalyptic eschatology and (2) maintaining moral conduct, virtue, self-control, godliness, true love, and so forth (1:5-7) in response to God's saving and purifying action in Christ (1:3-4, 9).

Jude (interpreted by Gerhard Krodel) has an epistolary prescript, but the first part of the body of the letter (vv. 5-16) reads like a polemical tract against (gnosticizing) libertines who wanted to be "with it," the "it" being a lifestyle that denies the "faith once for all delivered to the saints" (v. 3). Unfortunately they have gained entrance to communities and participate in their "love-feasts" (vv. 4, 12). But there can be no accommodation or coexistence with them. The faith delivered to the saints draws boundaries that exclude some beliefs and practices. Not every conduct or belief should be acceptable to the church that is grounded in "our common salvation" (v. 3) by God our Savior, through Jesus Christ our Lord (vv. 24-25). The second part of the letter (vv. 17-23) addresses the members of the church in terms of remembering the predictions of the apostles about scoffers. It is the scoffers, the worldly people, not you, who create divisions (v. 19), if you expel them. Second, Christian life consists of growth in faith, in prayer "in the Holy Spirit," remaining "in the love of God"; this includes an appropriate lifestyle, and it also includes a future hope, eternal life, when it will be clear who God is and who we are (vv. 20-21). Prior to that, try to save some heretics but be alert (vv. 22-23).

The three Johannine letters are interpreted by R. Alan Culpepper, Professor in the Department of Religion, Baylor University, Waco, Texas. He masterfully surveys the issues posed by these three writings and the interpretations that have been presented in recent commentaries and articles. He considers the probable historical contexts of these three writings, their literary structures, their canonical context, and, finally, their theological contributions. First John is not really a letter since it lacks all epistolary features. If it were a tractate, as some interpreters have suggested, one would expect a focus on a specific topic. It is not a homily either, because it does not refer to texts from Scripture. Hence in his magisterial commentary Raymond Brown declines to identify the genre of 1 John. The overall structure of 1 John also presents difficulties that have resulted in a variety of proposals, none of which has gained widespread acceptance. Yet the aim of 1 John is clear—to warn against false teachers (2:18-25; 4:1-6; etc.) who denied that Jesus is the Christ, the Anointed One, and that he has come in the flesh. They may have reputed the atoning effect of Christ's death (2:1; 4:10; 5:6), holding that they were without sin (1:6-10) because they possessed the Spirit, and hence they may have regarded themselves as anointed ones. Moreover, they failed to practice the commandment to love one another (2:7-11). But the identity of these false teachers is anything but clear; Culpepper summarizes various hypotheses. His concluding sections on the distinctive contribution of 1 John to the doctrines of God, Christ, the Spirit, to soteriology, ecclesiology, and eschatology illumine the theology and abiding significance of this writing.

According to their form 2 and 3 John are Hellenist private letters. Second John warns the community against teachers who do not confess that Jesus Christ "has come [present participle in Greek!] in the flesh" (v. 7) and seeks to establish a firm boundary against those who do not follow "the truth," which is "the doctrine of Christ" (vv. 4, 9-10). The elder demands that the community avoid any contact with them.

Third John is addressed to an individual, Gaius, who is praised because he has offered hospitality to the emissaries of the elder and he is encouraged to continue rendering hospitality in spite of the opposition of Diotrephes, who is apparently the leader of the community. Diotrephes has rejected the elder's authority, is spreading false charges against him and his group, and has excommunicated those who have welcomed the elder's emissaries.

While many questions remain unanswered, these three Johannine writings are windows to the struggles in which the Johannine communities were involved. The General Epistles and Hebrews challenge us to think anew about the ground of Christian truth and its defense in polemics, the drawing of boundaries, the relationship of truth and polemics to the love commandment, and the ground of love in God, Christ, and the Holy Spirit.

Gerhard Krodel
Professor Emeritus of New Testament
Lutheran Theological Seminary
Gettysburg, Pennsylvania

ABBREVIATIONS

AB	Anchor Bible
ABD	D. N. Freedman, ed., *Anchor Bible Dictionary*
AnBib	Analecta Biblica
ANRW	*Aufstieg und Niedergang der römischen Welt*
BAGD	W. Bauer, W. F. Arndt, F. W. Gingrich, and F. W. Danker, *A Greek-English Lexicon of the New Testament*
BDF	F. Blass, A. Debrunner, and R. W. Funk, *A Greek Grammar of the New Testament*
CBQ	*Catholic Biblical Quarterly*
EKKNT	Evangelisch-katholischer Kommentar zum Neuen Testament
HNT	Handbuch zum Neuen Testament
HNTC	Harper's New Testament Commentaries
ICC	International Critical Commentary
JSNTSup	Journal for the Study of the New Testament—Supplement series
KJV	King James (Authorized) version
LEC	Library of Early Christianity
LXX	Septuagint
MNTC	Moffatt New Testament Commentary
NCBC	New Century Bible Commentary
NEB	New English Bible
NICNT	New International Commentary on the New Testament
NIV	New International Version
NovT	*Novum Testamentum*
NRSV	New Revised Standard Version
NTS	*New Testament Studies*
RevExp	*Review and Expositor*
RSV	Revised Standard Version
SBLDS	Society of Biblical Literature Dissertation Series
SBLMS	Society of Biblical Literature Monograph Series

SBT	Studies in Biblical Theology
SE	*Studia Evangelica*
WBC	Word Biblical Commentary
WUNT	Wissenschaftliche Untersuchungen zum Neuen Testament
ZNW	*Zeitschrift für die neutestamentliche Wissenschaft*

REGINALD H. FULLER

HEBREWS

Introduction

The King James Bible entitles our document, "The Epistle of Paul the Apostle to the Hebrews." Unfortunately, every one of these claims is questioned or refuted by modern scholarship. Our document is not an epistle, it is not by Paul, it is not by an apostle, nor can it be said without qualification that it was written to the Hebrews.

Hebrews does not begin like an NT epistle. There is no opening formula such as "A to B, greetings." Instead, Hebrews plunges straight into its theological discussion with a formula recalling the prologue of John: "Long ago God spoke in many and various ways . . . in these last days he has spoken to us by a Son" (1:1-2). There is no thanksgiving for the recipients' progress in Christian faith and life as there is in Paul's letters, with the notable exception of Galatians. After the opening christological formula the author develops an argument about the superiority of Christ over the angels with a string of OT quotations. As we read the first chapter, the impression we get is that Hebrews is not a letter, but a theological treatise. Treatises, however, tend to be abstract, not geared to a specific situation like a letter. As soon as we begin chapter two we find the author has a very specific situation in view: "We must pay greater attention to what we have heard, so that we do not drift away from it" (2:1). All through the document we find christological exposition preceded or followed by very concrete exhortation. These exhortations clearly have in mind a very specific community, or more likely a close-knit group within a larger community. But at the end we are in for another surprise. Although Hebrews does not begin like a letter, it ends like one, with personal notices, greetings, and blessings. No wonder some have thought that the epistolary conclusion was added by a later hand to dress up a treatise like a letter, while others have thought our document originally had an epistolary beginning which was cut off later. But there is no manuscript evidence for either view. Hebrews is a literary anomaly, the opposite of James, which begins like a letter but does not end like one. And both documents differ from 1 John, which neither begins nor ends like a letter.

What then is the literary form of our document? The constant alternation between christological argument and practical exhortation, and the fact that the christological argument almost invariably takes the form of an extended exposition of an OT text (e.g., Ps. 95:7-11 in Heb. 3:7—4:11), suggests that our document originated as a sermon or a course of sermons. This seems to be clinched by the reference in chapter 13 to what has gone before as a "word of exhortation" *(logos tēs paraklēseōs). Paraklēsis* is almost a technical term for pastoral preaching as opposed to evangelism *(kerygma)* and baptismal instruction *(didachē, didaskalia,* or *katechēsis).* Moreover, the author refers to himself several times as "speaking" rather than writing (2:5; 8:1; 9:5). Perhaps 13:20-21 is the doxology at the end of the sermon, although this is less likely since, as we shall see, the whole of chapter 13 is probably a later appendage. If we are right in thinking that our document was originally designed as a sermon, how are we to explain the epistolary conclusion? Is it a not too successful attempt to dress up our document to make it look like a Pauline letter (G. Buchanan)? If so, the ending would be as fictitious as the Pastorals, with their personal elements of a Pauline character. But that only shows the difference, for we would have expected to have an epistolary beginning as well. So with most recent commentators we take the epistolary conclusion to be genuine. What then was the author's connection with Timothy? We will take up that point a little later when we consider the document's date.

Generally speaking, the ancient Eastern church accepted Hebrews as a letter of Paul. A notable exception was Alexandria. The West, however, for a long time rejected the Pauline authorship of Hebrews, not from scholarly doubt or historical evidence, but because it did not like some of its teachings. It was especially uncomfortable with the denial of a second repentance, a point which we will pick up later. This denial was particularly awkward for the Western church when it was fighting against the Novatianists and Donatists. These heretics wished to exclude permanently all who had apostatized in time of persecution. More interesting, however, is the objection of the Alexandrian scholars. Trained in the classical tradition of literary criticism, they could not believe that Hebrews was by Paul. Its style and content were too different. Hebrews contains some of the best Greek in the NT, equalled only by that of the author of Luke-Acts when he has a free hand, untrammeled by the use of sources. As for content, the great Pauline themes are significantly absent (e.g., justification by grace alone through faith, or the church as the body of Christ). Pauline categories such as faith are used in a very different sense. Although the kerygma of both Hebrews and Paul is centered upon the cross, Paul's theology derives its imagery from the law courts and salvation history (righteousness, justification), whereas the imagery of Hebrews is drawn chiefly from the Levitical cultus, the Day of Atonement. We cannot do better than to stick by Origen's scholarly verdict, "Who wrote it, God knows."

Attempts have been made in antiquity, at the Reformation, and in modern scholarly discussion to find some other well-known author of the apostolic age for Hebrews. Thus Tertullian suggested Barnabas; Luther and T. W. Manson proposed Apollos, a rather more plausible hypothesis. Even Luke has been considered. The mention of Timothy in the epistolary conclusion seemed to support such theories. But clear indications that the recipients belonged to the second or third Christian generation rule out such attempts. Hebrews 2:3 provides unmistakable evidence that both author and recipients belonged to the subapostolic age, like the author of Luke 1:1-4. There was first the period of Jesus' earthly life, then the time of the original witnesses, and finally the age of the author and recipients. Hebrews 13:7 provides another pointer for the subapostolic date: the original leaders, who brought the gospel to the recipients, have since died.

Another factor which used to play a major role in determining the date of the document (e.g., B. F. Westcott) and which is revived from time to time (T. W. Manson, W. Manson, G. Buchanan) is the *prima facie* assumption that the temple was still standing when the work was written. The author speaks of the Levitical high priests performing their services in the sanctuary in the present tense. If this argument were tenable, it would presuppose a date before 70 C.E., although there is some possibility that sacrifices continued on the site of the temple between 70 and 135 C.E. The trouble with this argument is that the author is expounding Scripture. He is speaking of what the priests do in the book of Leviticus, not what was going on in the temple. The sanctuary he refers to is the tent in the wilderness, not the temple at Jerusalem.

A more sophisticated attempt to date Hebrews earlier than 70 has been made by G. W. Buchanan. He believes that the recipients were Christian Zionists who had literally come to Zion, the heavenly city, before its destruction (12:22-23). For the moment we simply note this view and will deal with it more fully later. Hebrews 13:10 does, however, seem to speak of current priestly activities on the Day of Atonement, rather than of the temple in the wilderness. But the argument may still be a theoretical one. It is unlikely that first-century Jewish priests claimed admission to the Christian Eucharist!

Like other authors of the subapostolic age, the author of Hebrews writes with a quasi-apostolic authority. Though not himself an eye-witness or an apostle, he presumes to address a local church or a group within it over the heads of the local leaders. The same thing happens in the Johannine Letters and in the Pastorals. All in all, the atmosphere in Hebrews suggests the early subapostolic age and the period of emergent catholicism. More of this will become evident as we proceed.

Properly speaking, "Hebrews" would be Aramaic-speaking Palestinian Jews. In Buchanan's theory (see above) the recipients did live in Palestine, but they were Jews from the Diaspora who had returned to the homeland. Were they actually Diaspora Jews? The use of the LXX points in this direction. Most of the OT quotations come either from the LXX as we know it, or from a lost version of the text. Of course, many gentile converts were familiar with the LXX, but the central concern for the Levitical priesthood and its sacrifices suggests a deep commitment to the LXX as verbally inspired Scripture. Nairne's view that the recipients were a group within a congregation has much to commend it. In 13:24 they are asked to greet "all the saints." They should by now have become teachers (5:11-14). They were neglecting attendance at the Christian assembly (10:25).

Can we be any more certain of the domicile of the recipients? Several considerations speak in favor of Rome. There are greetings to "those from Italy." The author seems to have people with him who are away from where the recipients live. Hebrews 10:32-34 alludes to an earlier persecution in terms which nicely fit Tacitus's descriptions of the Neronian persecutions in Rome back in the sixties *(theatrizomenoi)*. The evident tension between the recipients and the larger congregation bears some similarity to the tensions in the Roman church which Paul writes about in Romans 14–15. Finally, the first writer to quote Hebrews was Clement of Rome (96 C.E.).

Structure

Ancient writers did not divide their works by chapter and verse, but had other ways of indicating their structure. The author of Hebrews uses the methods developed in Jewish midrash. One of his favorite devices is the use of *inclusio*. The last words in the section repeat words which were used at the beginning. A good example of *inclusio* is 3:1—4:16, a midrash on Ps. 95:7-11. Several key words are introduced at the beginning: Jesus, high priest, and confession (3:1). The same words occur in 4:14. Two French scholars, L. Vaganay and A. Vanhoye, have worked out a structural analysis of the whole document, using the criteria of *inclusio* and catchwords. Here is an adaptation of their analysis:

   I.   1:1-4. Introduction: the basic Christian confession or *homologia*
   II. 1:5—5:10. Preparation for the main argument
       A. 1:5—2:18. Jesus' superiority over the angels
       B. 3:1-6. Jesus' superiority over Moses
       C. 3:7—4:16. Jesus' superiority over Joshua, including a hortatory midrash on Ps. 95:7-11
       D. 5:1-10. Jesus' qualifications for high priesthood

III. 5:11—10:39. Major christological exposition: Christ the high priest
  A. 5:11—6:20. Introductory paraenesis
  B. 7:1-28. Christ's high priesthood after the order of Melchizedek
  C. 8:1—9:28. The eschatological perfection of Christ's high priesthood
  D. 10:1-18. The eschatological efficacy of Christ's high priestly work
  E. 10:19-39. Concluding paraenesis
IV. 11:1—12:29. Major exhortation
  A. 11:1—12:2. The heroes of faith
  B. 12:3-13. Exhortation to endurance
  C. 12:14-29. Exhortation to holiness
V. 13:1-25. Appendix
  A. 13:1-18. Ethical injunctions
  B. 13:20-21. Concluding benediction
  C. 13:22-25. Epistolary conclusion

It is idle to ask which was the more important in the author's eyes, the christological exposition or the ethical exhortations. The two are inseparably connected. Faith must lead to conduct, and conduct must be based on faith. No doubt the author began with the situation of his audience. They were sluggish and stagnant, so they required exhortation. But a mere pep talk was not enough. If the recipients (and the original audience, too) were to reach maturity in conduct, they must first develop a deeper insight into the confession of faith which they had made at their baptism.

The Use of the Old Testament

The original confession, reproduced in 1:1-3, also contained a reference to Christ's session at the right hand of God after the completion of his saving work. The imagery of the heavenly session was derived from the primitive use of Ps. 110:1 in kerygma and apologetic. Taking this as his starting point, the author will develop throughout his work an extended interpretation, a midrash on this psalm (Buchanan). The first verse of the psalm leads him naturally to verse 4 which speaks of the messianic king enthroned as high priest after the order of Melchizedek. Within this major midrash covering the whole of chapters 1–12, there are several minor midrashim. In 2:5-9 there is a midrash on Ps. 8:4-6. Another, as we have noted, is on Ps. 95:7-11 (3:7—4:11). There are two on Jer. 31:31-34 (8:8-13; 10:15-18), and another on Ps. 40:6-8 (10:5-10). In the major parensis there is a short midrash on Hab. 2:3-4 at 10:37-38 and a more extended one on Prov. 3:11-12 at 12:5-11. Typical of the midrash method is the way in which one OT passage can be interpreted with the help of others. All the minor midrashim contribute to the interpretation of the principal one,

Ps. 110:1-4. We should also note Ps. 2:7, which is quoted at 1:5 and 5:5-9 to establish Christ's appointment by God as high priest. Psalm 8:4-6 is used at 2:5-9 to make the point that Christ's temporary humiliation on the cross was a necessary precondition of his exaltation. Hence, his humiliation by no means implies his inferiority to the angels.

Without a direct quotation, the story of Abraham's encounter with Melchizedek (Gen. 14:17-20) is reproduced at some length in 7:1-10 to prove the superiority of the high priesthood according to Melchizedek over the Levitical. This argument is hardly likely to convince the present day reader, but it was typical of the midrashic technique. Today, we may accept the conclusion without buying the argument!

Another important text which enriches the interpretation of Psalm 110 is Jeremiah's prophecy of the new covenant. It demonstrates that the OT itself was fully aware of the ineffectiveness of the Levitical priesthood and of God's plan to replace it eventually with a better priesthood. Note here that the author regards both the covenant and the law as the institution of a priesthood. Its moral purpose or its function as a summons to repentance are completely disregarded. In chapter 9 the Levitical legislation for the Day of Atonement is summarized without direct quotation (9:7-10). Then, resuming the covenant theme, the author expands the picture by an allusion to the covenant sacrifice offered by Moses in Exod. 24:6-8. Thus we have a confusion of typologies. The author is untroubled by this. He wants to bring out two different, though related aspects of the effects of Christ's death.

Psalm 40:6-8 plays an important role in the Christology of Hebrews (10:5-10). The author calls attention to the singular reading of the LXX, "A body you have prepared for me." The Hebrew text has "you have given me an open ear"—to hear God's commandments and obey God's will. The whole purpose of the incarnation ("when Christ came into the world") was that he should have a body to offer in sacrifice. This would qualify him to fulfill the role of high priest after the order of Melchizedek. Once more, a subordinate text supports and amplifies the main text (Ps. 110:4).

Later the author reverts to Jeremiah's prophecy to demonstrate that under the new covenant God will "remember no more" (i.e., punish) the sins of his people (10:16-17). This proves the finality of Christ's atonement. Under the old covenant, God did remember sins, and Jeremiah looked forward to their final removal. This has now been achieved, and so there is no longer any need for atonement. Christ's priesthood is eternal, not one whose service must constantly be repeated, whether in the daily sacrifice or annually on the Day of Atonement. In the major paraenesis Hab. 2:3-4, a *testimonium* also used at Qumran and by Paul, is cited for quite a different purpose. The Christian must hold on until the final consummation.

The last text, Prov. 3:11-12, is used (12:5-6) to assure the readers that persecution throws no doubt on the validity of their salvation. God chastises his trueborn children so persecution is a sign that they are not illegitimate.

The High Priesthood of Christ

We now come to the central doctrine of Hebrews and its signal contribution to Christology. Was the author the first to use this title? Some have thought that 3:1 ("high priest of our confession") indicates that the baptismal confession of the community already contained the title. This, however, is doubtful. The exact wording of the confession, as G. Bornkamm has shown, is to be found in 1:1-3. This culminates in the statement that when he had made purification for sins, Christ sat down at the right hand of the majesty on high. The *homologia* thus contained an allusion to Ps. 110:1, but not to 110:4. The earlier kerygma had used verse 1 atomistically. The author takes a new step by applying the psalm as a whole to Christ. Thus the *homologia* implied that Christ is high priest after the order of Melchizedek.

But was the substance of this Christology new? Not altogether. Quite early on, the liturgical tradition had interpreted Christ's death as a sacrifice (1 Cor. 11:24, *hyper hymōn:* Mark 14:24, *ekchynnomennon hyper pollōn*; Mark 10:45, *lytron anti pollōn*). In his own theologizing, Paul had preferred the imagery of the law court and the battlefield, though sometimes he drew on liturgical formulas which spoke of Christ's death as a sacrifice (cf. also 1 Cor. 5:7). The author of Hebrews is clearly aware of this liturgical tradition. By combining this tradition with the extension of Ps. 110:1 to verse 4 he arrived at his new doctrine.

It is also possible that the author was influenced by Jewish precedents. Long before he wrote, the Hasmonean priestly rulers had supported their pretensions by an appeal to Psalm 110. The eleventh cave of Qumran has yielded a scroll which shows that the covenanters looked for the coming of Melchizedek as a messianic figure (11QMelc). Philo identified the logos as a high priest. Clearly the notion of a priestly Messiah after the order of Melchizedek was, so to speak, in the air in contemporary Judaism, especially in some of its sectarian forms. There were currents of thought originating in Palestine which spread to Hellenistic Judaism, both in its Philonic form and in a Christian form in Hebrews. This will be an important point to remember when we consider the author's intellectual milieu.

The author, however, was not interested in theological speculation for its own sake. It was the situation of his readers, as evidenced in the hortatory sections, that led him to elaborate his doctrine:

> You have become dull in understanding. For though by this time you ought to be teachers, you need someone to teach you again the basic elements of the oracles of God. You need milk, not solid food (5:11-12).

Nevertheless, the writer will give them solid food: "Therefore let us leave the elementary doctrines of Christ" (6:1 RSV). The high priesthood of Christ is a mature doctrine, a further indication, incidentally, that it was not part of the original baptismal confession. The doctrine of Christ's high priesthood would lead the readers into maturity and overcome their sluggishness and stagnation. How will it do this? The author sets up a comparison between the recipients and Israel in the wilderness. The Israelites of the exodus had also grown tired. They too had murmured, and wanted to return to the fleshpots of Egypt instead of holding on until they reached the promised land (midrash on Psalm 95 in 3:7—4:11). Like the children of Israel, the community of the new covenant lives between the times. The former lived between the bondage of Egypt and the freedom of the promised land, the latter between the first and second comings of Christ. For each interim God has provided a priesthood and a sacrificial system to enable the wanderers to enter into the promised rest. Hence it will be seen that the doctrine of Christ's high priesthood was not intended as an abstract piece of theologizing. It was a matter of life and death for the original recipients of the document.

For the same reason it was important that the sacrifice of Christ should be final. There was no place for any other. If they turned their backs on this salvation, the readers would get no second chance. There was no further sacrifice for sin. This denial of a second repentance will be discussed later in these pages.

The author expounds his new doctrine by a point-by-point comparison between the Levitical high priesthood and that of Christ. Why does he take this line? There is really no suggestion that the recipients were in danger of returning to the temple sacrifices. Probably the temple had been destroyed by then and the temple sacrifices were hardly a live option for them, especially if, as we think, they lived outside of Palestine. This comparison is motivated by two considerations. First, there is the author's scriptural orientation. He believes that the OT is not only the inspired word of God, but was written in direct reference to his own day. Second, there is the analogy between the wilderness generation and the church of the new covenant, as already noted.

If the whole epistle, as we have claimed, is an extended midrash on Psalm 110, this will mean that the document in its entirety is related to that text, and to the exposition of Christ's high priesthood. This is obvious in the central section (5:1—10:39), and fairly obvious in the major exhortation (11:1—12:29). It is less obvious in 1:1—4:16. But there are, to begin with, three references to Christ as high priest in these opening chapters. The first occurs in 2:17, in the section which demonstrates Christ's superiority over the angels. Has the author planted this first reference arbitrarily or does it have an integral connection with Christ's superiority over the angels? We suggest that it has. The old "message" (i.e., the Mosaic law or old covenant) was "declared through angels" (2:2). This was a common notion in contemporary Judaism and it was also taken up by Paul in Gal. 3:19 and by the author of Luke-Acts in Stephen's speech (Acts 7:38, 53), but for different purposes. The author of Hebrews is concerned with the law simply and solely because it instituted the Levitical priesthood and its sacrifices. In demonstrating Christ's superiority over Moses, therefore, the author is preparing his readers for his thesis that Christ's high priesthood is superior to the Levitical. Wherever we read of angels in the first two chapters, we must conceive of their function in this way.

The second enunciation of the main theme occurs at 3:1. This is the opening verse of the section which deals with Christ's superiority over Moses. Moses is introduced as the "servant" of the house (i.e., the house of Israel; Num. 12:7). It is also said that Moses testified "to the things that would be spoken later" (v. 5). What things are these? The usual interpretation is that they are the revelation to be brought later by Christ and his apostles (so Thomas Aquinas). However, Moses is always a negative witness in Hebrews. He represents solely the Levitical priesthood which is done away with in Christ. When the author needs prophecies of Christ and his work, he does not refer to Moses (i.e., the Pentateuch) but almost exclusively to the Prophets and Psalms. So the "things" of 3:5 must be the revelation of the law which Moses was soon to give according to Num. 12:8. The NRSV "later" is not in the Greek text. Remove that, and put yourself at the point of time when Moses went up the mountain to receive the law and the difficulty disappears. Once more, the point of the argument is the superiority of Christ over Moses as the instituter of the old covenant and the Levitical priesthood. Hence the priesthood of Christ is superior to that which Moses instituted.

The midrash on Psalm 95 (chap. 4) focuses similarly on Christ's superiority over Joshua. The name Joshua is "Jesus" in the Greek. The first Jesus did not bring Israel into the eschatological rest but only into the earthly promised land. Only the second Jesus did that. Therefore his high priesthood is more effective than Joshua's leadership. The Joshua passage is significantly followed by the third enunciation of the main theme (4:14). This confirms that the comparison with Joshua is related to the high priesthood of Christ.

The author is now ready to tackle his subject head-on. But first he must establish what was not obvious—that Jesus had the proper qualifications to be a high priest. It was not obvious because the necessary requirements were duly set out in the Pentateuch, and only the descendants of Levi could fulfill them. Nevertheless, Jesus does fulfill the essential qualifications. The high priest must be chosen from among humans for his sacred functions. He must share the weakness of those on whose behalf he functions. Only so can he sympathize with them. He must not take this honor upon himself, but must be called by God.

Jesus measured up to all these points, as is proved by a combined quotation of Ps. 2:7 and Ps. 110:1 (5:5-6). The argument is clinched by yet another enunciation of the main theme (5:10).

Before embarking on a point-by-point comparison between Christ and the Levitical high priests, the author inserts a long exhortation (5:11— 6:20), which serves to remind the readers once more of the practical purpose of the christological exposition. It indicates that what follows is to be advanced teaching for the mature.

Skillfully, the author steers his exhortation back to the major theme by discussion of God's promise to Abraham (6:13-20). It was a promise given under oath. Hence the readers can have confidence that they will enter where Jesus has gone before, a high priest after the order of Melchizedek. This is the fifth and final enunciation of the theme.

At last we are ready for the central argument (7:1—10:18). First, there is a discussion of the story of Abraham and Melchizedek as related in Genesis 14 (7:1-10). The transition was made smooth by the previous discussion of God's oath to Abraham. The Genesis story does not mention Melchizedek's father, mother, or genealogy, not does it say anything of his death. This suggests that he is a mysterious figure from eternity, and so he "resembles" the Son of God as a priest forever. Melchizedek is thus not a type of Christ, for types have a historical reality. Rather, he is a shadowy *Doppelgänger* of the Christ (7:1-3).

In the next section (7:4-10) we get a proof from the Genesis story that Scripture itself recognizes the superiority of Melchizedek's—and therefore Christ's—priesthood over Levi's.

Verses 11-14 illustrate the indispensable role of Melchizedek in the argument. Psalm 110:4, written later than the Pentateuch, shows that the Levitical priesthood is not the only one. So, in spite of his descent from Judah rather than Levi, "our Lord" could nevertheless occupy a priestly office.

There are two more reasons why Christ is superior to the Levitical priests (7:15-19). His priesthood is not based on physical descent, nor on an ineffective law. The old priesthood could not achieve "perfection." Here we have a key term of Hebrews which will be discussed later.

The next point (7:20-22) is that there is no oath in connection with the appointment of the Levitical priests, but there was for the Melchizedek priesthood. This is clear from Ps. 110:4, though it is not clear when the oath appointing Jesus was sworn. No doubt it was implied in the exaltation of Christ to the right hand of God.

There was a constant succession of Levitical priests. When one died, another took his place. Once again, it is clear that the author's argument is purely scriptural. Had he been talking of the high priests of Jerusalem of the first century C.E., he could not have avoided mention of their frequent deposition for political reasons! But Jesus has no successor. His tenure is permanent. Therefore he lives to make perpetual intercession for his own, that they too may gain access to the presence of God (7:23-25).

Christ, moreover, was sinless. He did not have to offer sacrifice every day for his own sins and those of others. Note how the author shifts from the Day of Atonement to the daily sacrifices. The reason is the point he is making: he wishes to emphasize the constant repetition of the Levitical ministrations. Christ's sacrifice is superior because he was offered once and for all and its effects last forever (7:26-29).

The scene of the ministrations of the two priesthoods is also different (8:1-7). The Levitical priests ministered in the tent in the wilderness; Christ performs his priestly liturgy in heaven. He could never have exercised his priesthood on earth since the office was already occupied (v. 4). The earthly sanctuary was a mere copy of the true, a point which prepares the ground for the next argument. Even the OT recognized the inadequacy of the first priesthood (v. 7).

That inadequacy was pointed up by Jeremiah's prophecy of a new covenant. There would have been no need for a new one if the old one had done its job properly (8:8-13). With evident fascination, the author enumerates every detail of the furniture in the earthly sanctuary (9:1-5). He would have loved to give a typological interpretation to every item, but unfortunately he had no time. So he focuses at once on the ritual of the earthly sanctuary (9:6-10). That ritual was ineffective because it could deal only with external breaches of the ceremonial law. It could not remove the barrier between humanity and God, the barrier of sin. That, however, is just what Christ's work did (vv. 11-14). He entered into the very presence of God, taking with him not the blood of animals, but his own blood.

The core of the argument is contained in these two sections, 9:6-10 and 11-14. The first paragraph describes the work and effects of the Levitical high priesthood, while the second (the central paragraph of the whole document) describes the work of Christ and *its* effects. The high priest performs his office on earth, but Christ performs his in heaven; the high priest offered the blood of animals, but Christ offered his own blood. The high priest took the blood into the earthly sanctuary, Christ took his into heaven itself. The Levitical sacrifices covered only ritual impurity, Christ's sacrifice took away sin, enabling the worshipers to serve the living God.

In 9:15-22 the theme of the two covenants reappears. The inauguration of the first covenant (and with it the Levitical priesthood) is contrasted with the death of Christ. Here again we see that the author is not concerned with the Day of Atonement per se, but with the saving work of Christ. While the Day of Atonement is the most helpful image, there are other images too, like the daily sacrifice which we have already encountered, and the inaugural sacrifice of the covenant at Sinai in this section. The point which the author wants to make is that covenants have to be inaugurated by a death. He reinforces the argument by a play on the word *diathēkē*, which can be both a covenant and a will. Wills come into force only when the testator dies.

Hebrews 9:23-28 contains a curious argument: Just as the furniture in the earthly sanctuary had to be cleansed on the Day of Atonement, so the heavenly things of which the earthly are only a copy require purification. It is not clear what the heavenly things are, or why they required purification. The author has been carried away by his argument.

The section 10:1-4 contains no new arguments but underlines points already made: the shadowy nature of the old ritual, its ineffectiveness and need of constant repetition, the inability of animal sacrifices to take away sins. But these verses do prepare the way for something new, the introduction of Ps. 40:6-8 into the picture (10:5-10). The nature of Christ's sacrifice was an act of obedience to the will of God. This does not mean that it was a purely ethical act. The will of God for Christ was precisely that he should die as a sacrificial victim. But as we shall see later, this use of Psalm 40 does open up the possibility of a modern reinterpretation of Hebrews' central thesis.

With 10:11-18 the theological exposition is rounded off. Once more, the author contrasts the two sacrificial systems. Once more he alludes to the daily oblation, and contrasts it with the singularity of Christ's sacrifice and the finality of its effects. No more sin, no more offering. The problem of postbaptismal sin, apart from the unforgivable sin of apostasy, is simply not raised.

As our structural analysis shows, 10:19-39 concludes the christological exposition with an exhortation corresponding to the initial exhortation in 5:11—6:20. Key words from the exposition are introduced here, such as "enter," "sanctuary," "blood of Jesus," "way opened up for us through the curtain," "great priest," "approach," "confession." These catchwords rivet together the exposition and the parenesis and show that the latter belongs here and not to the major exhortation, which begins in 11:1.

Some Residual Theological Problems

Christ's Sacrifice: At Calvary or in Heaven?

Since the Reformation there has been much debate over the scene of Christ's sacrifice. On the one hand, some exegetes, mainly Protestants, have tried to locate that sacrifice exclusively on the cross. In favor of this interpretation one may cite the tremendous emphasis on the once for all (*eph' hapax*) character of Christ's sacrifice and its interpretation in terms of obedience (10:7). Also Christ's session at the right hand of God indicates the completion of his work. The verb *prosphero* invariably occurs in the aorist tense. On the other hand, many argue that the real scene of Christ's sacrifice is in heaven. It is there that he presents his blood to the Father. And this he does continuously for the atonement of our sins. The following arguments are used in support of this position: In the sacrificial system of the OT the real moment of sacrifice was not the slaying of the victim but the manipulation of the blood after it had been slain. That the author of Hebrews presumes this rationale is indicated by his curious insistence that the cult objects in the heavenly sanctuary must be cleansed by an application of the blood. Hence Christ's priesthood is eternal, and his sacrifice goes on in eternity. Those who argue for this position frequently interpret Hebrews on Platonic lines (e.g., M. Bourke). It will be noted, however, that this is only an inference and is by no means certain. The only specific activity ascribed to Christ in heaven is that of making perpetual intercession for us (Heb. 7:25), or appearing in the presence of God on our behalf (9:24). The author, as we have noted, is careful to put the words about Christ's self-offering in the aorist. There must be some reason for this.

Whatever the original understanding of sacrifice in the OT was, Hebrews clearly regards the slaughter of the victim as an essential moment in the ritual, along with the presentation of the blood in the sanctuary. Accordingly, what happened at Calvary was no mere preliminary, but an essential part of the sacrifice. That sacrifice, however, is not confined to Calvary. It includes the presentation of his blood in heaven to the Father. But this happened once and for all, not eternally. It must therefore have happened at the moment of his entry into the heavenly sanctuary. The *eph' hapax* of his self-oblation embraces the death and exaltation as a single, indivisible event. Of course, Christ continues his high priestly work in eternity, yet that work is not eternal self-oblation, but intercession and appearance before the presence of God for his own on the grounds of his once-for-all self-offering (7:25; 9:24). Although Hebrews does not use the term, it would probably be legitimate to say that he eternally "pleads" his once-for-all sacrifice.

The Contemporary Meaning of Sacrifice

There is a tendency among some scholars to write off the Christology of Hebrews as meaningless for contemporary faith so far as the doctrine of Christ's high priesthood and sacrifice are concerned. Our understanding of that Christology depends upon an experience of the sacrificial cultus which we do not have today. One is reminded of Sir Edwyn Hoskyn's once expressed desire that an ox might be sacrificed annually in the court of Corpus Christi College, Cambridge, preferably on a hot summer's afternoon. That would teach theological students what sacrifice was all about! Unfortunately it would be a curious and disgusting spectacle, rather than an existential experience.

But is such an existential experience really necessary? We do use the term sacrifice today, and we use it in a sense transformed by the sacrifice of Christ. We speak of soldiers making the supreme sacrifice for their country, an act which a popular hymn refers to as a "lesser Calvary." We speak of a mother sacrificing her life in a fire to rescue her child. The OT prophets taught that the real sacrifice God required was ethical obedience. This ethical reinterpretation of the concept made great strides in Hellenistic Judaism, and found its way into the NT (Rom. 12:1; Heb. 13:16; 1 Peter 2:5, 9). But if God demands that kind of sacrifice, human beings are incapable of rendering it. When the prophets sought to ethicize the concept of sacrifice, they were perhaps insufficiently aware of the problem. But the very continuation, nay, elaboration of the sacrificial system in postexilic times was a witness to this impossibility (O. C. Quick). Thus the OT prophets unconsciously pointed forward to the need for God to do for humanity what it could not do for itself. This was done, according to Hebrews, by Christ, the "apostle" of God at Calvary, and in his exaltation. Hebrews does not draw its understanding of Christ's redeeming work exclusively from the obsolete sacrificial system. After all, our document was not describing a living rite of which his hearers had an existential experience, but the scriptural arrangements for the tent in the wilderness. Now, as we have seen, Hebrews also draws upon one of the psalms which encapsulates the prophetic protest against cultic sacrifice:

> Sacrifices and offerings you have not desired, but a body you have prepared for me; in burnt offerings and sin offerings you have taken no pleasure. Then I said, "See God, I have come to do your will, O God," (in the scroll of the book it is written of me). (10:5-6)

Of course, as we have already said, the author did not intend to eliminate the cultic element in sacrifice. This is clear from his repeated use of the term "blood of Christ." But he does open up the possibility of interpreting

Christ's sacrifice in ethical terms today. After all, sacrifice is only one of the images used to interpret the meaning of Christ's death. Matthew speaks of Christ's life in its totality as the fulfillment of all righteousness. Paul speaks of the perfect obedience of the last Adam which reversed the disobedience of the first. The cross is the climax of the total life of obedience, and acquires its significance from the quality of the life that preceded it. By that perfect obedience to the will of the Father, Christ did for humanity what it could not do for itself. God required total obedience; Christ rendered it, and Christ alone. This is the truth in the controversial, yet scriptural, doctrine of satisfaction. It is not, however, as has often been thought, an immoral doctrine, as though Christ offered the sacrifice and we can get off scot-free. It is not that since Christ has offered his sacrifice of perfect obedience we have nothing to do at all. Rather, it means that Christ has opened up the way of obedience for us. Now at last we can fulfill what the prophets demanded. Christ takes up our imperfect obedience into his perfect obedience:

> Look Father, look on his anointed face,
> and only look on us as found in him.

Christ in Hebrews is the pioneer, the one who went before that we might follow. Two analogies may help us to understand the relation between Christ's obedience and ours. C. S. Lewis once compared the situation to that of a child trying to make his first letters. The father puts his own large hand over the child's small hand and traces the letters with him. E. Schweizer compared the situation to an experience of his own childhood. In the alpine snows his father would walk ahead making footsteps in which the child could follow. In this way it does seem possible to make homiletical sense of a Christology which originally depended for its comprehension upon an understanding of the sacrificial cultus which we no longer share.

Other Aspects of Hebrews' Christology

While the high priesthood of Christ forms the central concept of Hebrews' Christology and its original contribution, there are other titles and concepts as well. The opening hymn uses the title Son of God to cover the three stages of preexistence, earthly life, and exaltation. The preexistence part of the formula is based upon the concept of the heavenly wisdom, similar to that found in other hymnic formulae (Phil. 2:6-11; Col. 1:15-20; John 1:1-18). Unless the reading *hyios* ("Son") is original at John 1:18, the Hebrews formula is the only one which directly identifies the preexistent with the Son.

The author never makes it quite clear where he locates the moment at which the preexistent Son became incarnate. One would naturally think, of course, of the birth or conception and this certainly seems to be suggested by 1:6, especially when it is read as the liturgical Epistle on Christmas Day. However, this is probably not the author's meaning. The quotation from Deut. 32:43 (LXX) is framed by two other OT quotations which refer to the enthronement of Jesus at the exaltation (Ps. 2:7 in v. 5 and 45:6-7 in vv. 8-9). Accordingly it seems best to take "into the world" as a translation of lĕʿôlām. In this passage the term "Son of God" is used to express the dignity of the exalted One. We have here a combination of a three-stage Christology of the gentile mission with a more primitive two-stage Christology of Hellenistic Jewish Christianity, as in Phil. 2:6-11. As applied to the exaltation, the title Son of God acquires a special nuance in Hebrews from the high priesthood Christology. This is especially clear in 4:14 where the two titles are brought together.

Between preexistence and exaltation comes the incarnate life. As has often been noted, Hebrews lays extraordinary emphasis upon the humanity of Jesus. He shared the flesh and blood of humankind (2:14). God prepared a body for him (10:5). He assumed the seed of Abraham and became like other humans in every respect (2:16-17). Is this a particular emphasis upon Jesus' Jewishness? Probably not, for in the context the human qualities specified are quite general, liability to temptation, suffering, and death. As a christological title, "Son of God" covers the incarnate life. Though he was a Son, Jesus learned obedience through suffering (5:8). This passage, with its emphasis on Jesus' prayer for deliverance from the terrors of death, is almost certainly based on the synoptic traditions of Gethsemane. It seems to portray Jesus as the suffering servant of Deutero-Isaiah. Thus Hebrews has a three-stage Christology, each stage of which is covered by the title Son of God.

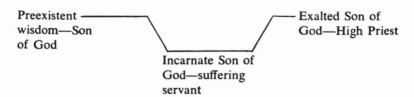

Preexistent
wisdom—Son
of God

Exalted Son of
God—High Priest

Incarnate Son of
God—suffering
servant

Nothing is said of Jesus' Davidic descent, and Buchanan thinks Hebrews deliberately rejected it. This is improbable. In primitive Christology Jesus' Davidic descent was not in itself a christological concept, but a necessary qualification for the exalted messiahship. It was inappropriate for the exalted state as Mark 12:35-37 makes clear. This pericope cites Ps. 110:1, which is also the main text of Hebrews. Hebrews' attitude to the title son of David was probably the same as that of the Synoptic pericope. Like it, our author probably took for granted Jesus' Davidic descent as a necessary qualification for his messiahship. But the main weight of his Christology lay upon the exaltation.

In a citation of Ps. 8:4-6 Hebrews once applies the title Son of Man indirectly to Jesus in his earthly existence (2:5-8). The author of Hebrews was evidently aware of the Synoptic use of "Son of Man" as a self-designation of Jesus in his earthly activity and humiliation. This tradition enabled him to apply Psalm 8 christologically to Jesus. "Son of Man" as a christological title for Hebrews expresses humiliation as the pathway to exaltation.

The Major Exhortation, 11:1—12:29

This section balances the major christological exposition. It sets forth the appropriate ethical response to Christ's saving work, and defines that response as faith. Faith for Hebrews is very different from what it was for Paul. For Paul it denoted the moment of passivity in which the believer accepts Christ's saving work as a gift from God. For Hebrews, it is a human virtue (11:1) closely related to endurance (*hypomonē*) and hope (*elpis*). Faith also involves holding fast the confession of faith, the *homologia*. Thus faith is also becoming a matter of affirming dogmatic propositions. It is *fides quae creditur* rather than *fides qua creditur,* the faith which is believed rather than the faith by which we believe. These developments (faith as virtue and as "the" faith) in the meaning of faith are signs of the author's subapostolic, early catholic outlook.

In chapter 11 our author draws upon a traditional recital of Israel's salvation history similar to that in Stephen's speech (Acts 7). This need not imply a direct literary connection between the two recitals, as W. Manson thought. It means only that both authors drew their traditions from a similar milieu, probably Hellenistic Jewish. This type of recital was developed in the wisdom literature. Earlier recitals in the OT praised Yahweh for his mighty acts. The later recitals praise the heroes of the past for their mighty deeds. Typical is the *exordium* of Sirach 44, "Let us now sing the praises of famous men." So Hebrews praises the heroes of the past for their faith. Its perspective on salvation history again suggests an early catholic standpoint.

The first two verses of chapter 12 are a redactional link between the recital of chapter 11 and the exhortations based upon it (12:3-29). Verse 2 looks like a christological hymn, and serves to join the ensuing exhortation with the major christological exposition. Note especially the reference to Christ's session at the right hand of God. This is the only occurrence of the word "cross" in Hebrews, a fact which suggests a Paulinist origin for the hymn, similar to that in Phil. 2:6-11. Jesus is the supreme hero of faith, conceived as endurance. To take the cross of Christ as an ethical example in this way is again typically subapostolic, and recalls 1 Peter 2:21-25. The author wishes to exhort his readers to pursue the same virtue of faith at a time of persecution. He develops his point by means of a midrash on Prov. 3:11-12 (12:5-11). This midrash is followed by a more general exhortation to holiness (12:12-17), a requirement of all the baptized (cf. 1 Peter 1:14-16). Once more, the imperatives are grounded on an indicative (12:18-24). The Christian assembly is compared to the gathering of the old community at Sinai which received the law. Once more, we must remember that for our author the "law" meant specifically the institution of the Levitical priesthood. These verses are important for the author's understanding of Christian worship (cf. also v. 28). The liturgy is an earthly foretaste of the eschatological worship in the heavenly Jerusalem. Verse 24 provides another link with the major christological exposition, while verses 25-29 offer a concluding warning.

Appendix: A Brief Catechesis and
Epistolary Conclusion

With the conclusion of chapter 12 the main body of the document is completed. Chapter 13 is an appendix. Some (e.g., Spicq, Vanhoye, and Buchanan) consider it an addition from a later hand. Buchanan believes it was added quite late and that its intention was to dress up the letter as a Pauline epistle in order to secure its acceptance in the NT canon. But there is little in the chapter to suggest a different hand. It exhibits the same concern for Christian worship that we found in chapter 12 (see 13:10-16). The "city that is to come" (13:14) recalls the heavenly Jerusalem of 12:22. The same situation of a church faced with persecution is presupposed (13:3). True, there are some minor differences. Only chapter 13 mentions marriage (v. 4), a point Buchanan uses to support his thesis that the original document was addressed to a monastic community. That, however, is an argument from silence. Verses 1-5a look like a catechesis similar to those in the hortatory parts of other NT epistles. Note the similarity in style between this passage and Rom. 12:3-21. In both passages imperatives are expressed by nouns and adjectival complements without a copula. Another difference is that the closing benediction (13:20-21) mentions the resurrection, whereas the main part of the document speaks invariably of Christ's exaltation. This difference, however, is probably due to the use of a traditional formula.

Finally, we have a proper epistolary conclusion in verses 22-24. "Briefly" is surprising after chapters 1-12, but it may refer simply to chapter 13

(Buchanan). If this is the case, "word of exhortation" will likewise refer only to chapter 13.

What then is the author's purpose in appending chapter 13? The most probable explanation is that he was adapting a sermon or series of sermons which he had already composed or preached, and sent it off to another congregation for whose needs he considered it to be relevant. And with it he sends a special exhortation particularly adapted to them, with a blessing and epistolary conclusion.

Residual Ethical Problems

Four problems call for a particular discussion. These are:
1. The meaning of "perfection" in Hebrews.
2. The sacrificial nature of Christian worship.
3. The denial of a second repentance.
4. The concept of the rest which awaits the people of God.

Perfection

This term has both christological and ethical significance. Christ achieved perfection through suffering (5:8-9), and the Christian likewise must grow toward perfection (6:1; cf. 12:2).

Perfection (*teleiōsis*) means etymologically to achieve a *telos* or goal. For the author of Hebrews it is primarily a religious and only secondarily an ethical category. As a religious term it means to attain the goal of all religion, which is access to the presence of God in worship. Christ through his self-oblation entered into the presence of God and won eternal redemption for us. His perfection or achievement of his goal was reached when he sat down at the right hand of God. As the pioneer he passed through the veil which cut us off from the presence of God and opened up for us the way to achieve the same perfection. In each case there is an ethical element involved. For Christ, this consisted in his perfect obedience to the will of God, as expounded in the midrash on Psalm 40 (10:5-10). In our case ethical perfection consists of holiness, without which none will see the Lord. It includes purity from all defilement of sin. Here as elsewhere the indicative implies an imperative.

The Sacrificial Nature of Christian Worship

No author has insisted so strongly on the once-for-all character of Christ's sacrifice. It was from his teaching that the Anglican reformers composed their prayer of consecration: "Who made there by his one oblation of himself once offered, a full, perfect and sufficient sacrifice, oblation and satisfaction for the sins of the whole world." At the same time our author does speak in his appendix about a sacrifice which Christians have to offer.

It is twofold. One aspect is liturgical, a sacrifice of praise: "the fruit of lips that confess his name" (13:15). The other aspect is ethical: "to do good and to share what you have, for such sacrifices are pleasing to God" (13:16). Our author can even say that the Christians have an altar in which they partake (13:10). He is clearly talking about a different kind of sacrifice from the salvific, atoning sacrifice of Christ. The Christian sacrifices have no atoning value. Rather, they are a *response* to the atoning sacrifice of Christ. Do these sacrifices include the Eucharist?

> F. F. Bruce quotes with approval Bengel's pithy comment on Heb. 13:10, *"nil de missa."* But surely, the sacrifice of praise is present in the Eucharist, since it was preeminently at the Eucharist that a confessional recital of the redemptive acts of God in Christ was presented. But, of course, this does not exclude other offerings of praise outside the Eucharist. Thus Hebrews justifies our using sacrificial language for the Eucharist. The word *altar* in 13:10 may well, despite Bengel and Bruce, *also* refer to the Eucharist (so Bornkamm, Michel). For in that liturgical action thanksgiving is offered for Christ's redeeming work, and that redeeming work thereby becomes a present reality. The author does not draw this deduction himself, but he may well imply it. It is not inconsistent with his teaching about the once-for-all character of Christ's atoning sacrifice. Hebrews is thus already developing a line of thought which was to become explicit a few years later in the *Didache*, where for the first time the Eucharist is actually called a sacrifice. In this respect, too, Hebrews is a document of emergent Catholicism.

The Denial of a Second Repentance

One of the greatest difficulties in Hebrews is its denial of the possibility of a second repentance (6:4-6; 10:26-31 and its use of the example of Esau in 12:16-17). When the Western church was locked in combat with Novatianists and Donatists, it refused to accept Hebrews into the canon because of this teaching and denied its Pauline authorship. The mainline church wanted to receive apostates back into the fold when persecutions were over and found the teaching of Hebrews embarrassing. How are we to interpret this teaching and what authority does it have for us today?

First, we may agree with R. Williamson that the author restricts his rigorism to the ultimate sin of apostasy. This is clear from the language of 6:6. He does not extend it to cover all postbaptismal sin, contra Buchanan, who sees here another expression of the author's monastic sectarianism.

Even so, does this mean that apostasy is for all time unforgivable? Is this a permanent law for the church? The issue becomes problematical whenever a persecution ceases. It became so in the German churches after the *Kirchenkampf*. Generally, the church has taken a compromise position. Apostates have usually been put on probation and allowed to work their passage home. But is this consistent with the teaching of Hebrews? Or do we reject it on this point? In answering this question we must pay due attention to the context of Hebrew's rigorism. The author lays down his principle not after apostasy has occurred, but before. What he is saying is that no one should bank on being taken back later if he or she apostatizes. One should face up to the serious consequences of a proposed line of conduct. The denial of a second repentance is analogous to the preaching of hellfire. In the NT it is used as an ultimate sanction before a contemplated line of behavior is adopted. It is not a situationless dogma with a general validity of its own.

The "Rest" That Remains for the People of God

Strictly speaking, the term *rest* in Hebrews is a soteriological concept rather than an ethical one. Nevertheless it has ethical implications, and we will therefore discuss it here. In the midrash on Psalm 95 (Heb. 3:7—4:11) the author elevates the concept to a central position in his ethical exhortation to perseverance.

> E. Käsemann made it the key to his interpretation of Hebrews. While acknowledging the typological framework, Käsemann sought the substance of the concept in Gnosticism. The rest, which corresponded to entering into the promised land, was the rest of the soul which had achieved the fruition of Gnosis. But the rest is for God's *people* (4:9).
>
> At the other extreme, G. Buchanan has connected the idea of the rest with his notion of Christian Zionism. For him, the rest means peace and prosperity in the *earthly land of Canaan*, the same land God promised his people in the time of Joshua, a promise still unfulfilled. Christ's work has taken away the sins which prevent God's people from appropriating rest in the land of Canaan. If they hold on, they will eventually enjoy peace and prosperity in the holy land. This is a most improbable interpretation. The promise was in fact fulfilled when Israel entered the promised land and all its enemies were defeated. At the very latest, it was fulfilled when David consolidated the monarchy and gave peace and prosperity to the land. The "rest" of which the author speaks is not the same rest which was held out before the wilderness generation, but the typological fulfillment of their entry into the promised land, Canaan. Canaan is a type of the rest which is both future and transcendent. It is both because the author thinks simultaneously of two ages and two worlds (see below). Second, if Christ the high priest is our pioneer, the one who goes before us and enables us to enter where he is, then it follows that the rest will be the heavenly sanctuary where he is enthroned at the right hand of God. Third, if our author were addressing Christian Zionists who returned to Palestine, they would be already enjoying it, not still awaiting it.

With primitive Christianity in general, the author regards the Christ event as the fulfillment of the exodus. Hebrews has the same perspective on the heavenly rest as is implied in 1 Cor. 10:1-13 and John 6:25-59. All three writings seem to be drawing upon a common tradition in Hellenistic Jewish Christianity.

The Milieu of the Author

It has often been held that the author of Hebrews was a Platonist. Although the view has been seriously questioned, it still finds advocates, most recently M. M. Bourke. According to this view, Hebrews operated with a scheme of two worlds, an upper world of ideal realities and an earthly world where every empirical entity was a copy or shadow of its ideal counterpart. The Platonic interpretation can appeal to such passages as 9:24, which speaks of the earthy sanctuary as a "copy" of the "true," with its contrast of "shadow" and "reality." Usually this line of interpretation is coupled with a stress on the affinities between the author of Hebrews and Philo of Alexandria. This association is particularly plausible in view of Hebrews' other affinities with Philo (e.g., the use of Melchizedek).

Against this view we should note the following: Hebrews does not have a Platonic worldview in general. It is not concerned with the correspondence between all earthly entities and their ideal counterparts. Its language, insofar as it is Platonic, is confined to the correspondence between the earthly tent in the wilderness and the archetypal sanctuary in heaven. Moreover, this doctrine is not derived from Platonism, but is already suggested in the Pentateuch itself (Exod. 25:9) and was later developed in apocalyptic and rabbinic Judaism. Hence it is fair to conclude that Hebrews owes nothing to Platonism except the Greek terminology which it uses to describe this typological correspondence.

The dualism of Hebrews is a complex one. On the one hand it speaks about a correspondence between the earthly tent in the wilderness and the tabernacle of God's presence in heaven. On the other hand it operates with the dualism of two ages. This is indicated by 10:1, where Christ is called the high priest of the good things *which are to come*. The priestly institutions of the OT are a shadow of these good things which are yet to come, not merely of good things up in heaven. If the author were a thoroughgoing Platonist, Christ would have been performing his high priestly office from eternity. It could hardly have been inaugurated by a once-and-for-all event here on earth. This complex dualism of two worlds and two ages is found also in the Dead Sea Scrolls, and in apocalyptic and rabbinic writers.

Another suggestion for the author's milieu, popular in the Bultmann school, is that Hebrews is influenced by Gnosticism (Käsemann; see above). On this view, the Christology of Hebrews is based on the Gnostic concept of the *Urmensch* or primeval human. A modified form of this view was proposed by G. Bornkamm, who deduced from 13:9 that the recipients of

Hebrews were syncretists. But the author himself is opposed to these tendencies. His Christology is entirely explicable as a development within Christianity. Its combination of wisdom's preexistence with royal exaltation Christology, and its emphasis on the human history of Jesus, its understanding of salvation as redemption from sin rather than illumination of our heavenly origin, is quite different from Gnosticism.

The Dead Sea Scrolls produced in the 1950s a kind of Qumran fever. It was suggested that the recipients were Essene Christians (C. Spicq, J. Daniélou, D. Flusser, H. Kosmala, and Y. Yadin). We have already noted the importance of the Melchizedek scroll. Buchanan sought to refine these theories by his theory of Christian Zionism.

What are we to make of all this? A clearer distinction needs to be drawn between the original audience of the midrashic sermons, the recipients of the written document, and the author. If the original audience was attracted to Qumran ideas, were the final recipients too? And how far did the author go along with either party? Was he reproaching them for not being better Christians of a Qumran type, or was he trying to wean them away from Qumran ideas? Probably the most judicious conclusion would be that none of the three parties was directly influenced by Qumran. Each of them emerged from Hellenistic Jewish Christianity somewhere along lines of development which led from Jewish sectarianism to later Gnosticism. Philo seems to stand upon a parallel trajectory of similar origin.

JAMES

James is one of the more useful books in the NT, even though it has never been a very popular one. It has always prompted misgivings, and the reasons are plain to see. One does not have to read far into the letter before being struck by the glaring absence of central tenets of Christian faith. In particular, one looks in vain for any reference to the life and ministry of Jesus, or to his death and resurrection. There are but two brief, unelaborated references to Jesus in the letter (cf. 1:1 and 2:1). Moreover, the letter has much to say about the importance of "works" in the Christian life, and thus has had the misfortune of appearing to contradict the NT's preeminent apostle, Paul—who maintained that we are "justified by grace through faith *apart* from works of the law" (Rom. 3:28). For all of these reasons, Martin Luther denounced it as an "epistle of straw." The stigma of his condemnation haunts the letter to this day.

Much of the uneasiness that attends a reading of the letter is laid to rest, however, when one important fact is understood: in terms of literary form, James is "paraenesis," or ethical exhortation in the guise of a letter. "Paraenesis," from the Greek word *parainesis* (which means "advice" or "counsel"), is instruction concerning how or how not to live. Martin Dibelius provided this key insight in his classic commentary on James and it is crucial for interpretation, for once the letter's paraenetic nature is acknowledged, its purpose comes into clear focus. It does not preach the kerygma; instead, it calls readers to live the Christian life. It is not a missionary document, and so does not undertake to present the whole of Christian truth. It is a document for use within the church, and is addressed to folk who have already embraced the gospel and who are familiar with the central tenets of Christian faith. Its purpose is to help believers see the implications of Christian faith for how they live their lives.

James is not the only place at which one finds paraenesis or ethical exhortation in the NT. The Letter of James has formal parallels, for example, to the paraenetical sections that usually conclude Paul's letters (cf. 1 Thessalonians 4–5; Galatians 5–6; Romans 12–14), in which Paul provides concrete admonitions, direct advice as to how people who have embraced the gospel should live. James, however, is paraenesis through and through. As Sophie Laws observes, it is "the most consistently ethical document in the New Testament" (Laws, *Epistle of James*, 27)—the NT's most persistent reminder that genuine Christian faith has implications for how we live our lives.

For this reason, John Calvin found great value in James and was not inclined to reject it as Luther did. Calvin maintained that if James seems to preach less of the grace of Christ than we might prefer, "we must remember not to expect everyone to go over the same ground." Moreover, he found it to be "full of instruction on various subjects, the benefit of which extends to every part of the Christian life." What Calvin appreciated about James is its practical teaching, which has relevance for everyday existence. James deals almost exclusively with the social and practical aspects of Christianity. It reminds its readers of the everyday problems with which Christians struggle and maintains that Christian faith touches every aspect of life, transforming routine pursuits into opportunities for discipleship. Viewed from this perspective, the observation of a nineteenth-century commentator, Johann Gottfried Herder, is germane: "If the epistle is 'of straw,' then there is within that straw a very hearty, firm, nourishing, but as yet uninterpreted and unthrashed, grain."

The Milieu of the Letter of James

The author of the letter speaks not as a preacher but as a teacher (cf. "we who teach" in 3:1)—as one who was responsible for guiding the early Christian community in many aspects of its life (cf. Eph. 4:11-13). In instructing the Christian community, he draws on a wide range of resources at his disposal. Indeed, his moral exhoration, like most first-century Christian paraenesis, is traditional and eclectic in nature. As Dibelius notes, the teacher who speaks through the letter is "more a witness than a creator"; he is "not a thinker, a prophet, or an intellectual leader, but rather a pedagogue, one among many, who appropriates and distributes from the property common to all" (Dibelius, *James*, 21, 25). Thus, it is important to consider the larger milieu of which the letter is a part. Three different currents of thought—Jewish, Hellenistic, and Christian—inform it in significant ways.

First of all, one observes immediately that James is the most *Jewish* of all the NT writings. Distinctively Jewish concepts pervade the letter. The letter is addressed to "the twelve tribes in the Dispersion" (1:1); it refers to the Christian congregation in 2:2 as a synagogue (*synagogē*; NRSV "assembly"); and in affirming that "God is one" (2:19), it sounds the central tenet of Jewish faith. Furthermore, the letter takes a positive attitude toward Torah (1:25; 2:8-13; 4:11-12); it quotes the OT as authoritative

(2:8, 11, 23; 4:6; 5:11); and it lifts up OT heroes and heroines such as Abraham, Rahab, Job, and Elijah as exemplars of faith (2:21-25; 5:11; 5:17-18). James also echoes the OT prophetic writings when it calls for conversion (4:8-10); when it attacks rich oppressors (5:1-6); and when it insists that believers effectively care for widows and orphans in need (1:27).

James's clearest affinities with the world of Judaism, however, are with Israel's wisdom tradition. Like the sages whose voices are heard in the canonical books of Proverbs, Job, and Ecclesiastes and the deuterocanonical books of Sirach and Wisdom of Solomon, the author of James, too, seeks to provide instruction in the art of living. James shares the sages' practical and ethical focus—their concern to order and maintain life in a manner that acknowledges the sovereignty of God. Moreover, James's often proverbial style is reminiscent of the writings of the sages, as are some of its central themes—in particular, control of the tongue. The letter itself features prominent references to wisdom in 1:5 and 3:13-18, which it knows to be a gift of God. Moreover, like the sages before him, the author of James proves to be a keen observer of nature, in which he finds instructive analogies to human experience. The letter is remarkable for its nature imagery. Insight can be gained, for example, from observation of the forest fire (3:5ff.), the mist that appears and then vanishes (4:14), the flower of the field (1:9ff.), or the wind-tossed wave upon the sea (1:6). In many respects, then, James's paraenesis is rooted in Israel's wisdom tradition. James is the wisdom book par excellence in the NT canon.

The author of James, however, is also at home within the world of *Hellenism*, as were Israel's cosmopolitan sages. It may be observed, for example, that the letter is written in relatively polished Greek language and style, and that it opens with the form of greeting (1:1) that was customary of the Hellenistic letter. Moreover, the letter makes considerable use of the diatribe, a popular form of Hellenistic moral address in which the author instructs his readers by engaging in debate with a straw person— an imaginary addressee (cf. 2:18; 3:10; 4:13). Moreover, there are references to Hellenistic philosophical terms ("the implanted word" in 1:21 and "the cycle of nature" in 3:6), and to Hellenistic science (cf. the astronomical allusions in 1:17); and some of the letter's striking images (e.g., the horse and the ship in 3:3-4) have little biblical background, though they are well known in Greek and Latin literature. Moreover, James's extensive OT quotations and allusions are drawn from the Septuagint, the Greek translation of the Hebrew Scriptures.

Still, for all its affinities with both Jewish and Hellenistic currents of thought, the letter of James is also decidedly *Christian*. To be sure, it makes scant reference to Jesus, and no mention at all of his death and resurrection. For this reason, L. Massebieau (1895) and F. Spitta (1896) proposed that James was originally a Jewish document that was appropriated with only minor editing (in 1:1 and 2:1) for use by Christians. This opinion, however, has found little support; for although Jesus is mentioned only twice (1:1; 2:1), specifically Christian connections pervade the letter. For example, there is no textual warrant for eliminating the two references to Jesus Christ in 1:1 and 2:1, and the references to him as the "Lord Jesus Christ" (1:1) and the "Lord of Glory" (2:1) certainly presuppose the resurrection (see also 5:7-8, 14-15). Moreover, James alludes to baptism in the name of Christ (2:7) and speaks explicitly of hope of his second coming (5:7ff.). The Christian community is termed the "church" (*ekklēsia*, 5:14); and the discussion of "faith and works" in 2:14-26 presupposes some familiarity with Paul.

Most striking, however, is that the letter is filled to the brim with echoes of the teaching of Jesus. The observant reader will note, for example, that James's prohibition of oaths in 5:12 closely resembles that of Jesus in Matt. 5:34-37; its emphasis on hearing and doing the word in 1:22 echoes Jesus' instruction concerning the wise person who builds a house on rock instead of sand in Matt. 7:24-26; and the command in 2:8 to love the neighbor as oneself from Lev. 19:18 is also highlighted by Jesus in Matt. 22:39, Mark 12:31, and Luke 10:27. Parallels between James and Matthew's Sermon on the Mount are particularly striking and suggest that the author of James is well acquainted with the oral tradition of Jesus' teachings (cf. James 1:2 and Matt. 5:11-12; James 1:4 and Matt. 5:48; James 1:5 and Matt. 7:7; James 1:20 and Matt. 5:22; James 1:22 and Matt. 7:24; James 2:10 and Matt. 5:19; James 2:13 and Matt. 5:7; James 3:18 and Matt. 5:9; James 4:4 and Matt. 6:24; James 4:10 and Matt. 5:4; James 4:11, 21 and Matt. 7:1-5; James 5:2ff. and Matt. 6:19; James 5:10 and Matt. 5:12; James 5:12 and Matt. 5:33-37). Indeed, James is permeated by the thought and sayings of Jesus more than any other NT writing outside the four Gospels, (cf. Patrick Hartin, 215–17).

Parallels to other NT authors suggest that James also reflects developing patterns of Christian ethical instruction. Notable in this respect are James's many points of contact with 1 Peter (cf. James 1:1 and 1 Peter 1:1; James 1:2 and 1 Peter 1:6; James 1:3 and 1 Peter 1:7; James 1:10-11 and 1 Peter 1:24; James 4:6-10 and 1 Peter 5:5-9; James 5:20 and 1 Peter 4:8). For all of these reasons, James's character as a Christian document is no longer seriously disputed.

The Epistle of James, then, represents a meeting of Jewish, Hellenistic, and Christian worlds of thought. The early Christian teacher who speaks through this letter draws from rich and varied resources at his disposal to instruct the Christian community in many practical aspects of its life.

Author, Date, Recipients

The specific identity of the teacher who speaks in the Letter of James is a matter of debate. In the opening verse of the letter, the author is designated simply as "James, a servant of God and of the Lord Jesus Christ." The five Jameses who are mentioned elsewhere in the NT thus present themselves as candidates: (1) James, the son of Zebedee (Mark 1:19; 3:17 par.; Acts 12:2); (2) James, the father of Jude (Luke 6:16; Acts 1:13); (3) James, the son of Alphaeus (Mark 3:18 par.); (4) James the younger (Mark 15:40); and (5) James, the brother of Jesus (Mark 6:3 par.; 1 Cor. 15:7; Gal. 1:19; 2:9, 12; Acts 12:17; 15:13; 21:18; Jude 1). Only one of these candidates, however, was of sufficient stature and authority within the early church to be identifiable with so brief an ascription as in 1:1. That would be James, the brother of Jesus, whom Paul refers to as one of the "pillars" of the early Christian church in Jerusalem (Gal. 2:9). The letter thus appears to be attributed to this James. But did he in fact pen the letter?

From the time of Origen in the third century, church tradition has held that James of Jerusalem was the author of the epistle. This position continues to find some support, for what is known of James of Jerusalem is thought to cohere with the character of the letter. One thing that is known for certain of this James is that he was a dedicated advocate of Jewish-Christian piety. References to him both within and without the NT are consistent in presenting him as a Christian who attached great importance to observance of the Jewish law. Thus, that the letter is strikingly "Jewish" in many respects continues to persuade some scholars of Jacobean authorship to this day. Since James of Jerusalem is known to have been martyred in 62 C.E., his epistle would then be one of the earliest writings of the NT. As Hartin concludes in a recent study, "James shows the heritage of Judaism flowering forth into the new world of Christianity" (244).

A majority of scholars, however, are not persuaded that James of Jerusalem composed the letter. Indeed, a number of factors are held to argue against it. (1) First, the letter is written in relatively polished and literary Greek. Although Greek was the lingua franca of the first-century world, there is some question as to whether the cultured language of the epistle would have been in the command of James of Jerusalem, an Aramaic-speaking Palestinian Jew. (2) Nowhere does the author indicate that he is the Lord's brother or that he knew Jesus personally. One cannot help but wonder why a Christian with such a special relationship with the Lord, who also was a witness to his resurrection (1 Cor. 15:7), would make such scant reference to him. (3) The discussion of "faith" and "works" in 2:14-26 seems to presuppose Paul's theological activity. As we will see, James's discussion seems to stand at some remove from the resolution of Paul's struggle with this issue in the mid-50s of the first Christian century and to be a response to a popular but sloganized misunderstanding of Paul's position. (4) One of the most serious objections to Jacobean authorship, however, concerns the letter's view of the law. James of Jerusalem's devotion to the Jewish law, which was well known, placed a high priority on cultic-ritual matters. In Acts and Galatians, for example, James figures prominently in discussions of gentile observance of the law, the decree of the council of Jerusalem, and concern for temple ritual (cf. Acts 15:13-21; 21:18-24; Gal. 2:12). Cultic-ritual concerns, however, are never mentioned in the Epistle of James. When the letter enjoins its readers to embrace religion "that is pure and undefiled before God" (1:27), the injunction is not related to circumcision, Sabbath observance, table fellowship, and purification laws—precisely the concerns that seem to have been significant to the historical James. The letter's own appeal to Torah is limited to the Decalogue and the "law of love" in Lev. 19:18 (cf. James 2:8-11). Therefore, the "law of liberty" (1:25; 2:12) or the "royal law" (2:8) of which James speaks—that is, the law of the kingdom—apparently refers not to the ritual observances but to the moral teaching of Torah. (5) Finally, it was only slowly and in the face of opposition that the Letter of James came to be included in the Christian canon in the earliest centuries of the church. Interestingly, its late canonization was due to doubts about its apostolic origins. Thus, early on, the letter does not appear to have been universally regarded as the work of the Lord's brother, and therefore as apostolic and canonical.

For all of these reasons, a majority of scholars regard the letter as pseudonymous. An unknown teacher, following a common, acceptable literary practice, has provided his work with the mantle of apostolic authority by writing in the name of the revered leader of the Jerusalem church. The author himself, who appears to have been well acquainted with Hellenistic culture, was probably a member of a Christian community that grew out of Diaspora Judaism. It is impossible to date his letter with any precision, but he is generally thought to have written toward the end of the first century, well after Paul's activity in the mid-50s, and after the death of James of Jerusalem in 62—at a time when the martyred James of Jerusalem had become a revered figure of the past.

Neither do we know to whom the letter was first addressed. The church has regarded James as one of the "general" or "catholic" (i.e., universal) epistles. Unlike Paul's letters, which are addressed to particular congregations in specific places, the catholic Epistles such as James, Jude, and 1 and 2 Peter are identified by the name of the author rather than of the recipients, because the catholic Epistles appear to be addressed to Christians in general rather than to a specific community at a particular place. They appear to have been written for general distribution and to address issues in the wider church. James 1:1, for example, greets "the twelve tribes in the Dispersion." The "twelve tribes" is a way of referring to the Jewish nation, and Jews in the "Dispersion" lived outside Palestine, scattered among the nations. "The twelve tribes in the Dispersion," however, is likely a reference to all Christians as heirs of the Jewish tradition, for the early Christians freely applied Jewish titles to themselves. James would appear, then, to address the whole of God's people scattered throughout the world. It addresses a wide audience and speaks of general rather than particular situations. Still, as Dibelius reminds us, James's discussion does relate to historical reality, in that it indicates those areas of life in the early Christian community that the author found to be most urgently in need of direction and regulation (Dibelius, xi).

It must be said, however, that advances in redaction criticism and in sociological study of the early church have begun to take issue with this "generalist" position. It has become increasingly apparent, for example, that James addresses Christians who perceived themselves as poor (1:9; 2:5) and who have experienced economic hardship at the hands of the rich (1:10-11; 2:6; 5:1-6). Structurally, the Christian communities may also be administered by "elders" (5:14), and are probably located "in the Dispersion" (i.e., outside Palestine). As research continues, more will no doubt be able to be said about the situation of the churches to which James is addressed.

Theological Perspective

The great form critic Martin Dibelius provided an invaluable key to understanding James when he identified its literary form as that of paraenesis, or ethical exhortation. He wrongly concluded, however, that as paraenesis, James is a miscellaneous collection of teachings from various sources without any internal coherence or theological unity. James, Dibelius declared flatly, has no theology. Many have shared this perspective, referring to James as "a handful of pearls" or "an ethical scrapbook," devoid of any unifying theme. Redaction critics, however, have taken issue with this position. Although James is short on Christology, it has become increasingly apparent that James is among the richest of NT writings in its reflection upon God—its theology.

James's perspective is decidedly theocentric. It may be observed, for example, that God is the ground of Christian existence: "In fulfillment of God's own purpose [God] gave us birth by the word of truth, so that we would become a kind of first fruits of [God's] creatures" (1:18). It is God's own word that has been "implanted" in us (1:21). It is "the wisdom from above" that God so generously provides (3:17; 1:5), God's own spirit that dwells within (4:5), that directs Christian living. Indeed, James maintains that God is a gracious presence in human life. Is there anyone lacking in wisdom? Simply "ask God," James advises, "who gives to all generously and ungrudgingly, and it will be given you" (1:5). James notes, in fact, that "every generous act of giving, with every perfect gift, is from above, coming down from the Father of lights"—from the constant and ever-faithful God (1:17). "Draw near to God," James exhorts readers, knowing that God is eager to draw near to you (4:8).

It may also be observed that every aspect of Christian life of which James speaks is related to the God who is creator, sustainer, savior, and judge. Why, for example, is it inappropriate to curse one's brother or sister? Because that brother or sister is made in the image of God (3:9). Why is it inappropriate to fawn over the well-heeled visitor to the Christian assembly and shuffle the shabby visitor aside? Because in dishonoring the poor, one dishonors those whom God has honored and chosen to be heirs of the kingdom (2:5-6). Why is it arrogant to assume that life consists in doing business and making money, and that human calculation can secure the future? Because the future is not in our control and we do not know what it will bring—in everything, we depend utterly upon the living God (4:13-17). Like Israel's sages, James seeks to order and maintain life in the context of God's sovereignty.

Interest in the theology of James is growing, and recent studies have highlighted the richly theocentric nature of the epistle. Luke T. Johnson, for example, maintains that the theological linchpin of the letter is found in 3:13—4:10, where James squarely sets two alternatives, two measures, two standards of reality before its readers and asks them to choose: between friendship with the world or friendship with God (cf. Johnson, *Discipleship in the NT*, 166–83). Friendship, as Johnson notes, was not a casual affection in the first-century world. It was one of the most-discussed and highly esteemed relationships. Friends were considered "one soul." Friendship meant "at the least, to share the same attitudes and values and perceptions, to see things the same way" (ibid., 173). Furthermore, he notes that by the term "world," James refers to ways of thinking and systems of values that do not take God's existence and God's claims into account. The worldly disposition is one that places self and the pursuit of pleasures at the center of one's aspirations and activities, and it results in a lifestyle that is largely destructive of persons (3:14-16; 4:1-3).

God, however, has made available another way of viewing and measuring reality. God's word has given us birth (1:18), has been "implanted" in us (1:21); and we can receive it and become "doers of the word" (1:22). Empowered by God's "wisdom from above" (3:17), by the "spirit that God has made to dwell in us" (4:5), we can live out the demands of "the royal law" (2:8; 1:25; 4:12), that is, the law of the kingdom, which is a law of love that directs us beyond self-concern to love of neighbor (2:8).

So which will it be? Will we the readers share the attitudes and values and perceptions of the world? Will we live as though God had no claim on our lives? Or will we embrace the attitudes and values and perceptions of God? Will we acknowledge God's claim on our lives in faith and action as did Abraham (2:23) and be a friend of God? James's target is the "double-minded person" (1:8; 4:8), who wants to be both a friend of the world and a friend of God at the same time—who looks to both God and the world for values and security. But James insists that these two ways of life are simply incompatible; they are mutually exclusive. Indeed, James states rather emphatically that "whoever wishes to be a friend of the world becomes an enemy of God" (4:4). Johnson maintains that this choice, enunciated clearly at the midpoint of James in 3:13—4:10, provides the conceptual framework for the whole letter.

Likewise, Sophie Laws highlights the theocentric nature of James when she suggests that a discernible motive underlies much, if not all, of James's ethical teaching: the motive of the imitation of God (cf. Laws, *SE* 7 [1982]: 299–305). She observes that two themes are juxtaposed throughout the letter. On the one hand, James emphasizes the "singleness," the unity, the constancy, the integrity of God. James affirms, for example, that "God is one" (2:19), and notes in 1:5 that God is a generous and wholehearted giver. Indeed, in 1:17 James underlines the constancy of God's goodness and love: "Every generous act of giving, with every perfect gift, is from above, coming down from the Father of lights, with whom there is no variation or shadow due to change." First-century people observed with keen interest the movements of the heavenly bodies and their waxing and waning. What James affirms is that their creator and governor is exalted above any such change. Unlike the created heavenly bodies that shift in position and are darkened by the shadows of eclipse, God neither changes nor is changed by anything outside God's own self. James notes, moreover, that the singleness of God is also the sanction for obedience to the whole law, for "the one who said 'You shall not commit adultery,' also said, 'You shall not murder' " (2:11); and as there is one lawgiver, so also there is one judge (4:12). James underlines the oneness, the unity of God.

On the other hand, James repeatedly chastises disunity and inconsistency in human behavior. Human creatures are torn apart with conflicting desires (4:1) and therefore lift up ineffective prayers (4:3). They are often plagued by doubt and fail to approach God in a wholehearted manner (1:6-8). Moreover, disunity afflicts human relationships, for James chastises "acts of favoritism," particularly discrimination between the rich and the poor

(2:1-9); failure to carry through word and belief into action (1:22-24; 2:14-26); and the forked tongue, since "with it we bless the Lord and Father, and with it we curse those who are made in the likeness of God" (3:9). Indeed, James's characteristic pejorative adjective is *dipsychos* or "double-minded" (1:8; 4:8), a word found only in this epistle in the NT and unknown in Greek literature. From James's perspective, doubleness is the essence of sin (4:8), and it would appear that James's hope is that readers will achieve a state of wholeness, singleness, or integrity. Laws observes that while these two major themes (the singleness and consistency of God, and the doubleness and inconsistency of humans) are not explicitly connected in the letter, they are juxtaposed. Thus, the imitation of God may well be the motive behind much of James's ethical teaching. Although Christian authors more characteristically emphasize the imitation of Christ as a motive for ethical instruction (John 13:15; 1 Cor. 11:1; 1 Thess 1:6; 1 Peter 2:21), James would not be the only NT author to sound this theme (cf. Eph. 5:1; Matt. 5:48; Luke 6:36; 1 Peter 1:15-16.). Whatever the case may be, Laws's discussion, like Johnson's, demonstrates that James is by no means devoid of theology.

Integrity is a central emphasis of the epistle, implicit in every line. James's hope is for the wholeness and integrity of Christian life. To see that theme embodied in the life of the church is the letter's primary goal as well. James's hope, expressed in the opening verses of the letter, is that readers may be "mature and complete, lacking in nothing" (1:4). James challenges readers to be persons of integrity—consistent in all they see, say, believe, and do. From the first verse to the last, readers are called to behavior consistent with their convictions. Readers are urged to live out their faith. The letter develops this emphasis by means of three principal lines of discussion: faith and works, control of the tongue, and wealth and poverty.

Faith and Works

The Letter of James is best known for its insistence on the inseparable connection between faith and works. It is a central theme that undergirds all the ethical exhortation in the letter. Whether James speaks of ministering to widows and orphans, or meeting the needs of the poor, or resisting discrimination, or controlling the tongue, it speaks of "works"—works that are intrinsically related to faith and are in fact its proper expression.

James has much to say about the relationship between faith and works: "Be doers of the word, and not merely hearers who deceive themselves" (1:22). Or "what good is it, my brothers and sisters, if you say you have faith but do not have works? . . . Faith by itself, if it has no works, is dead" (cf. 2:14-26). But if this is the theme for which the letter is best known, it is also the theme that has gotten it into the most trouble. Consider 2:24, the most controversial verse in the whole letter: "You see that a person is justified by works and not by faith alone." It is words like these, more than anything else, that prompted Luther to say: "I almost feel like throwing Jimmy into the stove."

Luther was concerned, as others too have been, that James here seems to contradict a central biblical affirmation: that of justification by grace through faith alone. James has been frequently accused of standing in direct contradiction to the apostle Paul and to the very heart of Christian faith. In Rom. 3:28, Paul states emphatically that "we hold that a person is justified by faith apart from works prescribed by the law." Indeed, Paul's affirmation that we are brought into right relationship with God by God's grace alone and not by meritorious works sparked the Protestant Reformation in the sixteenth century, and is central to both Protestant and modern Roman Catholic faith. Thus, when the author of James insists that "a person is justified by works and not by faith alone" (2:24), is he not proposing a new way of salvation? Is he not distorting the very heart of Christian faith?

Before one jumps to any such conclusion, one should note that Paul and James addressed themselves to different struggles, and each intends quite different things by "works." On the one hand, Paul addressed himself to the starting point of faith—to the question of how one is brought into right relationship with God. He battled the notion that one must perform meritorious works to earn God's acceptance and approval. The works to which he referred were "works of the law," and included such things as compliance with food laws, circumcision, purification rites, and ritual prescriptions. None of these things, Paul argued, is a requirement for salvation, for salvation is a gracious gift of God, to be accepted by faith alone, apart from any such works of the law. On the other hand, the Letter of James addresses itself not to the initial experience of acceptance by God but to the continuing life of the believer. It does not speak of "works" as meritorious deeds aimed to win God's approval, but rather as the outgrowth or fruit of Christian faith. Moreover, when James speaks of "works," it refers not to "works of the law," legal observances, but to acts of love on the neighbor's behalf. Therefore, works, for James, include such things as the care of widows and orphans, respect for the poor, feeding the hungry, clothing the naked, and control of the tongue. From James's viewpoint, genuine faith cannot exist without producing these kinds of works as the fruit of obedience.

It is also important to note that James insists upon the inseparability of faith and works throughout the discussion in 2:14-26. At no point does it contrast faith and works. Instead, it contrasts two kinds of faith: genuine faith (of which works are a sign) and counterfeit faith (which finds no expression in works and thus cannot really be "faith" at all). Faith, when it is genuine, is inseparable from works, which are its proper expression. Therefore, in 2:14 the reader is not asked "What good is it if you have faith but do not have works?" but rather "What good is it if you *say* you have faith but do not have works?" To James's way of thinking, faith that fails to issue in works is not deserving of the name "faith" at all. Thus, when James insists that "a person is justified by works and not by faith alone," one must bear in mind that James speaks of works that are grounded in faith and are the proper expression of it. James speaks of "faith alone" as counterfeit faith, because it does not produce the fruit of faith. Works by themselves are not saving; they are saving only because they manifest genuine faith.

One final important difference between Paul and James concerns use of the word "justification." When Paul spoke of "justification," his eyes were focused, as we have noted, on the starting point of the Christian life. When the author of James speaks of "justification," however, his eyes are focused on the final judgment. He speaks of "justification" in connection with the last day, when it will be determined whether believers have embodied in their lives the possibilities the gospel offers (cf. Matt. 25:31-46; and the emphasis on eschatological reward and punishment in James 1:9-10, 12; 2:5, 12; 3:1; 4:10, 11-12; 5:1-6, 7-9, 12).

Thus, while their emphases differ and cannot be harmonized, Paul and James do not stand as directly in opposition to each other as they might appear at first glance. James's discussion in 2:14-26 presupposes Paul's theological activity, for it employs Paul's language (faith or *pistis*, works or *erga*, and justification or *dikaiousthai*), Paul's illustration (Abraham; cf. Galatians 3, Romans 4), and Paul's thesis ("faith, not works"). Most scholars concur, however, that James is not responding directly to Paul at all, but rather to an area of the church in which Paul's slogan of "justification by faith" was being used and distorted to argue that "faith alone" was all that counted, without any accompanying moral fruit or transformation of life. Indeed, the author of James does not appear even to have been acquainted with the letters of Paul themselves, for he does not appreciate that the "works" over which Paul struggled were "works of the law," legal observances. He is familiar only with the use and misuse of Paul's slogans, and apparently combats a distorted "Paulinism" that has emerged within the early Christian church.

It is often noted that James fails to scale the heights and depths of Paul's theological vision. That may well be the case. The author of James writes as a teacher and as a moralist, who calls his readers to behavior consistent with their convictions. His voice deserves a continued hearing, for it is a

bulwark against what Bonhoeffer deemed "cheap grace"—a constant reminder that Christians are called to be disciples and that genuine faith finds
expression in a lifestyle that is compatible with one's convictions. An apt
analogy in 2:26 summarizes James's point. The word *pneuma* or "spirit"
(which is found in many English translations of the verse) can also mean
"breath," and this is probably James's intention. Just as breathing is a sign
that the body is alive, so are works a sign that faith is alive. When the
body is without breath, it is a corpse. So faith without works is also dead!

Control of the Tongue

Disciplined speech, one of James's most persistent themes, is also an
important theme in Jewish ethical instruction. Israel's sages recognized
that the tongue has extraordinary power to lift or to destroy, to build or to
maim. James stands squarely in the tradition of Israel's wisdom literature
with its reflection on the power of speech and the evils perpetrated by the
tongue. Consider some of the keen insights about the tongue found in the
writings of Israel's sages:

> When words are many, transgression is not lacking,
>   but the prudent are restrained in speech. (Prov. 10:19)
>
> Rash words are like sword thrusts,
>   but the tongue of the wise brings healing. (Prov. 12:18)
>
> A soft answer turns away wrath,
>   but a harsh word stirs up anger. (Prov. 15:1)
>
> Pleasant words are like a honeycomb,
>   sweetness to the soul and health to the body. (Prov. 16:24)
>
> A fool takes no pleasure in understanding,
>   but only in expressing personal opinion. (Prov. 18:2)
>
> A slip on the pavement is better than a slip of the tongue. (Sir. 20:18)
>
> Many have fallen by the edge of the sword,
>   but not as many as have fallen because of the tongue. (Sir. 28:18)
>
> Make balances and scales for your words,
>   and make a door and a bolt for your mouth.
> Beware lest you err with your tongue. (Sir. 28:25-26)

If one listens to Israel's sages and then turns to James, one will hear
familiar echoes, for James speaks repeatedly of disciplined speech (cf.
1:19, 26; 2:12; 4:11-12; 5:9, 12), and a large central section of this short
letter is devoted entirely to the dangers of the tongue (3:1-12). Of all the
sins by which people stumble, those of the tongue are the most difficult

to avoid. James maintains that disciplined speech, therefore, should be of utmost concern to Christians. In order to impress this upon the reader, the letter sets forth a series of dramatic images in 3:1-12 to illustrate the astonishing potential of the tongue, which exercises a power and influence far out of proportion to its small size. Like the bit in the mouth of a horse, or like a rudder guiding a wind-tossed ship, the tongue also is small in size but great in its effect (3:3-5).

The great power of the tongue can, however, be turned to evil purposes. This potential is clearly at the heart of James's concern for, with a spiraling series of remarkable images, the letter graphically portrays the destructive effect of undisciplined speech. First, the tongue is likened to a fire, which, though small, is capable of wild and far-reaching devastation: "how great a forest is set ablaze by a small fire!" (3:5b). Moreover, James decries it as "placed among our members as a world of iniquity" (3:6)—that is, "it represents among our members the world with all its wickedness" (NEB). Not only does it thus defile the whole body, rendering the individual unclean before God; it also sets on fire the "cycle of nature" or "wheel of birth" (*ho trochos tēs geneseōs*)—a peculiar phrase with which James appears to suggest that the tongue's devastating effect is felt throughout the entire course of human life, from the cradle to the grave (3:6). And no one can tame it! James underscores the inability of humans to discipline their speech. Although human beings, who have been given dominion over the earth (Genesis 1), exercise mastery over the whole animal world, they cannot master their own unruly tongues (James 3:7-8). The tongue alone is beyond control. Indeed, it is "a restless evil, full of deadly poison," akin to the venomous tongue of a snake (3:8). James sharply censures the duplicity that characterizes the forked human tongue (3:9-12), thereby calling readers to restore integrity and discipline to Christian speech.

James's imagery is severe and exaggerated to be sure—the better to impress upon the reader the dangerous potential of uncontrolled speech. Dramatic, exaggerated language and illustration are employed here and at many points throughout the letter to grasp the reader's attention, to make an impression, and to goad into action (cf. 1:2; 2:2-4, 15-16). Thus, the graphic language in 3:1-12 should not be pressed too literally. The language is that of hyperbole, and its intended effect is to exhort the readers to make every effort to check the dangerous potential of their tongues—to do exactly what is said to be impossible to do. From James's perspective, change is possible for believers, else the author would not have expended so much energy on this topic of disciplined speech. One will not accomplish change, however, by one's own efforts alone, but in reliance upon the wisdom and power of God, to whom James points in the opening verses of the letter— the God who "gives to all generously and ungrudgingly" that we may be "mature and complete" (1:4-5). Here and throughout the letter, the author of James maintains that God's grace in Jesus Christ comes to us not only as mercy but also as power for renewed and transformed life.

Rich and Poor

In addition to faith and works, and disciplined speech, a third principal line of discussion is interwoven throughout the letter: James speaks pointedly and vigorously about economic realities. The letter manifests deep sympathy for "the poor" (cf. 1:9-11, 27; 2:1-7, 15-16; 5:1-6). Moreover, one gets the distinct impression that the author is not positively inclined toward "the rich." For example, 1:9-11 issues a warning against the transient nature of riches; 2:6-7 disparages the rich as oppressors of the poor; and in 5:1-6, there may be no doubt about the author's animosity, for he unleashes his fury in fierce denunciations. The rich are invited to "weep and wail" for the miseries that are coming upon them, and in harsh, graphic language reminiscent of the OT prophets, they are warned of the disasters that surely await them on the judgment day.

What is one to make of this emphasis? Two questions have dominated the scholarly discussion of wealth and poverty in James, and are central for interpretation. First, does James use the concept "poor" (*ptōchos*) as an economic description or as a spiritual designation? Many scholars point out that by the time the letter was written, poverty had become a religious concept. As a result of Israel's experience of downfall, exile, and Hellenistic invasion, "poor" and "pious" merged as parallel concepts. The "piety of the poor" was then nourished in the language of the Psalms (cf. Pss. 69:32-33; 86:1-2; 113:7-8.), the prophets (cf. Isa. 41:17; 49:13; 61:1ff.; Amos 2:6-7; 5:10-13; 8:4-6; Ezek. 16:49), and the intertestamental literature (Sir. 4:1-10; 13:2-8; *1 Enoch* 94–105; 108:7-15; *Psalms of Solomon* 5, 10, 15, 18). Jewish "piety of the poor" is also encountered at Qumran (1QpHab 12:3ff.; 6QD 6:16ff.; 1QM 14:7), and found a continuing heritage in the preaching of Jesus (cf. Luke 6:20-21, 24-25; 12:13-21; 16:19-31; Mark 10:25, 28-30). Thus, Dibelius, one of the chief representatives of this view, maintains that the statements in James about the rich and the poor "show our author to be an energetic representative of the ancient, recently revitalized pride of the Poor" (Dibelius, 45).

Other commentators, however, insist that James's language must not be spiritualized (and rendered palatable) in this manner. After all, the letter speaks pointedly of lawsuits, discrimination, business practice, the withholding of wages from agricultural laborers, oppression, anger, and envy. Such references suggest that the author is deeply concerned about the great gulf between the rich and the poor with all of its attendant problems, and that he addresses readers who have in fact experienced economic hardship at the hands of the rich. It may not be necessary, however, to take an either/ or position on this matter. The letter of James may draw on a conventional equation of poverty and piety. As Sophie Laws observes, however, "it is arguable that the tradition of the poor as the righteous was most fervently maintained by those who were in fact actually poor" (Laws, *Epistle of James*, 7–8). "James's language may, then, give some indication of the social situation or social attitudes of himself and his readers" (ibid., 9).

The second question that has dominated discussion is the question of whether "the rich" of whom James speaks are Christians. In 5:1-6, for example, is the author of James attacking wealthy members of the Christian community? The letter does not say. But a great deal of ink has been spilled discussing this question, and scholars tend to agree that he is probably not. It is doubtful that "the rich people" he censures were Christians. In each of the three texts in which "the rich" (*hoi plousioi*) are mentioned (1:9-11; 2:6-7; 5:1-6), they appear to be regarded as "outsiders"—people who are not members of the Christian community. There is no attempt to influence the rich. James's condemnation is absolute. There is no call to repentance.

More than likely, the Christians with whom the author of James was familiar were largely from the lower end of the economic spectrum. Indeed, the harsh warning to rich oppressors in 5:1-6 appears to be an apostrophe (a literary device in which people who are not present are personally addressed). In other words, at this point in the letter the author flings open a window of the sanctuary and begins to shout toward the manor house: "Come now, you rich people, weep and wail for the miseries that are coming to you." In 5:7 he resumes his address to the Christian congregation: "Be patient, therefore, beloved, until the coming of the Lord." A number of scholars suspect, then, that the harsh words of condemnation in 5:1-6 aim to give comfort and consolation to people who were on the low side economically and who seem to have experienced hardship at the hands of the rich (cf. 2:6-7). Of course, these words also serve as a word of warning to them about the danger of riches.

Thus, it may be no coincidence that James's first words on poverty and riches in 1:9-11 are juxtaposed to words about experiences of trial (1:2-4, 12-18). Economic hardship may have been among the chief trials with which most of James's first readers struggled. Still, there were probably some people of means within these congregations. Small merchants, for example, appear to be addressed in 4:13-17—though interestingly, they are not designated as "the rich." Moreover, it does appear from 2:1-7 that rich visitors were beginning to frequent worship services—indeed they were being fawned over—and the author feared this development. He chastises them harshly for such discriminatory behavior. Some scholars argue that paraenetical illustrations such as one finds in 2:1-7 should not be pressed for historical connections; but illustrations, to be effective, must bear some relation to the readers' actual experience.

James's reflections on wealth and poverty are not the easiest of words for many North American Christians to ponder. Still, this emphasis represents one of James's most relevant themes. James continues to remind its readers that Christian faith affects not only one's personal and private life but also one's social life and perspectives. Furthermore, James reminds us that God wills justice for the poor and hears the cries of the oppressed. Martin Luther King Jr. once observed that "any religion that professes to be concerned with the souls of men [and women] and is not concerned with the slums that damn them, the economic conditions that strangle them, and the social conditions that cripple them is a dry-as-dust religion." It is an observation much in the spirit of James. "Faith by itself, if it has no works, is dead" (2:17).

Structure

The structure of James is a puzzle that continues to be a matter of scholarly debate. While James begins as a typical Hellenistic letter with a statement of sender, recipient, and a greeting (1:1), this is its only standard epistolary feature. There is no thanksgiving or closing statement; and the body of the "letter" consists of loosely connected admonitions (in 1:2-26 and 5:7-20) and short essays or *topoi*—that is, extended paraenetical statements focused on particular themes (in 2:1-13; 2:14-26; 3:1-12; 3:13—4:12; 4:13—5:6). As we noted in the opening paragraphs, James is paraenesis, or ethical exhortation, in the guise of a letter. But the overall structure of James's counsel is by no means self-evident.

Can any plan or logical progression of thought be discerned? Some scholars maintain that the letter evidences no continuity of thought, and that this, in fact, is the nature of paraenesis—it should not be pressed too hard for a logical, orderly progression of thought. Other scholars, however, have tried to discover an overarching plan. Various proposals have been proffered, yet none has won a significant following. The continuing discussion suggests, however, that James may have more order and structure than appears at first glance. It is possible, for example, that chapter 1, which consists mainly of loosely connected aphorisms and which seems especially dense and disconnected, might in some sense be a table of contents for the whole letter. As several scholars have noted, themes announced in chapter 1 are elaborated upon in the chapters that follow. The theme of trials, for example, announced in 1:2-4, 12-15, reappears in 5:7-11; the theme of rich and poor announced in 1:9-11 is resumed in 4:13—5:6; the theme of disciplined speech announced in 1:19-21, 26 is elaborated upon in 3:1-12; the theme of doing the word announced in 1:22-26 is focal in 2:14-26; and the theme of true wisdom, announced in 1:5-8, 16-18 is sounded again in 3:13—4:10. Continued work in rhetorical criticism, which draws parallels between the NT and Greco-Roman rhetoric, promises to shed further light on the puzzle of the structure of James.

Postscript

Multicultural voices enrich one's reading of this long-neglected letter and demonstrate how relevant it can be. Cain Hope Felder of Howard University, for example, in his book *Troubling Biblical Waters: Race, Class, and Family*, observes that James 2:1-13 provides what is perhaps the NT's strongest castigation of class discrimination—or for that matter, any discrimination based on outward appearance—and that these words have particular pertinence for African Americans who still experience such discrimination daily (Felder, 118–19). Likewise, Elsa Tamez, a Mexican scholar, highlights James's contemporary relevance when she observes that if the Letter of James were sent to the Christian communities of Latin America today, it would probably be intercepted and censored by the national security forces in certain countries. Why? She suspects that it would be branded as subversive because of the paragraphs that vehemently denounce exploitation of workers by landowners (5:1-6) and the carefree life of merchants (4:13-17). Moreover, she suspects that the passage that affirms that "pure, unspoilt religion in the eyes of God our Father is this: coming to the help of orphans and widows when they need it, and keeping oneself uncontaminated by the world" (1:27) would be criticized as "reductionism" of the gospel or as Marxist-Leninist propaganda (Tamez, 1). Indeed, she maintains that the problem is that James has been intercepted and censored throughout Christian history—branded as theologically inferior, an epistle of straw.

But as Peter Rhea Jones has observed, if one attends carefully to this letter, James "could actually bring off a renewing of the Christian life. There will be a recurring temptation to tame the powerful social message of this flaming letter, to domesticate it and calm its biting, all too relevant message into palatable terms. If the message of James is allowed to go out unmuffled, it will rattle the stained glass windows" (Jones, "Approaches to the Study of James," *Rev Exp* 66 [1969]: 426). We Christians would do well to chew on that straw together, giving thanks for the opportunities that James sets before us to enter ever more fully into the experience of God's grace.

GERHARD KRODEL

1 PETER

The Purpose of the Letter

What did the author intend to accomplish when he sent this circular letter to Christians in five provinces of Asia Minor? In 5:12 he tells us that his purpose was twofold. One, he wanted to exhort (encourage, console) them. Two, he wanted to "testify [to them] that this is the true grace of God"; and he added an imperative: "stand fast in it." His letter was meant to communicate exhortation, encouragement, and consolation, on the basis of the grace of God, to Christians under duress. Mere exhortations would not suffice. Exhortations need to be grounded. They must be based on a reason, or reasons, why one should behave in one way and not in another. In 1 Peter, the exhortations are grounded in God's call to a new life and above all in God's supreme new deed, the death and resurrection of Jesus Christ and in the ultimate future that will reveal the glory of Christ and of his followers who are now the objects of defamation and persecution. Moreover, Scripture, the example of Christ, and the will of God undergird the exhortations of this letter and offer reasons why Christians should conduct themselves in the manner set forth by the author. In short, the exhortations of this letter are grounded "in the true grace of God" (5:12).

The author's testimony to the grace of God is a testimony to the God of all grace (5:10) whose foreknowledge (1:2) spans the ages (1:20). The prophets of the OT had already spoken about "the grace that was to be yours" (1:10). His grace is present (1:2; 5:12) with his elect people, who are sanctified by the Spirit (1:2), reborn to "a living hope" (1:3), a hope set "upon the grace that is coming to you at the revelation of Jesus Christ" (1:13). Christian husbands and wives are "joint heirs of the grace of life," both now and forever (3:7). God's grace manifests itself in the believers' lives as they bear undeserved suffering. "It is grace" when a person, suffering unjustly, bears afflictions because his or her conscience and commitment are grounded in God (2:19, 20; Greek *dia syneidesin theou*; the NRSV translates *charis* with "credit" and "approval"; cf. Luke 6:32, 33). For Paul, God's grace is his power "made perfect in weakness" (2 Cor. 12:9). For Peter, God "gives grace to the humble" (5:5) and this grace finds expression in the endurance of undeserved suffering, which is acknowledged as "grace before God" (2:20). God's gracious "power" guards his people in the present for the salvation to come (1:5), and therefore in his salutation the author wishes that God's grace "may abound" among the recipients of his letter (1:2). He recalls for his readers that "each has received a gift of grace" from God (Greek *charisma*) and hence they are "stewards of God's manifold grace" (4:10). Until the future grace is revealed at Christ's parousia, the believers live by faith and hope, grounded in God's redemptive act through Christ (1:18-21; 2:24-25; 3:18-22). They are a new people, God's alternative to society around them, and their mission is to "proclaim the mighty acts of him who called you out of darkness into his marvelous light" (2:9).

Therefore, they live like "aliens and exiles" within their own pagan culture, and yet in this culture they must live. No withdrawal into a desert community that is cut off from the world! But simultaneously they must retain the new life and "conduct in Christ" (3:16). There is to be no cultural assimilation. The people of God may not become society on Sunday. Therefore, the author wrote his letter of exhortation, encouragement, and consolation, grounding his exhortations in God's grace in its past, present, and future dimensions. He draws a sharp line between what they formerly were and what they are now: formerly, "you were no people, but now you are God's people" (2:10); formerly, you lived in "ignorance" (1:14), in the "futile ways inherited from your ancestors" (1:18), which expressed themselves in various vices, from licentiousness to idolatry (4:3). But now you have been "born anew" individually (1:3) and corporately you are "the people of God" with a mission (2:9-10). Just as God makes his assault upon the world through the mission of his people, just so the world makes its assault upon the people of God and tribulations are a consequence for them. Local hostility, defamation, and undeserved suffering are the lot of the people of God, and hence they are like aliens within their own society. The author of this letter seeks to act against the debilitating effects of unjust suffering as well as against the temptation to assimilate in order to avoid suffering. He therefore exhorts his readers to maintain nonconformity with their culture (4:3-4) no matter what the consequences might be. The distinctive Christian faith, hope, and identity may not be compromised or surrendered.

Simultaneously, the author exhorts them to "do good" within the structures of society, including bearing unjust suffering in accordance with Christ's example, or to follow Sarah's example (2:18—3:7). Even a pagan society, though it exhibits vices and idolatry, is aware that vices ought to be avoided and that "doing good" is what ought to be. "Doing good" means conducting oneself in accordance with the will of God (2:15). Their good deeds may even be noticed by their pagan neighbors (2:12) and may lead them to "glorify God on the day of visitation" (2:12). Good conduct may lead to the conversion of unbelievers (3:2), because deeds often speak louder than words. In short, believers can fulfill some, not all, conventional expectations by "doing good" (2:15; cf. 4:4).

The exhortations of 1 Peter are supported by the doctrine of judgment according to works (1:17; cf. 4:17-18; Rom. 2:6-11; 14:10-12; 2 Cor. 5:10; Gal. 6:7-8). The final judgment discloses whether Christian freedom was used as a "pretext for evil" (2:16) or as an opportunity for "doing good." The imperative: "conduct yourselves with reverent fear" (toward God) indicates that the Father is also the judge (1:17-21). Reverent fear is not terror in view of the impending judgment, but reverence and awe toward him whom humans do not control. It is the opposite of the arrogance which takes for granted that he will forgive us, because that is his business. "Stand fast" in God's grace (5:12). This exhortation receives its urgency because the end was believed to be imminent and the final judgment was already beginning (1:5; 4:5, 7, 17). Signs of the final judgment, which begins with the people of God, are the messianic woes that they are already experiencing (4:12-19). Therefore the author's witness to God's grace and his exhortations are also, in part, consolation to Christians facing the "fiery ordeal" (4:12). The author consoles them not only by recalling God's gracious acts and their new identity, but by connecting their suffering with Christ's passion and vindication, and with his glory in which they will share. This letter, by witnessing to God's grace, lays the foundation for exhortation, encouragement, and consolation.

The Greek verb *parakalein* (2:11; 5:1) can mean to encourage, to exhort, to console, and so on (see BAGD, 617). One encourages a person to continue to do what he or she is doing (e.g., "stand fast" in the grace of God, 5:12). One exhorts someone who is, or might contemplate, doing what is not right, telling that person to do the right thing (e.g., "stand fast . . ."). One consoles those who suffer by offering them a new perspective; consolation is effective especially if the speaker also suffers (cf. 5:1). "Stand fast" in the grace of God can also be heard as consolation. To some degree it will depend on the readers whether they perceive 1 Peter primarily as consolation, exhortation, or encouragement. To some degree! Not everything in this letter can be understood in terms of consolation (e.g., 2:11).

Content and Structure

In his commentary on 1 Peter, J. Ramsey Michaels identified the genre of this letter as "an apocalyptic diaspora letter to 'Israel' " (XLVI–XLIX). Just as the prophet Jeremiah had sent a letter to the exiles in Babylon (Jer. 29:1-23), so 1 Peter is addressed to the "exiles of the Diaspora" of Asia

Minor. But a "Diaspora letter" is not a literary genre. A letter's type is dependent on its content, not its destination. The content of 1 Peter deals with exhortation. Letters of exhortation and advice played an important role in Greek moral instruction, as Stanley Stowers has shown (91–151). Such letters can include warning, encouragement, praise, admonition, and consolation. They can make use of examples to be followed or to be avoided. The frequent use of imperatives, the presence of "I exhort you" (2:11; 5:1, 12), the instructions on conduct given to different groups, to slaves, wives, husbands, elders, and young people (2:18—3:7; 5:1-5), the general exhortations for good behavior in the world (2:13-17; 3:8-12) and within the community of believers (4:7-11), the teaching on unjust suffering (3:13-17; 4:12-19), and the use of positive and negative examples for conduct (2:21-23; 3:5-6; 4:3-5) all indicate that 1 Peter is a letter of exhortation.

As a letter of exhortation 1 Peter uses quite a few imperatives. But the RSV and NRSV, together with other modern translations and commentaries, frequently translate adverbial participles as imperatives, provided the context does not forbid it (e.g., 1:8). An example of the translation of Greek participles with English imperatives occurs at 1:13. The NRSV reads: "Therefore prepare your minds for action [Greek participle; English imperative]; discipline yourselves [Greek participle; English imperative]; set all your hope on the grace . . . [imperative in Greek and English]." It is generally held that in 1 Peter many Greek adverbial participles are imperative equivalents. This state of affairs is believed to be the result either of poor style, or of an ellipsis of the imperative of "to be" (BDF, para. 468) or of the Hellenistic development of Greek (thus Moulton), or of the influence of rabbinic Hebrew (thus Daube). With Troy Martin, I hold that Greek adverbial participles are not substitutes for imperatives but are subordinate to the main verb. For example, in 1:13 the two participles are subordinate to the imperative "set your hope" and I would translate: "Therefore [referring to 1:3-12] *since* you have prepared your minds for action, *since* you are alert, set your hope completely on the grace that will be brought to you when Jesus Christ is revealed." Adverbial participles are rather vague; instead of "since" one could also translate "if," or "as," but participles should not be understood as imperatival equivalents.

When a participle is used adverbially then it is not preceded by an article. It modifies some other verb in the sentence and should be translated by an appropriate adverbial clause, which is to be deduced from the context. The context implies whether an adverbial participle is the equivalent of (1) a final clause (e.g., Acts 3:26, "in order to bless you"), or (2) a causal clause (e.g., Acts 12:3), or (3) a temporal clause (e.g., Matt. 14:14), or (4) a conditional clause (e.g., Gal. 6:9), or (5) a concessive clause (e.g., Acts 13:28). Moreover, adverbial participles may denote means, or manner, or attendant circumstances (e.g., Matt. 6:27; Acts 2:13; Luke 4:15). In short, adverbial participles are somewhat ambiguous, but the general consensus that they can function as substitutes for imperatives, especially in 1 Peter, should not be maintained. The hearer or reader who meets such participles *prior to the leading verb* would hardly understand them as imperatives (see 1:13, 14, 22; 2:1, 4, etc., where participles *precede* imperatives). If the author had intended these participles to be understood as imperatives then he would have had to add the imperative of *eimi* ("to be"). Lauri Thurén's suggestion that the ambiguity of the adverbial participles results from the author addressing two different social groups in this letter does not solve the problem, because, in distinction from Troy Martin, he still accepts the idea of participles as imperative equivalents.

An example of the confusion in translations, introduced by the notion that participles can be surrogates for imperatives, occurs in 2:1-5. Verse 2 and probably also verse 5 contain Greek imperatives ("long for" the pure milk; "let yourselves be built" into a spiritual house). The two participles, "having put away" (v. 1) and "having come" (v. 4), are also translated in the NRSV as imperatives, just as in the commentary of Brox and others, for a total of *four* imperatives in these verses. At the other extreme the KJV and the commentaries by Kelly and Davids have only *one* imperative (v. 2), though at other times Kelly and Davids also interpret participles as imperatives. The commentary by Michaels and the NIV translate the participle of verse 1 as imperative, but not the participle of verse 4 (!), thus having *two* imperatives in this section. Furthermore, they translate the verb in verse 5 as an indicative, not as an imperative, as is probable (thus Bigg, et al.). To complete the confusion caused by these participles, Bo Reike's commentary has *three* imperatives in 2:1-5.

It is hoped that a second edition of the NRSV would at least indicate where participles are translated as imperatives. I would hold that such translations do not properly relate adverbial participles to explicit imperatives. Such participles indicate the attendant circumstances, conditions, and causes for fulfilling the imperatives. Greek imperatives in 1 Peter occur in:

1:13 (set all your hope)
1:15 (be holy yourselves in all your conduct)
1:17 (conduct yourselves with reverent fear)
1:22 (love one another earnestly)
2:2 (long for the pure spiritual milk)
2:5 (let yourselves be built into a spiritual house)
2:13 (be subject to every human creature [rather than "institution"])
2:17 (honor all people, love the brother- and sisterhood, fear God, honor the emperor)

3:3 (let not yours be the outward adorning)
3:10 (let him keep his tongue)
3:11 (let him turn away from evil . . . let him do good . . . let him seek peace . . . let him pursue it)
3:14 (have no fear . . . nor be intimidated)
3:15 (in your hearts sanctify Christ as Lord)
4:1 (arm yourselves with the same insight)
4:7 (be sober-minded and be self-controlled)
4:12 (do not be surprised at the fiery ordeal)
4:13 (but rejoice . . .)
4:15 (let none of you suffer as a murderer)
4:16 (let him not be ashamed, but . . . let him glorify God)
4:19 (let those who suffer . . . entrust themselves to a faithful creator)
5:2 (tend the flock of God)
5:5 (submit to [the authority of] the elders)
5:6 (humble yourselves therefore under the mighty hand of God)
5:8 (be self-controlled, be watchful)
5:9 (resist him)
5:12 (stand fast in it [the grace of God])
5:14 (Greet one another)

The reader may choose to underline the above imperatives in her or his NT, because the imperatives determine the structure of the sections and subsections of this exhortation. Space does not permit a thorough argument as to why participles are not surrogates for imperatives nor to show how translations of particular participles in 1 Peter differ from each other. We now turn to the structure of this letter.

Like other letters in the NT, 1 Peter begins with a *prescript* (1:1-2), followed not by a thanksgiving but by a *blessing* (1:3-12), as in Ephesians. The prescript as well as the blessing set forth themes that are elaborated in the body of the letter (e.g., the theme of suffering in 1:6-7 and then in 2:18—3:6; 4:12-19) and clarify the identity of the persons addressed. They are elected, chosen, and destined by God, sanctified by his Spirit, and cleansed by the blood of Christ for a definite purpose, namely, for obedience to Jesus Christ (1:1-2). Moreover, their identity is based on a new birth, which entails both membership in a new family as well as a living hope grounded in the resurrection of Christ from the dead (1:3). This hope looks forward to receiving an indestructible inheritance, the salvation that is to be revealed in "the last time" (1:4-5, 8-9). Simultaneously, in sharp contrast to their status as the chosen people of God with a glorious future, the people addressed exist as "exiles of the Dispersion" (1:1) in five provinces of Asia Minor. They live by faith, not by sight (1:8), and experience suffering caused by various trials "for a little while" (1:6). Through suffering, the genuineness of their faith is tested (cf. Wis. 3:5-6a; Sir. 2:5). Only "in the last time" (1:5), "when Jesus Christ is revealed" (1:7), then their faith, tested by trials, will "result in praise and glory and honor" (1:7). Even the prophets of old foretold this pattern of suffering and subsequent glory with respect to Christ and for the benefit of believers (1:10-12). Since the prophets spoke "by the Spirit of Christ," prophesying "of the grace that was to be yours," our author regarded the OT as a witness to Christ and to the Christian faith. The citations, allusions, and use of phrases from the OT in 1 Peter are grounded in the author's conviction that the Spirit of Christ was present in the prophets of old.

The prescript and the blessing (1:1-12) serve as introduction to what follows. In the past, the addressees have received a new birth from God. Their new status gives them a new identity (and family) and a new hope (1:3) for the ultimate future. In the present, however, they are confronted by suffering (1:6), to which they must respond in faith, hope, and love. Both faith and hope are related to their future vindication. "The outcome of your faith is the salvation of your souls" (1:9). God's power guards them in the present "through faith for a salvation" yet to be revealed (1:5).

With the first imperative the *theme* of this exhortation is stated in 1:13. The conjunction "therefore" connects this verse with the blessing of 1:3-12 and draws an inference. Because of their dialectical status as people who are reborn, who are not made of the stuff the world is made of, and who simultaneously must live like exiles in the world and suffer under the pressures of the world, our author exhorts them: "Therefore, as [or 'if'] you have prepared your minds for action, as ['if'] you are self-controlled, *set your hope* completely on the grace that Jesus Christ will bring you when he is revealed." Grace refers to the future salvation, to the indestructible inheritance of glory yet to come (1:4, 9), and hope is what must be maintained in the present. The note of "grace" is sounded twice at the end of the letter and forms an inclusion with 1:13. "The God of all grace who has called you (chosen you) for his eternal glory in Christ will himself restore, support, strengthen and establish you" (literally, "give you a foundation"; 5:10). The last imperative in this exhortation (prior to the greeting; 5:14) is also related to "grace," just like the first: this letter is written "to testify that this is the true grace of God. *Stand fast in it.*"

The body of the letter (1:14—5:12) can be divided into the following sections:

1. 1:14—2:10: The Household of God

Five metaphors indicate the identity of believers as members of the household or temple of God; five imperatives exhort them to appropriate conduct; and five reasons are given why they should heed the exhortations. In short, this section states *who* the believers are; *what* they must do; and *why* they should do it.

a. 1:14-16. Believers are "obedient children" of God. As such they do not conform to the passions that they "formerly had in ignorance." But (first reason) because God who called them "is holy," therefore the exhortation applies to them: "be holy yourselves in all your conduct." A second reason for this imperative lies in the scriptural warrant of Lev. 11:44-45.

b. 1:17-21. Believers have God "as Father" of the household and they "invoke" him. This Father, however, is not a grand old man in heaven who lets sleeping dogs lie and does not bother. Rather he is the one "who judges all people impartially according to their deeds" (cf. Matt. 16:27; 25:31-46; Rom. 2:5-10, 16; 14:10; 2 Cor. 5:10; 2 Thess. 1:5-10; 2 Tim. 2:14). Hence the exhortation: "Conduct yourselves with reverent fear during the time of your exile." The reason for such conduct is known to them (1:18-21). They have been "ransomed . . . with the precious blood of Christ." He has paid the price for their new status. His salvific action is the reason why they should conduct themselves "in reverent fear" toward their Father and judge. The result of Christ's death and resurrection is that their "faith and hope are set on God." For the Christology of this subsection see the section on traditions below.

c. 1:22-25. Believers have "purified" their souls from hypocritical love by "obedience to the truth," that is, by accepting the word of God in faithful obedience. As children of God's family they are a new sister- and brotherhood. Hence the exhortation: "love one another deeply from the heart" (1:22). The basis and reason for such love is their new birth, accomplished through the word of God (1:23). Reciprocal love in God's family is the horizontal implementation of their new status effected vertically by God's word. His "living and enduring word" (1:23) prompted the author to quote from Isa. 40:6-9, which contrasts frail, mortal human nature with "the word of the Lord" that abides forever. He added his interpretation: "that word is the good news that was announced to you" (1:25) and accepted in "obedience" (1:22).

d. 2:1-3. "Having put away all malice, guile, and hypocrisy," believers, "like newborn infants," are in need of nourishment and growth. Hence the exhortation: "long for the pure, spiritual milk," which refers to spiritual nourishment through hearing the word of God, through worship, instruction, and the like. They should "long for" it, just as babies long for their mother's milk. The purpose of such longing is growth toward and into the ultimate future; that through God's word "you may grow into salvation."

What is striking in this subsection is a list of vices connected with newborn infants (2:1-2). But we should remember that "newborn infants" is a metaphor applied to adult members of the church. The author, however, insists that the imperative "long for" (spiritual nourishment) can be fulfilled only if the vices enumerated in 2:1 have been "put away" by them. The rationale for the imperative, "long for," interestingly enough, contains a condition: "if indeed you have tasted that the Lord is good" (Ps. 34:8, as adapted by the author). This condition links up with the participle of 2:1. If the addressees have not put away all malice and so forth, if they have not experienced the kindness of the Lord, the imperative "long for" (spiritual nourishment) would be inappropriate for them. Finally, verse 4, which is connected to verse 3 by a Greek relative pronoun, will make clear that "the Lord" of verse 3 is Christ and that the Greek *chrestos ho kyrios* is a play on words.

e. 2:4-10. The previous subsection spoke of the spiritual growth of individual believers. Attention now turns to the community and its growth under the metaphor of building the "spiritual house" of God, which is his true temple. The notion that the people of God themselves are the true spiritual house, the temple of God, has antecedents in Judaism (1QS 8:5-10; 9:3-6). Moreover, the citation of Isa. 28:16 in verse 6 (also used in v. 4) attracted two other "stone" passages, Ps. 118:22 (used in vv. 4 and 7) and Isa. 8:14 (used in v. 8). Probably our author himself made this threefold combination of texts (cf. Rom. 9:33; 10:11) and he added his interpretation. It is interesting to note that this subsection does not polemicize against the Jews. Christ, "the living stone," who in God's sight is "chosen and precious," is said to be rejected not by Jews but "by men" in general (Greek *hypo anthrōpon;* NRSV "by mortals," in the light of 1:24). His rejection by men does not disgrace him; it disgraces them (2:8). The OT already knew that some people would "stumble" and "fall" on account of Christ, because they "disobey the word." Even their disobedience occurred according to God's grand design (2:8c). His purpose is not negated by human rejection.

"As you come to him, to that living stone, rejected by people" (2:4) but precious in God's sight, you, who are reborn and therefore are "living stones," must hear the exhortation, given in the form of an imperative passive: "Permit yourselves to be built into a spiritual house." Its purpose is: "to be a holy body of priests" (Elliott) that offers "spiritual sacrifices acceptable to God through Jesus Christ." Our author does not indicate what he meant by that expression. But his emphasis on holiness in daily conduct (1:15-16; cf. Rom. 12:1), on prayer (3:7c, 12b; 4:7), on glorifying God (4:16; cf. 2:12), and on the true beauty of the inner self (3:4) would seem to include these among the spiritual sacrifices as well as the proclamation of the mighty acts of God (2:9). Their spiritual worship is acceptable to God "through Jesus Christ."

The rationale why believers should "let themselves be built" into God's spiritual temple is found in Scripture (v. 6). In quoting from Isa. 28:16, that God is laying a precious and chosen cornerstone (which is Christ) in Zion and that "whoever believes in him will not be put to shame," our author states the reason why believers should permit God to incorporate them into his spiritual temple. In verse 7 he contrasts them with the unbelievers, with those builders who rejected the very stone that "has become the head of the corner" (Ps. 118:22). Adding from the "stone" saying of Isa. 8:14-15 he concluded that unbelievers "stumble because they disobey the word, as they were destined to do" by God (v. 8).

The last two verses (2:9-10) apply attributes and titles of honor, once reserved for Israel, to the community of believers in Christ. The verses announce the identity of the church, "a chosen race [chosen by God], a royal priesthood [belonging to God the king], a holy nation [set apart by God who is holy], God's own people" (his treasured possession; see Isa. 43:20-21; Exod. 19:5-6; 23:22 LXX; cf. Rev. 1:6; 5:10). Their task is to proclaim and sound the praise of God's mighty acts in word and deed (cf. Isa. 42:12) and they are reminded of their past. "Once [they] were no people" (cf. Hos. 1:6-9; 2:23), but now they are "God's people." The reason for their new identity has already been stated: they have been ransomed by "the precious blood" of the lamb "without blemish or spot" (1:19; cf. Isa. 53:7; Exod. 12:5). The metaphors of verses 9-10 highlight the identity as well as the election and holiness of the community of believers in Christ.

2. 2:11—3:12: Ethics for Exiles Within the Structures of This World

This section begins and ends with exhortations addressed to *all* believers (2:11-15; 3:8-12). Sandwiched in between are *specific* groups—slaves, wives, and husbands—who are addressed directly (2:18—3:7). But before they are addressed the author announces the theme of this section (2:15-16), which is expounded in the following three examples.

a. 2:11-15. In stark contrast to their exalted status in the sight of God (2:9-10) is their status in the world, where they are like strangers in their own land, like exiled Israel in Babylonia. The word translated "aliens" refers to resident aliens who have settled down; "exiles" means temporary aliens, such as visiting foreigners with no permanent home in the land. Both metaphors depict the transitoriness of Christian existence on earth. The direct address "beloved" signals the beginning of a new section (cf.

4:11) which contains two exhortations. The first is introduced with "I exhort you" (Greek *parakalō*) followed by an infinitive; some Greek manuscripts have an imperative (p 72, A, C), which does not change the meaning of the sentence but would rescue the author from a grammatical slip. (An infinitive would require *echontas,* accusative.) "I exhort you (to) abstain from the desires of the flesh that wage war against your soul." These passions, or desires, may include sexual sins but may just as well refer to different forms of self-centeredness such as arrogance. How does one abstain from those desires? By "maintaining good conduct" (participle) among the Gentiles. Note that the identity of the church, as the people of God, requires that, from the theological perspective of this letter, those outside the church's boundary are considered to be "the Gentiles" even though the sociological background of the letter's recipients was gentile, not Jewish (cf. 1:14b, 18; 4:2-4). The motivation for abstaining from negative expressions of behavior and for maintaining good conduct is found in verse 12b. Should outsiders malign Christians, the author hopes that the good conduct of Christians may be recognized even by them (cf. Matt. 5:16). The accusers themselves might see that their accusations are false—on the basis of the believers' good conduct rather than their preaching—and they might join the praise of God, if not now, then "on the day of visitation," which is the day when the final salvation and judgment are revealed (cf. 1:5; 4:17).

The second exhortation is: "Submit to every human creature" (2:13). I understand the Greek word *ktisis* to mean "creature," rather than "institution" (thus NRSV; NIV: "every authority instituted among men"). The context does not speak of institutions but of people. Just as believers should "submit to *every* human creature" (2:13), just so they are commanded: "Honor *all* human beings" (2:17). The rationale for submitting to everyone is stated at once: "for the sake of the Lord" (2:13). This Lord is Jesus Christ (cf. 2:3; 3:15). He submitted by bearing our sins in his body on the tree (2:24) and leaving an example for all Christians to follow (2:21). Verse 15 gives a second reason: "*For* it is God's will that by doing good you should put to silence the ignorance of the foolish." Doing good includes submitting to those who occupy a higher station on the social ladder, be it "the emperor" or "governors." It is understood that such submission is not absolute. For instance, should emperor worship be demanded, then "doing good" would mean "resisting the devil" (5:8-9; cf. Acts 5:29). Here, however, the point is that Christians should be good citizens and obey the laws of their rulers rather than exhibit obnoxious behavior. They should conduct themselves in such a way that they can show false accusations against them to be charges made by foolish people. If their good conduct is not acknowledged in the present time, then it will be "on the day of visitation" (2:12).

b. 2:16-17. The theme for the following subsections is stated by the introduction of the new metaphor "as free persons." Troy Martin has shown that the domestic code of 2:18—3:6 depends grammatically on the imperatives of 2:17 (200–206). His translation of 2:16-17, slightly adapted, reads: "As free persons, and not as persons who use their freedom as pretext for evil, but as persons who are slaves of God, honor all people" (201). He also points out that the contrast in verse 16 is not between free persons and slaves of God, but between free persons who are slaves of God and those who misuse freedom in terms of license. Only slaves of God are free persons and vice versa. This, however, means that the now popular social interpretation of "free persons" misses the point. The following subsection unfolds the code for Christian slaves, who by definition are not socially free people. Yet theologically they too are free men and free women if they are "slaves of God," who fear, love, and trust in God above all else. Verse 17 contains four imperatives. The first, "honor all people," is an aorist imperative, which, according to Martin, dominates the other three present-tense imperatives. "They are subsidiary ideas of the command to honor all" (204). I doubt this interpretation. For theological reasons, the imperative "fear God" can hardly be subsidiary to "honor all people." Moreover, the imperative "love the sister/brotherhood" is explicated in 3:8-12. Finally, the imperative "honor the emperor" forms an inclusion with the first one: "Honor all people." It seems to me that all four imperatives set the theme for the subsequent domestic code.

c. 2:18—3:12. The domestic code here gives three examples of honoring (or: respecting) people: loving the community of sisters and brothers, fearing God, and respecting Caesar's laws.

2:18-25: By accepting the authority of their masters Christian slaves render honor to them. Simultaneously they respect Caesar's laws. Moreover, they express their reverent fear toward God (2:18). The NRSV and NIV, which translate *phobos* with "deference" or "respect" and relate it to slave masters, are incorrect for two reasons: (1) The prior verse (2:17) distinguishes clearly between honor rendered to humans and reverent fear (Greek *phobos*) directed toward God and him alone. (2) Other texts, such as 1:17; 3:2, 6, 14, 16, show that fear or reverence (*phobos*) has God as its object, not humans. "Have no fear of them," even if they can inflict unjust suffering (3:14). Slaves express reverent fear toward God by following in Christ's footsteps as they bear the pain of undeserved suffering. In so doing they live as free persons because their existence as slaves is not determined by the viciousness and capriciousness of their earthly masters. Their love of the brother- and sisterhood remains unimpaired by their social status as they exhibit a Christlike "humble mind" (3:8). What is said to Christian slaves applies to all believers. Slaves, like Christians, are subject to unjust punishment. If punishment is undeserved and quietly borne, then it has "God's approval." But evil conduct by Christians, be they slaves or not, receives what it deserves. The great christological section (2:21-25) depicts Christ as example and as Savior (see the section on traditions below) and serves as rationale for enduring unjust suffering. It also indicates that what is said to slaves applies to all. The concluding verse 25 alludes to Isa. 53:6, 40:11, Psalm 23, and other OT texts and contrasts their past with their present state under "the shepherd and guardian of your souls."

3:1-6: Wives were, by Caesar's law, subject to their husbands, even as prior to marriage they were subject to their fathers. Here, wives "likewise" become examples for all when they render honor by being submissive to their (unbelieving) husbands who through their wives "may be won over without a word" to the word of God and the community under that word. This can happen when husbands "see (the) pure behavior in reverent fear (toward God)" of their spouses. External adornment with fancy clothing, jewelry, and makeup is contrasted with a woman's true inner beauty of a "gentle and quiet spirit, which is very precious in God's sight." The motivation for such good conduct is found in the examples of OT women, particularly of Sarah, who honored and obeyed her husband by "calling him lord." "You are now Sarah's children as [or 'if'] you do good and as [or 'if'] you fear no intimidation."

3:7: "Likewise you (believing) husbands show honor to your wives by living considerately" with them. Reason: "you are joint heirs of the grace of life." Hence husbands should treat their wives with tender loving care, "so that nothing may hinder your prayers." In short, a husband's good conduct toward his wife is his response, as husband, to the four imperatives of 2:17. The examples of slaves, wives, and husbands illustrate how Christians should maintain their identity and conduct themselves as aliens within a more or less hostile culture.

3:8-12: With the idea of being "joint heirs" in the previous verse, the Christian community has come into view. What applies to the marriage of two Christians is true also for life in the community. The imperative "Love the sister- and brotherhood" includes "all of you" who should exhibit "unity of spirit, sympathy, love for brothers and sisters, a tender heart and a humble mind, not returning evil for evil" (cf. Rom. 12:9-21). "For to this you were called" points back to 2:21 and indicates that what has been said in the three examples of slaves, wives, and husbands applies to all believers. All, like the slaves, should "do good" (2:20) when confronted with unjust suffering; they should not return evil for evil, but rather bless

(3:9). In terms of conduct, believers are called "to do good," which includes not retaliating but blessing. In terms of soteriology, believers are called to inherit eternal life, salvation, and glory (1:3-5; 2:9; 5:10). Moral conduct and final salvation are, however, not two unrelated tracks (cf. 1:17). On the contrary, those who bless rather than revile (3:9b) shall themselves obtain a blessing as their reward (cf. Luke 6:37, "forgive and you will be forgiven," etc.). The reason for this is given in the author's favorite psalm, which he changed slightly (Ps. 34:12-16). For the author "life" in this psalm is the same as "the grace of life" in 3:7—eternal life, not just a long and happy life. To "see good days" means to be part of the future time of salvation. Participation in God's future requires that a believer should now keep his or her tongue in check (cf. 3:9), turn from evil, and "do good." The Lord's "ears are open to their prayer" (cf. 3:7), "but his face is against those who do evil." These are not only intemperate, obnoxious Christians but also the opponents of God's people. Note where the author breaks off quoting from this psalm. Psalm 34 has more to say about the fate of the ungodly. It is characteristic of 1 Peter that it does not dwell on God's judgment of the enemies of his people, in contrast to Jewish apocalypses (cf. 3:16-17; 4:5, 18b; 5:5).

3. 3:13—4:11 Conduct of Christians Facing Suffering

After exhorting his readers how to conduct themselves individually and corporately, the author now focuses on the theme of Christians facing suffering. This theme has already been brought to their attention in prior sections (1:6; 2:12, 19-21) but it is now explicated at length. If their new existence involves the call to follow in the footsteps of the suffering Christ (2:21), then suffering will be part of their lives. Because as free persons they are slaves of God, those who are slaves to sin will abuse them.

a. 3:13-22. Do not fear them, but sanctify Christ as Lord in your hearts. These imperatives are placed within the context of the righteous sufferer who "will be blessed" (3:14; cf. Wis. 2:10—3:10). The model of the righteous sufferer in 1 Peter is Christ, "who has gone into heaven" after his suffering, vindication, and victory over demons (3:18-22).

Picking up words from Psalm 34 (doing evil, v. 12c; to do good, v. 11a; seek and pursue, v. 11b), the author asks a rhetorical question that functions as an indirect exhortation: "Now who will harm you, if you are zealous to do what is good?" But at once he modifies his question with a beatitude. "But even if you do suffer for righteousness' sake, you are blessed" (cf. Matt. 5:10; James 1:12). The optative mood used in the beatitude does not imply that suffering is merely a possibility for the people addressed. The point is that in enduring undeserved suffering you are blessed and not forsaken by God. Suffering caused by other people evokes fear, and fear is the enemy of faith and hope. The exhortation "have no fear of them, nor be intimidated" comes from Isa. 8:12 and is similar to exhortations in the Synoptics (Matt. 10:26a, 28, 31). Believers are not to fear their persecutors. Instead they are to "sanctify Christ as Lord" in their hearts (Isa. 8:13 LXX). To "sanctify" here means to acknowledge him as holy in the heart, to set him apart as one's Lord from all other humans. The opposite is fear of persecutors and slanderers arising in the heart, choking and dominating it. How does one sanctify Christ in the heart? By being "ready to make a defense at any time to any one who requests an accounting from you of the hope that you have" (3:15). But such a defense needs to be done with "gentleness" toward opponents and with "reverent fear toward God." Moreover, to sanctify Christ in the heart implies keeping one's "conscience clear" (3:15). The enemies of the faith who "revile your good conduct in Christ" will be put to shame by God on the day of judgment (cf. 2:6-7). Those who now request an accounting from believers and attack their good conduct as evil will themselves have to render an accounting before him who judges justly (1:17) and be "put to shame" (3:16). To be put to shame in the final judgment is the alternative to bearing unjust suffering in the present. "It is better to suffer for doing good" than to be put to shame "for doing wrong" (3:17). Those who suffer unjustly now are blessed (3:14) and will rejoice when Jesus Christ is revealed (1:7). The reason why suffering for doing good is preferable to suffering for doing evil is found in the example set by Christ. He suffered for doing good and is now at "God's right hand." This christological statement (3:18-22) will be discussed in the section below on traditions.

b. 4:1-6.   Freedom from sin: Two reasons enclose an imperative (4:1) followed by a result clause (4:2). "Since Christ suffered in the flesh, *arm yourselves with the same insight*—because the one who has suffered in the flesh [namely, Christ] is finished with sin—so as to live for the rest of your earthly life no longer by human desires but by the will of God" (cf. Dalton, 220). The author had interrupted his exhortation at 3:17 and he now returns to the theme of Christ's suffering (cf. 3:18) and its consequences for believers. One is tempted to read into this Petrine text Paul's understanding of baptism as sharing sacramentally in the death of Christ. But we should first seek to understand these verses on the basis of what we read in 1 Peter. In 2:24 the purpose of Christ's suffering, of his death, was "that we, having no part in the sins (which Christ carried in his body on the tree) might live for righteousness." The purpose of Christ's death is a clean break with sins by his followers. Moreover, 3:22 states that Christ has gone into heaven and therefore it can be said that he is "finished with sin." It is this purpose of Christ's suffering and death with which Christians should "arm themselves." They too should be finished with sin, having made a break with sin in baptism, which "now saves" as a pledge made to God from a clear conscience (3:21) to follow in the footsteps of Christ (2:21), who through suffering went into heaven (3:22). Those who follow Christ are finished with sin. Sin no longer determines their lives. That does not mean that they are sinless. If so they would not need exhortations. It means that "for the rest of [their] lives" they live "no longer by human desires, but by the will of God." His will, not sinful passions, controls their lives.

What those passions, or desires, are is spelled out next (4:3), and the surprise on the part of Gentiles at the conduct of Christians leads to slander and abuse of believers (4:4; cf. Wis. 2:12-20). For this they will have to answer to God, the judge of the living and the dead (cf. Wis. 3:10). The reference to "the dead" reminds the author of those believers who had died, be they suffering, righteous, OT believers who, in the "Spirit of Christ" speaking through prophets, heard the gospel of "the sufferings of Christ and his subsequent glory," or be they postresurrection believers (1:10-12). The author concludes this subsection in verse 6. We paraphrase: "for this is why the gospel was preached to those righteous sufferers who are dead, so that—even though they were condemned in the flesh before people [or 'according to the will of people']—they might live before God [or 'according to the will of God'] in the Spirit," when their hope is fulfilled at the revelation of Jesus Christ (1:13), or: "that they might live before God in [their] spirit" (cf. 1 Macc. 7:14; Wis. 3:14).

c. 4:7-11. Exhortations for life according to the will of God: The author had referred to the will of God and contrasted it with the desires of the Gentiles (4:2-3). Apart from stating that God's will for his people requires that they be "finished with sin" as the power controlling their lives, he had not explicated what he meant by living "by the will of God." This he does now in this subsection (Schutter, 71–72), which presents a radical contrast to the conduct of Gentiles (4:3-4).

The author begins with a statement that serves as the rationale for the following imperatives: "The end of all things is near" (4:7). Therefore, (imperatives) "be sober-minded and be sober for your prayers," which is the very opposite of what their gentile oppressors exhibit (4:3). The remainder of this subsection indicates the circumstances and conditions under which these imperatives are fulfilled. The notion that "love covers a multitude of sins" may be based on Prov. 10:12, but it now refers to mutual forgiveness in love (cf. 1:22). In that way members of the community are "finished with sin" (4:1). This subsection admirably describes the new community as an alternative to society. Mutual love, ungrudging hospitality, charismata (gifts, which each one has received) employed for the benefit of the common good, right preaching, and service "by the strength that God supplies" characterize the community of the end time that glorifies God through Christ in word and deed. The subsection ends with a doxology: "To him belong glory, and dominion for ever and ever." Whether the antecedent of "to him" is God, or Christ, or both is unimportant.

4. 4:12—5:11: Conduct of Christians Facing the Fiery Ordeal

The doxology at the end of the previous section and the new address, "beloved" (cf. 2:11), signal a new major section in which a total of six imperatives set the tone in 4:12-19. Never before have we met so many imperatives, apart from the citation of Psalm 34 in 3:10-12. Moreover, vocabulary from 1:5-7 is taken up in this section ("the time," 1:6; 4:17; "to rejoice," 1:6; 4:13; "a little while," 1:6; 5:10; the testing *[peirasmos]*, 1:6; 4:12; "fire"/"fiery ordeal," 1:7; 4:12; "glory," 1:7; 4:13, 14, 16; "revelation," 1:7; 4:13; "the will of God" *[ei deon thelēma]*, 1:6; 4:19).

But shifts in perspective are also noticeable. In 1:6 the rejoicing takes place *after* suffering; in 4:13a it takes place *in* sharing suffering. The suffering is now specified as the eschatological ordeal of the end time (4:12) and as the beginning of the final judgment (4:17). The suffering itself is interpreted as sharing in the messianic woes of the end time. These perspectives were absent prior to 4:12. The eschatological adversary, the devil, also makes his appearance (5:8). He is to be resisted in the knowledge that "the same experience of suffering," that is, of the messianic woes, is required of the whole church (5:9). Caesar's city receives the cryptogram "Babylon" (5:13) not just because it is a place for exiles in the Dispersion (cf. 1:1). Rome is "Babylon" also because it is an antagonist of Christians (cf. Rev. 17:5). Therefore 4:15-16 introduces a new situation. The author envisions legal proceedings against Christians, who are condemned, like criminals, because they are Christians. They are "reproached for the name of Christ" (4:14). The perspective of 2:14 has disappeared, where "governors" are meant "to praise those who do good." Pseudonymity prevents the author from being more specific with respect to the situation of those enduring the "fiery ordeal."

Even though all recent commentaries insist on the unity of 1 Peter, I still hold that at a time when the writer believed that the final judgment was not just "near" but already beginning (4:17; cf. 4:7) in the persecutions experienced by Christians in Asia Minor, he expanded an original writing, perhaps a homily to newly baptized Christians, by adding 1:1-2 and 4:12—5:13. The combination of the metaphor of "newborn babes" (literally; "recently begotten embryos") with the idea of their need for growth would seem to point to newly baptized persons, rather than to people who had been converted decades earlier. (A reference to Mark 12:42 is irrelevant, because this Markan text does not contain the idea of growth.) Irrespective of this hypothesis, however, I interpret the letter in its present form.

a. *4:12-19. The fiery ordeal; sharing in the messianic woes.* The opening sentence with the first imperative seems to introduce a new subject. The author had spoken of different kinds of chicaneries in 2:11—4:6. Does he now place them into an eschatological/apocalyptic perspective—or does he refer to some new ordeal? The text does not give an unequivocal answer. Reaching back to 1:6-8 he uses its language but gives it a new twist. Instead of "various trials" (plural, 1:6), which probably refers to the chicaneries mentioned in 2:11—4:6, he now speaks of the "test" in the singular (4:12; NRSV: "to test you"). The present participle *(ginomenē)* cannot have a future meaning here because the following verse distinguishes between present and future. In short, according to the author's point of view the fiery ordeal is breaking out in the present situation of the addressees. He therefore exhorts them: "do not be surprised" at it. Nothing "strange" is happening. In 4:4 we heard that Gentiles were "surprised" because of the strange conduct of Christians. Here the readers are exhorted not to be surprised at what is happening to them. The fiery ordeal is the eschatological "test" that was to be expected (cf. Prov. 27:21; Wis. 3:5-6; 1QS 8:3-4; 1QH 5:16; 1QM 17:9). It consists in sharing "the sufferings of *the* Christ." In 1:11, 2:21, 3:18, and 4:1, we heard of Christ's suffering during his earthly life. Here, "the sufferings of the Christ" do not refer to his passion and crucifixion but to the messianic woes of the end time. Therefore the author sees in them the beginning of the final judgment (4:17). The messianic woes are the birthpangs of the new age, an intense period of turmoil and suffering, in which not the Messiah but the people of God, or the inhabitants of the world, suffer distress (Dan. 7:21; 2 Esdr. 13:19; *2 Bar.* 25, etc.; Mark 13:8-9, 14-25; Matt. 24:6-13; Rev. 7:14, etc.; see Best, 162–63).

In the face of the fiery ordeal the exhortation is sounded: "Rejoice!" Rejoice "insofar as you share the sufferings of the Christ" (4:13), which is the final testing of believers before the final revelation of Christ's glory. His revelation in glory will also result in the rejoicing of all who have endured the test. The imperative "rejoice" has nothing to do with masochism. The author does not exhort the readers to be happy because they suffer. He exhorts them to rejoice because they share in the messianic woes that usher in the final salvation. Therefore all who are now "reproached for the name of Christ" are "blessed" (cf. Matt. 5:11-12). The reason for this beatitude is stated at once: "the spirit of glory, which is the Spirit of

God, rests upon you" (4:14; cf. Isa. 11:2b) Note that in distinction from Isa. 11:2 here the author uses a present tense, "rests," not a future tense, "shall rest." In the midst of their suffering and alienation from the surrounding culture, the eschatological glory of Christ and the Spirit of God transfigure their misery. Hence, they are "blessed."

The third imperative (4:15): "Let no one suffer as . . . a criminal" may indicate that Christians are reproached as criminals and are taken to task accordingly. The last word in this catalog is usually translated with "mischief maker" (NRSV), "busybody" (KJV), or "meddler" (NIV). The Greek compound word *allotri-episkopos* (the hyphen is inserted by me) was not used prior to 1 Peter. It probably means "obnoxious bishop." It is hardly likely that *episkopos* would be used by a Christian writer at the end of the first century without referring to a bishop. Whom or what exactly the author had in mind is not known, except that 5:2 will show how a leader of God's flock should function. At any rate, other words were available in Greek for busybodies, meddlers, and mischief makers (cf. 2 Thess. 3:11; 1 Tim. 5:12).

"If one suffers as a Christian, let him or her not be ashamed, but under that name let her or him glorify God" (4:16). In his first round of proceedings against Christians, Pliny, *Legatus pro praetore* (governor) for Pontus and Bithynia, provinces mentioned first and last in the prescript here and hence highlighted, had Christians executed simply because they were Christians. Later, when he found out that they were actually harmless he had second thoughts and wrote to Emperor Trajan for advice (*Epistle* 10.96). One cannot be certain that legal proceedings were involved in 4:16, but neither can one dismiss them, as most interpreters do. The cloak of pseudonymity prevented the author from being specific, and if he wrote from Rome he would probably not be aware of the details of the situation in Asia Minor. At any rate, some Christians suffer the fiery ordeal for no other reason than that they are Christians. Believers were already identified by that title in Antioch (Acts 11:26) and Nero was able to distinguish between Jews and Christians around 64 C.E. I am not suggesting that an edict had been issued by an emperor against Christianity as such, but that legal actions could be taken against Christians simply because they were Christians. "Let him or her not be ashamed," but "let her or him glorify God" refers, in the light of the Synoptic tradition, to confessing Christ publicly (Mark 8:38; Matt. 10:32; Luke 12:8).

First Peter 4:17-18 indicate that "the fiery ordeal" is also the beginning of the time of judgment, which is not yet the time of salvation but precedes it. That the judgment would begin with God's own people is found already in the OT (Ezek. 9:5-6; Jer. 25:29; Mal. 3:1-6; See also *T. Benj.* 100:8-9, etc.). The ultimate judgment begins with the people of God, God's own temple. Since God places the church, his own people, of the end time under the fiery ordeal, "what will be the end for those who do not obey the gospel of God?" The author does not answer his own question, because he is not interested in the temperature of hell (cf. Rev. 14:9-11). He closes this subsection with the sixth imperative: "Let those who suffer according to God's will entrust their souls to a faithful creator by doing that which is good" (4:19).

b. 5:1-5: Exhortations to elders, young people, and to all members of God's flock.   One might ask, why was the code concerning elders not placed in the section beginning with 2:18, for instance, between 3:7 and 3:8? Two possible answers suggest themselves. One, the elders did not belong to the recently baptized and hence exhortations to them prior to 4:12 would have been out of place. Two, the theme of participation in the present messianic woes and in the future glory is continued in this and the following subsection.

In view of the present fiery ordeal, "therefore I, as a co-elder myself and as a witness of the sufferings of the Christ as well as one who shares in the glory to be revealed, exhort the elders among you: Tend the flock of God that is in your charge, exercising oversight." The author is a witness of the sufferings of the Christ, not because he was an eyewitness to Jesus' passion, but because he himself is also a participant in the messianic woes of the end time (cf. 4:13) and therefore he shall share in the glory that is to come. The exhortation to elders reminds us of Paul's farewell speech to the elders of Ephesus in Miletus (Acts 20:28-33), which also used the image of "the flock," "overseer" (here the participle: *episkopountes*), to "tend," literally, "to shepherd." The promise of a crown of glory in 5:4 is parallel to the promise of "the inheritance among the sanctified" (Acts 20:32). The statement "I coveted no one's silver or gold or apparel" (Acts 20:33) has its parallel in 1 Peter, "not for shameful gain" (5:2; cf. 1 Tim. 3:8; Titus 1:7). In contrast to Protestant studies on structures of ministry, the NT emphasizes the ethos, the example, ministers must exhibit if they are to be fit for the function of ministry.

The question of whether the elders of 5:1 are holders of an office, or merely older men who have seniority with respect to their conversion, cannot be answered with certainty. At any rate, they have authority in the congregation. The question is *how* should they shepherd "exercising oversight" (thus NRSV; *episkopountes*, though missing from some manuscripts, should probably be retained; see Metzger, 695). Three contrasts, with negatives first, give an answer. Shepherd God's flock "not under compulsion but willingly." The flock belongs to God, not to the elders (cf. Acts 20:28, "God's church"; John 21:16, "feed my sheep"). Christ is "the shepherd and guardian of our souls" (2:25), "the chief shepherd" (5:4) and elders should remember that. Ministry should not be a quest for self-fulfillment (Kelly, 201), but joyful, voluntary service "according to the will of God." Second, ministry should not be a rip off of God's flock, performed for "sordid gain" (cf. Acts 20:33; 1 Tim. 3:3, 8; Titus 1:7), but it should be done "eagerly," enthusiastically, not with an eye on personal enrichment. Third, ministers should lead God's flock not by "lording it over" the people entrusted to their care but by "being examples" of moral conduct, especially of humility (cf. 1 Peter 5:5; Mark 10:43-44; Acts 20:19; 1 Cor. 4:16; 11:1; Phil. 3:17; 4:9; 1 Thess. 1:6; 2:14; 2 Thess. 3:9; 1 Tim. 4:12; Titus 2:7). The promise attached to faithful, exemplary ministry is the same promise that applies to all the faithful (cf. 1 Peter 1:4; 3:9). They receive a "crown," which is the wreath of victors, a sign of honor and praise, not of power and authority. This victory wreath consists of eternal "glory." That is why the wreath is "unfading," like the hoped-for inheritance of 1:4. This crown of glory will be received when "the chief shepherd appears"; then the hope of 1:13 is fulfilled.

The young members are exhorted to submit to the authority of the elders. All members, elders and the younger ones included, are exhorted to be humble toward one another. A Scripture passage undergirds the imperative and offers the reason why all should "clothe" themselves with humility: "God opposes the arrogant, but gives grace to the humble" (Prov. 3:34; James 4:6). The "arrogant" may refer to Christians like the *allotriepiskopos* of 4:15; it surely refers to those Gentiles who oppose the humble people of God. The present tense ("opposes" and "gives") also includes the future. By faith we know that in the present God opposes the arrogant, but they are still running rampant. Only the imminent future will reveal God's opposition to them, as 4:17b-18 state. God's grace is ours by faith, but his grace is also to be revealed at Christ's parousia (1:13). Hence, the next subsection has a future thrust.

c. 5:6-11: Present suffering and future glory. As in the previous subsection, the messianic woes experienced in the present are the background of this last group of exhortations. Taking up the theme of humility from Prov. 3:34, the author exhorts: "Humble yourself under the mighty hand of God, that in due time he may exalt you." The pattern humiliation–exaltation is found in the Synoptic tradition, in Paul, and in James (Luke 14:11; Matt. 18:4; 2 Cor. 11:7; Phil. 2:8-9; James 4:10). Here the readers should "humble themselves" under the hand of God, who, through the fiery ordeal of the messianic woes, is testing them. If they pass such testing, God will "exalt" them to glory "in due time." In the meantime they can cast their worries and fears on God (Luke 12:11). He controls their fate and he cares for his flock.

Three final imperatives focus attention on "the devil, (who) prowls around like a roaring lion, seeking someone to devour." While from one perspective the messianic woes are God's final testing of his people, from another perspective they are the evil work of arrogant men who oppose God and his flock. Behind them is the ultimate antagonist, the devil. "Your adversary" is like a roaring lion, ready to devour the sheep of God's flock. Therefore "be sober, keep alert" and "resist" the devil. For you know that "the same kinds of sufferings" (namely, the messianic sufferings that are the beginning of God's judgment; 4:13, 17) are experienced by sisters and brothers throughout the world (5:8-9). After enduring the messianic woes "for a little while, the God of all grace" will exalt you, because he "has called you to his eternal glory" in your new birth (1:3), a glory that is shared with Christ. A doxology concludes this section.

5. 5:12-14: Epistolary Postscript

The author adds two final imperatives. After stating the purpose of his letter, namely, "to exhort and to testify that this is the true grace of God," the author adds: "Stand fast in it!" The letter reaches them "through Silvanus," which probably means that he is the courier carrying this letter to the churches of 1:1, rather than the scribe, or secretary, who wrote it. "The sister church in Babylon [see the section below on author] chosen together with you, sends greetings; and so does Mark, my son" (Philem. 24; Acts 12:12, 25; 15:37; Col. 4:10; 2 Tim. 4:11). The last imperative expresses the familial love within the household of God: "Greet one another with the kiss of love" (1 Cor. 16:20; 2 Cor. 13:12; 1 Thess. 5:26). With a wish for "peace to all of you who are in Christ" the letter ends.

Author, Place, and Time

The author identifies himself as "Peter, an apostle of Jesus Christ" (1:1), and later he calls himself "a fellow elder and a witness of the sufferings of the Christ as well as a partaker in the glory that is to be revealed" (5:1). An apostle is a fellow elder in the same way in which a bishop is a fellow pastor. The postscript notes that the letter comes "through Silvanus, a faithful brother as I regard him." It seems to be sent from "Babylon," from which "the elect," the church, send greetings (5:12-13). No one in the early church questioned the apostolicity and Petrine authorship of this letter. Polycarp quoted from it around 130 C.E. (without, however, identifying his source as Peter's letter); Papias too knew it; and 2 Peter referred to it (3:1). Quite a few respectable modern scholars accept the traditional view that this letter was written by Peter; others leave the question of authorship open, and still others opt for pseudonymity. In agreement with the last group I would like to present briefly the chief reasons why the hypothesis that 1 Peter is a pseudonymous writing seems more probable to me than the other two alternatives.

1. An admittedly weak argument, but still an argument in favor of pseudonymity, is that in its style and vocabulary 1 Peter contains some of the best Greek found in the NT. The author was able to produce some striking phrases, for example, *aphthartos kai amiantos kai amaranthos* (1:4), our future inheritance is "untouched" (by death), "unstained" (by evil), "unimpaired" (by time; translation by Beare). He was thoroughly familiar with the Greek OT and did not only quote it, but wove words, phrases, and ideas from the Greek Bible into his argumentation with idiomatic ease. In short, the author shows considerable literary skill. Though Peter was perceived to be an uneducated, common country bumpkin in Acts 4:13, it is possible to hold that coming from bilingual Galilee he could at the end of his life write a letter like ours. Those scholars who have difficulty with this line of thought seem to forget that people whose mother tongue is not English can write fairly well in English, even though they did not learn this language in school. Moreover, there still remains the possibility that Silvanus could have been involved in the composition of this letter, even though normally "through Silvanus" would suggest that he is the carrier of the letter, rather than the secretary who composed it. Silvanus is not mentioned as coauthor, as in 1 and 2 Thessalonians. It would also be somewhat awkward if Silvanus had referred to himself as "faithful brother, as I regard him" (5:12). The argument in favor of pseudonymity on the basis of style seems to me to be weak, but it remains a persistent argument in discussions on the authorship of 1 Peter.

2. More important is the following point. If Peter had written this letter from Rome, then he wrote it at a time when Paul was either a prisoner or had just died a martyr's death. Then, however, the failure even to mention Paul's name in a letter that included two provinces in which Paul himself had worked becomes incomprehensible. This letter, after all, deals with "the fiery ordeal" that Paul, the apostle to the Gentiles, was experiencing or had just endured to the fullest, and he was known by sight to the Christians of Asia and Galatia. Some of Paul's coworkers may have sowed the gospel in other provinces as well. Yet 1 Peter has not one reference to Paul! What sort of a person would Peter be, if he had actually written this letter? He who broke fellowship with gentile Christians in Antioch, he whose action Paul publicly opposed (Paul probably lost in the showdown with Peter; Gal. 2:11-14), he now writes to gentile Christians at a time when Paul faces martyrdom or had crowned his mission by martyrdom, and he, Peter, does not mention Paul at all. What sort of a person does that make Peter, who now declares his solidarity with gentile Christians but treats the apostle to the Gentiles with total silence?

When Clement of Rome wrote to the Corinthians (47:1), when Ignatius wrote to the Ephesians (12:2), when Polycarp wrote to the Philippians (3:2, 9), they quite naturally referred to the apostle who had planted the gospel there. It is at this point that also the secretary hypothesis finally comes to naught. It is most improbable that Silvanus, Paul's coworker (cf. 1 Thess. 1:1), would compose a circular letter to be read also by Christians in Galatia and Asia and not mention Paul once.

3. Moreover, 1 Peter does not contain one single sentence that would indicate that its author had known Jesus. This fact makes Peter's authorship of this letter rather unlikely. What the author knows is the Synoptic Sayings tradition. Yet nowhere are the allusions to the Synoptic Sayings tradition introduced as words of Jesus (cf. 1 Cor. 7:10, 25). Nowhere are they treated like quotations from the OT. Material from the Synoptic tradition is simply woven into his argumentation in the same way in which he made use of catechetical and liturgical traditions. None of the parallels to the Synoptics in 1 Peter is closer to Mark's Gospel than to the other two, and yet Mark's Gospel is supposed to have a Petrine connection. On the issue of a Petrine connection to Mark's Gospel one should remember that it was Papias who introduced this idea (Eusebius, *Ecclesiastial History* 3.39.15). Since Papias was familiar with 1 Peter 5:13 (ibid., 3.39.17), the probability is rather high that it was Papias who constructed the relationship between Peter and Mark's Gospel on the basis of 1 Peter 5:13 because Papias supposed that Peter wrote our letter. Finally, one may not use 1 Peter 5:1 to argue that the author was an eyewitness of Jesus' passion and death (according to Mark and John he was not even present at the crucifixion), because the phrase in 5:1 repeats 4:13 and refers to the messianic woes experienced in the present by the author and the recipients of his letter.

4. First Peter is not dependent on any of Paul's letters, but it belongs in the broad stream of post-Pauline thought. The burning issue of the validity of the Torah for gentile Christians (cf. Gal. 2:1-14; Romans 1–14) is no longer an issue in 1 Peter, even as it is no longer an issue in other Deutero-Pauline letters. But the Apostles' Decree of Acts 15:20, 29, which according to Luke was propagated by James and Peter, also left no trace in 1 Peter. This decree, based on Lev. 17:8-12, demanded a minimum of cultic observations from gentile Christians, who are the recipients of this letter. Instead of cultic purity, 1 Peter demands moral holiness (1:16), which the author also bases on Leviticus (19:2). The demand to "abstain" from some kinds of cultic impurities (Acts 15:29) appears as moral exhortation in 1 Peter: "abstain from the desires of the flesh" (2:11). The historical Peter agreed with the promulgation of the Apostles' Decree, probably as a result of the controversy in Antioch (Gal. 2:11-14). Assuming Peter's authorship one would have to believe that some years later he could

write to gentile Christians for whom the decree was issued and not refer to it at all.

Parallel to the absence of the issue of the Torah and the Apostles' Decree is the absence of the problem of synagogue and church, of Jews and Christians in 1 Peter. The letter is addressed "to the exiles in the Dispersion"; they are "a chosen race, a royal priesthood, a holy nation, God's own people" (2:9). Yet the addressees are Gentiles (4:3) and the Jews are simply ignored in this letter, as if they did not exist. Even when he speaks of "the living stone" who is rejected (2:4), the author does not refer to Jews but to "men" in general. When he speaks about stumbling, the verb is in the present tense ("they disobey," 2:8); it is people in general, not Jews in particular, who are disobedient. The OT has become a Christian book and its prophets had "the Spirit of Christ" (1:11) speaking through them. All designations of honor of OT Israel are bestowed on the church of the Gentiles. The letter gives no indication that Jewish Christians were among its recipients. The issue of the status and future of old Israel is as irrelevant as the observance of the Torah, or of the Apostles' Decree.

In short, 1 Peter fits better into a post-Petrine and post-Pauline period than into the life of the prince of the apostles, and the presence of Paulinisms (such as "in Christ," charisma, grace, freedom, etc.) places it among the post-Pauline letters. To rescue a Petrine connection some scholars have postulated a Petrine "school," or circle. But 2 Peter is so strikingly different in its outlook from 1 Peter that a Petrine school becomes problematic.

5. The letter claims to be written from "Babylon," which is commonly accepted to mean Rome. Moule suggested that Babylon is a symbol for "the place of the exiles" (cf. Isa. 43:5-6, 14; Psalm 137). But the letter is addressed to "the exiles" (1:1), who would then likewise be living in Babylon. The address states clearly that these exiles live in five Roman provinces. Babylon in 5:13 must therefore refer to the exiles *in Rome*. But "Babylon" is used as a cryptogram for Rome only after 70 C.E., as Hunzinger has shown (*2 Bar.* 11:1-2; 67:7-8; 2 Esdr. 3:1-2, 28; Rev. 14:8; 16:19; 17:5). When Rome, like Babylon of old, destroyed the temple and persecuted the people, then and not before was this code name applied to it. Therefore, the cryptogram "Babylon" establishes the pseudonymity of this letter.

6. It also seems unlikely that the historical Peter would simply call himself "Peter," as unlikely as it would be if Jesus called himself simply "Christ," without the article. As an alternative to the hypothesis of Petrine authorship, I would like to suggest one that is admittedly farfetched. The name Peter appears only once, as the first word of this epistle. Names were commonly abbreviated in Greek manuscripts. The difference between "Peter" and "Paul" in abbreviations is minute, and changing "Paul" into

"Peter" involves erasing the light upward stroke of the capital *lambda* and putting a vertical stroke on it. This change could have happened by accident or by design and would have had to occur prior to the writing of 2 Peter. (If the change was made intentionally, the author of 2 Peter would be as good a candidate for it as any—cf. his condescending attitude in 2 Peter 3:15-16.) The hypothesis that 1 Peter was originally a pseudonymous Pauline letter would explain why Paul is not mentioned in it, why the author is in the company of Paul's coworkers, Silvanus (1 Thess. 1:1) and Mark (Philem. 24; Col. 4:10; 2 Tim. 2:11), and why Paulinisms abound. For the purpose of interpretation it makes little, if any, difference whether the first word of this letter was originally "Paul" or "Peter," since in either case it is a pseudonymous writing.

To discover the meaning of pseudonymity is difficult in each particular case. I would suggest that by placing his letter under the authority of an apostle, the author wished to express apostolic solidarity with the Christians in Asia Minor who experienced persecution. It is consoling to know that the church in Babylon/Rome and its great apostle cares about them, shares in their suffering (5:1), and interprets their suffering for them (4:12-19; 5:8). The author hoped that his letter would gain acceptance and it did.

It is possible that the letter was sent from Rome. At least equally possible is the hypothesis that its origin lay in one of the provinces of 1:1. If so, "Babylon" is part of the pseudonymity of this writing. The cryptogram and apocalyptic ideas may indicate a place of origin in proximity to that of the book of Revelation. The code name Babylon does not appear in *1 Clement*, written from Rome.

Establishing the time of origin for any pseudonymous letter is difficult. Since 2 Peter knew this letter and Polycarp cited from it, and since the cryptogram points to a time after 70 C.E., we are left with the period between 80 and 111 C.E. as the time of origin.

Persecutions

Though the NT contains many references to persecution, we owe our knowledge of Nero's savagery not to the NT but to Tacitus (*Annales* 15.38-44). Likewise, were it not for the publication of Pliny's letter we would be unaware of the executions of Christians in 111 C.E. in Bithynia. With the exception of the Apocalypse, early Christian writers, including Clement of Rome and Ignatius of Antioch, did not dwell on the subject of Roman magistrates as persecutors of Christians.

All interpreters of 1 Peter agree that, first, the suffering referred to up to 4:11 was caused primarily by defamation, vilification, suspicion, hostility, and perhaps occasional violence on the part of a hostile pagan populace. Suffering is caused primarily through verbal abuse, as texts such as

2:12, 15, 23; 3:9, 16; 4:4 seem to indicate. In the case of slaves it probably also involved occasional beatings. Second, there was no empirewide persecution during the first two centuries. The statement in 5:9 would therefore amount to rhetorical hyperbole, unless it referred to nothing more than verbal abuse and the like.

To Francis W. Beare and others before him, the situation of persecution envisioned by the author appeared to be different in the final section (4:12—5:11), and it also seems to me that some local or regional persecution, involving Roman magistrates, should not be excluded as the background for this section and as the occasion for sending this letter. The argument that 5:9 would then presuppose an empirewide persecution does not hold. What is important is not what actually happened but what the author thought was happening. He thought that the final judgment was already beginning in the experience of suffering by the churches addressed. He expressed his solidarity with Christians of Asia Minor by referring to the worldwide sufferings, the messianic woes of the end time that would involve the whole Christian brother- and sisterhood. We today know otherwise. We should also remember that the cloak of pseudonymity prevented the author from being specific with respect to the situation in which these churches found themselves. The author was quite aware that not all Christians in Asia Minor were enduring the messianic woes. Not all were subjected to persecution simultaneously and with the same intensity. Therefore he wrote: "Rejoice, *insofar as* you share the sufferings of the Christ" (4:13).

It seems to me that the following items deserve more careful consideration than they have received recently. First, Christians are still exhorted to persevere in performing good deeds (4:19), but why is the hope expressed in 2:12, 15; 3:13, 16 absent in 4:12—5:11?

Second, the reproaches heaped on Christians in 4:4 are caused by the surprise of Gentiles at the conduct of Christians and seem to consist primarily of verbal abuse. The final section, however, juxtaposes suffering for the name of Christ (4:14) with a series of criminal activities (4:15). Does this juxtaposition not suggest that legal action was taken against Christians because they confessed the name of Christ? If so, then being a Christian (4:15) constituted a crime.

Third, suffering, as testing (1:6-7), receives a new interpretation in 4:13. Suffering now signals the presence of the messianic woes that, for the author, are the beginning of the final judgment (5:12-19). One must ask: Is the outbreak of "the fiery ordeal" merely a continuation of verbal abuse and other difficulties, caused by pagan neighbors, with which 1:6—4:11 has already dealt? Or is the fiery ordeal an intensification of those difficulties?

Fourth, only in the last section is suffering connected with "the devil" (5:8-9) and only here does Rome appear as "Babylon." This designation characterizes Rome not just as a place for exiles but also as the city of the persecutors of God's people. Thus 2:13-14 in conjunction with 5:8-13 show a more differentiated approach to Roman government than either Paul or John of Patmos presented. For the author the function of emperors and governors is to punish those who do wrong and praise those who do good (cf. Rom. 13:1-7). Insofar as they do that, Christians freely submit to their authority and honor the emperor (2:13,17). But when this function is perverted, then "resist firm in your faith" (5:9). Rome becomes Babylon, an extension of the ultimate antagonist, the devil, if Christians are "reproached for the name of Christ" (4:14; cf. Revelation 13; 17). Is the apocalyptic imagery of the last section merely an indication of the author's rhetoric, or does it also indicate a new development to which he responds with apocalyptic rhetoric ?

Perhaps we will never agree on answers to these questions. But in closing I would like to indicate briefly that in his interpretation of persecutions the author is more in tune with the apocalyptic enthusiasts of 2 Thess. 2:2 and their oracle ("the day of the Lord has come") than he is with the pseudonymous author of 2 Thessalonians. The latter did everything he could to separate the present sufferings from the notion of messianic woes, by presenting an apocalyptic timetable in 2 Thess. 2:3-12. According to his timetable the present experiences of suffering (2 Thess. 1:5-10) are two steps removed from the end. In the present the *katechōn,* whoever he may be, is at work. Then, in the future, the *katechōn* is removed. With the appearance of "the lawless one," who will take his seat in the temple, and with the "apostasy," this apocalyptic scenario reaches a second stage, prior to Christ's parousia. Then follows the destruction of "the lawless one" at Christ's parousia (2 Thess. 2:3-12). The author of 2 Thessalonians contradicts the notion that the persecutions and tribulations experienced in the present constitute the messianic woes and the beginning of the final judgment as 1 Peter 4:12-19 would have it. In 1 Peter, the interpretation of present suffering in terms of messianic woes and in terms of the beginning of God's judgment (4:12-19) is more attuned to the slogan of the opponents of 2 Thessalonians (2:2) than it is with the author's point of view. Nonetheless, 1 Peter's insistence on "doing good," no matter what the circumstances may be (4:19), puts the author in agreement, on this point, with the author of 2 Thessalonians, who opposed the "disorderly" of that community. They were unwilling to work, but lived from the generosity of the Christian community (2 Thess. 3:6-15).

Traditions and Their Use

The author was not a theological innovator, but a traditionalist. His letter reads like a timeless document, reflecting the traditions of the church. He did not advocate a "new" ethics of freedom but articulated a theology of liberation paradoxically through submission to God and to one another in reciprocal love (5:5-7; 2:13; 1:23). He exhorted his readers to a lifestyle of freedom that had its touchstone in the freedom to share in the sufferings of the Messiah (4:13). Above all, he used his considerable literary and theological abilities in the service of the tradition.

To clarify what ethics means for exiles, he employed a rich variety of the traditions. From the Christian exegetical tradition of interpreting the OT comes the combination of texts from Isa. 28:16 and Isa. 8:14 with Hos. 2:23 in 1 Peter 2:6-10, a combination also found with the same textual changes in Rom. 9:33, 25. But the author expanded and reinterpreted this tradition by incorporating Ps. 118:22 (in 2:7) and by borrowing concepts from Isa. 43:20-21 (LXX), Exod. 19:6, and 23:22 (in 2:9). In addition to citing OT Scripture in support of an exhortation, he used individual words or phrases from the OT in order to develop a thought. Thus, for instance, while he cites a text from Leviticus in 1:16 in order to support his exhortation of 1:15, he gives no indication that in 1:17-18 many of his words are taken from the OT and had already been used in Christian tradition.

He also incorporated some sayings of Jesus from the Synoptic tradition, as well as concepts and ideas that were transmitted in Pauline communities. Texts that relate suffering to joy or beatitudes for righteous sufferers (3:14; 1:6; 4:13-14) reflect the use of early Christian traditions (Matt. 5:10; Luke 6:22; 1 Thess. 1:6; Rom. 5:3; 8:18; Col. 1:24; James 1:2, 12). The historical antecedents of joy in (after) suffering lie in Judaism (e.g., 2 Macc. 6:30; 4 Macc. 6:24-30; 2 Bar. 52:6; Tob. 13:14). Among the parenetic traditions that admonish Christians to proper conduct, we find catalogs of vices from which they should abstain (1 Peter 2:1; 4:3; cf. Gal. 5:19-21; Eph. 4:31; 5:3-4) and catalogs of virtues that they should practice (1 Peter 3:8; 4:7b-11; cf. Eph. 4:2; Phil. 4:8, etc.). The modern interpreter should not conclude that such vices were actually practiced by the churches addressed. As traditional material, they merely express what should under no circumstances take place among God's elect.

Space permits me to deal only with the christological traditions that serve, in 1 Peter, as the foundation and motivation for exhortations. A few comments on the social code follow.

Christological Traditions

> He was foreknown before the foundation of the world
> He was made manifest at the end of times.
> (1:20)

Its pre-Petrine form is recognizable in its participial style, in its pattern of eternal predestination–eschatological revelation, and in the tension between the author's eschatology and the eschatology of these two lines. The tradition uses the pattern "once hidden, but now revealed," a pattern present, for instance, in *1 Enoch.* There, the "Chosen One" (the Son of Man–Messiah "was *concealed* in the presence (of God) prior to the creation of the world and for eternity. And he has *revealed* the wisdom of the Lord of the Spirits to the righteous" (*1 Enoch* 48:6-7). In the tradition used in 1 Peter, the revelation is identical with the past appearance of Christ. His past appearance, which was the result of God's eternal decree, constitutes the revelation of God and signals the end of time. For the author of 1 Peter the revelation of Christ is a future event (1:5, 7, 13; 4:13; 5:1, 4). The writer used this tradition to show that redemption through Christ's death is anchored in God's eternal purpose that spans the ages, and he added to this tradition: "for your sake who through him are *believing in God who raised him from the dead*" (1:21). The words in italics are also a traditional creedal formula that summarized the content of the faith (cf. Rom. 4:24; 10:9b; Col. 2:12c, etc.). Through his addition he told his audience that they themselves are the beneficiaries of God's past revelation in Christ; that faith comes "through" Jesus Christ. Faith itself is the work of Christ (cf. Phil. 1:27); it is faith in God and his act of raising Jesus from the dead. Hence, faith in God is inseparable from faith in the resurrected Christ, and this faith is inseparable from "hope" in "God" (1:21c). Faith as well as hope are the result of God's redemptive work, and hope is directed to the future: "Set your hope fully upon the grace that is coming to you at the *revelation* of Jesus Christ." Thus 1:21c links up with the first exhortation of 1:13.

The liturgical tradition of 1:20 probably continued with 3:18d and ended with 3:22.

> He was put to death in the flesh,
> he was made alive in the spirit. . . .
> he went into heaven,
> subjected to him were angels, authorities, and powers.
> (3:18d, 22; cf. 1 Tim. 3:16)

As in 1:20 so here each line begins with a passive participle, and in 3:18d the two lines are also contrasted through a *men . . . de* construction. That verse 19 did not belong to the tradition is evident not only on account of the position of the Greek participle but also because the sentence is introduced by *en ho,* which is typical of the author's style (1:6; 2:12; 3:16, 19; 4:4). That the sentence of verse 22, "he is at the right hand of God," also apparently did not belong to the tradition is indicated by the present tense of its auxiliary verb and by the sequence of the Greek text in which the going into heaven follows the sitting at the right hand. (The NRSV changed the sequence into a logical order.) As in 1 Tim. 3:16, so here the antithesis flesh-spirit does not refer to Christ's human and divine natures but to the two modes of existence. He was put to death as a human being, but God made him alive by giving him a divine, Spirit-permeated mode of existence (cf. 1 Cor. 15:44-50). The climax of this hymn is found in Christ's ascension into heaven through which the conquest of all supernatural powers was accomplished. As in Ephesians (2:2; 4:8), so in this tradition, the spiritual powers reside between earth and heaven. With this hymn, which may have been used at baptism (cf. 3:21), the Christian community boldly affirmed Christ's cosmic victory and hence his lordship over the world. Those small, despised Christian groups knew and rejoiced in the world's true Lord (cf. Eph. 1:20-22; Col. 2:15; Phil. 2:9-11).

We now turn to our author's use of this hymn. He placed it in the subsection dealing with suffering (3:13—4:6). By announcing that the supernatural powers behind the pagan tormentors of God's people have already been defeated, this hymn provides the foundation for the beatitude of 3:14. "If you suffer for righteousness' sake, you are blessed." Such suffering is prelude to victory, to life "in the spirit" (4:6). The antithesis, "in the flesh" and "in the spirit," also provides the connection between Christ and the Christian in 3:18; 4:1, 6.

Christ's victory over demonic powers (3:22) was preceded by his death: "being put to death in the flesh" (3:18d). Another tradition explicates the meaning of his death.

> Christ died for sins once for all,
> the righteous for the unrighteous,
> that he might bring us to God.
> (3:18a-c)

This creedal tradition combines the interpretation of Christ's death as atoning sacrifice for sins (cf. 1 Cor. 15:3; Gal. 1:4; Heb. 9:26, 28; 10:12; cf. 2 Macc. 7:37-38; 4 Macc. 6:28-29; 9:24) with the interpretation of his death as vicarious representation. Thus, Christ's death is the unique, vicarious, saving sacrifice, and much more than an example of undeserved suffering. But an example it remains in that Christians who "suffer for doing right" (3:17) follow in Christ's footsteps (2:21).

His death is inseparable from his resurrection. In verses 19-21 the writer inserted his own commentary into the hymn of verses 18d and 22. His commentary connected Christ's victory over all demonic "spirits" with

Christian baptism, which was prefigured in Noah's salvation "through" water.

The "spirits in prison" to whom Christ preached are not the spirits of dead people in Hades, but the fallen angels of Gen. 6:1-4. In Jewish apocalyptic speculations these spirits caused the corruption of Noah's generation and all the subsequent corruption of humankind. In 1 Enoch 18:12-14 their "prison" is not below the earth, but at the "end of heaven and earth." However, being in prison does not stop them from being active on earth; it merely prevents them from approaching God. The spirits in verse 19 are identical with the demonic "angels, principalities, and powers" of verse 22 even as the verb "he went" refers in both verses to Christ's ascension (Dalton, 185–86).

The ascending Christ proclaimed his victory to those demonic spirits (v. 19), which means he subjected them to himself (v. 22). As God's judgment had fallen on Noah's generation, so it is now ready to consume the living and the dead (4:5). As God saved a few at Noah's time "by means of water," separating them from those who drowned in God's judgment, so "now baptism saves" (3:21). It saves because in baptism Christ's resurrection and victory over demonic spirits is effective. It saves "not as a removal of dirt from the body, but as a pledge made to God to maintain a good conscience" (or "as a pledge proceeding from a good conscience"; or "as a petition for a good conscience"). The person to be baptized apparently pledged that she or he would maintain a good conscience, that is, faith, love, hope, and good conduct.

Baptism does not save through this pledge but "through Christ's resurrection" (3:21), which is effective in baptism, even as rebirth is brought about by God "through Christ's resurrection" (1:3). But God's saving power effective through Christ's resurrection in baptism does not operate magically. It demands the obedient response made first in baptism and then continued "throughout the rest of the time of life in the flesh" (4:2). Negatively this pledge entailed abstaining "from the passions of the flesh that wage war against your soul" (2:11; cf. 1:14). Positively it meant to "be holy" (1:15-16), to belong to God's elect people (2:4-10), and to exhibit conduct appropriate to that election (2:12; 3:8; 4:7-10).

A great christological tradition serves as basis for the exhortation of slaves and facilitates the transition to our discussion of the domestic code.

Christ died [suffered] for us [for you]. . . .
He committed no sin,
No guile was found on his lips. . . .
He himself bore our sins in his body on the tree,
That we might die to sin and live to righteousness.
(2:21b, 22, 24)

The relative pronouns in verses 22 and 24, the style, and the fact that the christological section of 2:21-25 transcends the immediate context of admonition to slaves would seem to indicate the presence of a tradition. The use of the first person plural, "*our* sins," "*we* might live" (lines four and five above), suggest that the tradition in line one also had a first person plural pronoun "*us*" and probably had "died" instead of "suffered."

With three additions, the author connected the tradition to the undeserved suffering of slaves. (1) He substituted "suffered" for "died" and "you" for "us" in line one; (2) he added, "Christ . . . was leaving you an example that you should follow in his steps"; (3) he added, "by his *wound* [singular] you were healed." The beatings endured by slaves are related to the passion of their Savior. Moreover, the author explicated lines two and three in verse 23. There the verb tenses are no longer aorist, as in lines one to three, but imperfect. Finally, he added a concluding sentence (v. 25) that links up with God's call of verse 21 and interprets their conversion: "For you were straying like sheep [Isa. 53:6], but now you have returned to the shepherd and guardian of your souls."

This tradition is unique in that it concentrates exclusively on Christ's death, combining the idea of atonement for sins with the notion of vicarious representation and with the fulfillment of the role of the Suffering Servant of Isaiah 53. Quoting from Isa. 53:9, it also affirms Christ's sinlessness (cf. 2 Cor. 5:21). He did not die because of sins he had committed. Even as the suffering servant of Isa. 53:4, 5, 12 took upon himself the sins of many, so Christ carried them in his body on the cross, suffering the consequences of sins and making atonement for them (cf. 2 Cor. 5:21; Gal. 3:13; 1 Peter 1:18-19). Moreover, the effect of the death of Christ is not only atonement for previously committed sins but also deliverance from sin for a life of righteousness (1 Peter 2:24b; cf. 3:18c; 4:1).

In the context of the letter, Christ's suffering is an example with respect to his conduct (2:21-23). Then the salvific, redemptive effect of his suffering and death become the theme. It becomes clear that what is said to slaves applies to all Christians. All believers should show in their conduct the same uncomplaining behavior that Jesus exhibited in his passion. The mistreated and insulted Servant of the Lord surrendered his life in trust (or: he surrendered all insults, threats, and unjust suffering) "to him who judges justly" (2:23). The meaning of the text is not clear at this point. What Jesus "handed over" to God is either his own self or the mistreatment of those who afflicted him, leaving the judgment up to God (cf. Rom. 12:19). In either case he remains an example for all believers.

With verse 24 the tradition is taken up again, combining Isa. 53:4 with the tradition of the crucifixion. "He bore our sins in his body on the tree" (for "tree" instead of "cross" see: Gal. 3:13; Acts 5:30; 10:39; Deut.

21:23 LXX). If he carried our sins away and up to the cross, then we, the believers, are separated from them. The result and effect of the Suffering Servant's redemptive work is "that free from sins, we might live for righteousness" (cf. Rom. 6:11). Instead of "free from" (so NRSV) or "might die to" (so RSV), one should probably translate "separated from sins," namely, from those sins that Jesus carried away to the cross. There is a clear-cut separation in believers' lives with respect to sins (cf. 1:14; 2:11; 4:1-2). Separation from sins means, in a positive sense, to live for righteousness in the present (cf. Rom. 6:4c, 12-13, 18-19). Therefore "his wound" (singular; Isa. 53:5 LXX), his death, has brought healing from sins and with it a new life (2:24c). The next verse in Isaiah (53:6) uses the metaphor of straying sheep. First Peter 2:25 connects it with the previous metaphor of healing through the conjunction "for." To be healed means that those who were straying like sheep "have now returned to the shepherd and guardian of their souls." For God as shepherd of Israel, see Isa. 40:11; Ezek. 34:11-16; Psalm 23. For Christ as shepherd, see John 10:11-16; Mark 6:34; 14:27-28; Heb. 13:20; 1 Peter 2:25; 5:4. In 2:25 the shepherd and guardian *(episkopos)* is Christ as the risen one to whom God has called them (2:21).

Domestic Code

Parallels to the domestic code of 1 Peter 2:13—3:7 occur in Col. 3:18— 4:1; Eph. 5:22—6:9; 1 Tim. 2:8-15; 5:4-16; Titus 2:1-10; Rom. 13:1-7; in *1 Clement, Didache,* and Polycarp's *Letter to the Philippians.* One can detect some antecedents in Jewish and Hellenistic popular ethics. David Balch traced the origin of the domestic code back to Aristotle's *Politics* and *Ethics* (33–59). Comparing the NT domestic codes, we recognize that their wording and sequence had not yet been fixed by oral tradition. The common elements of the domestic codes are: (1) direct address; (2) exhortation, generally in the form of an imperative; (3) elaboration of the exhortation; (4) motivation for the exhortation.

Even though the end is believed to be near (1:5; 4:5, 7), the persons addressed are exiles who have to live in the world. The domestic code directs them to live within the social structures of the world where they must express their obedience and love. The exiles were not to make an exodus from the world, nor cultivate a privatistic spirituality by withdrawing from social obligations, nor contemplate the imminent coming of Christ with apocalyptic enthusiasm. The domestic code of 1 Peter has a function similar to the social legislation of the Pentateuch. The people of God who are separated from the world as God's possession must simultaneously live in an alien culture, and for this 2:13—3:12 gives some examples.

Balch contends that the notion of subordination is the basic ingredient of the domestic code. For him, "be submissive" may be viewed as the title of the whole code (2:13, 18; 3:1; 5:5). Between the imperative "submit" (2:13) and the domestic code of 2:18—3:7, however, four imperatives intervene in 2:17: "Honor everyone. Love the sister- and brotherhood. Fear God. Honor the emperor." The participles of the domestic code that follow (being submissive, 2:18; 3:1) depend on those imperatives, as Martin has shown (130). The imperatives of 2:17, not the notion of subordination, are primary in terms of grammar. The participles, "being submissive" (2:18; 3:1), indicate how slaves or women render honor, love of the sister- and brotherhood, fear of God, and respect for the emperor's law in their particular situations. "Likewise" husbands render honor and so on by treating their spouses with consideration (3:7), and all express honor, love of the sister- and brotherhood, fear of God, and respect for the emperor by exhibiting the flawless behavior of 3:8-9.

In 2:13 the imperative "submit" expresses the biblical presupposition that authority comes from God, not from the majority opinion of the people. It demands that one translate obedience to God and unselfish love into action within social relationships. To put it differently, the lordship of Christ, which is inseparable from suffering and victory through suffering, is to be made manifest not only in the worshiping community but also in social relationships of believers. Therefore, this imperative is broadened to the greatest possible extent. "Submit for the Lord's sake to every human creature." The imperative of 2:13, "submit to everyone," is parallel to the demand of 2:17, "honor everyone." Between 2:13 and 2:17 we hear that believers are "free persons" because they are "slaves of God" (2:16). This characterization of their identity is independent of their social status. Household slaves are free persons because they are slaves of God, and the same applies to husbands, wives, and all.

Therefore, in 1 Peter, submission to everyone does not mean doing what everyone says. For instance, according to Plutarch, the submission of wives to their husbands meant that wives must also worship the gods of their husbands (*Praecepta Coniugialia* 19). But that kind of submission is set aside in all NT domestic codes. First Peter went one step further and not only challenged wives to win their unbelieving husbands through good conduct (3:1-2), but also called upon women not to be intimidated by their husbands (3:6). Blind submission is exactly not what is demanded here.

In popular Greek ethics submission of the wife to her husband meant that the husband should dominate his wife. "Rule your wife" was a popular Greek maxim. NT domestic codes exclude domination of wives by Christian husbands. Ephesians 5:25 exhorts them to *love* their wives, an exhortation unheard-of in popular Greek domestic codes. First Peter demands of husbands that they be sensitive and tactful to their wives, to bestow honor on them, and to remember that both husband and wife are equally heirs of God's grace, which consists of a new life. If a husband's new relationship to God does not find expression in his relationship to his wife, if his home becomes a hellhole of dissent, then their prayers are "hindered," and his faith has become an illusion (3:7). The prayer found among Greeks and Jews alike: "Lord, I thank thee that thou hast not made me . . . a woman" is absent from NT traditions.

One should also note that the demand for submission is related to freedom (2:16) and fearlessness (3:6; cf. 3:14). Freedom is the presupposition for submission, and both are grounded in Christology and in reverence (of God; 2:17). Therefore, submission is rendered "on account of the Lord" (2:13), not under compulsion but in freedom (2:16). For the Lord's sake Christians should submit to governmental officials and honor them as they submit to and honor every person (2:13, 17). Consequently, the quotation from Prov. 24:21, "Fear the Lord *and the king*," is changed to "Fear God, honor the king." Christians do not fear their temporary masters precisely because they fear God. They are not servile pleasers of humans (cf. Col. 3:22), but they submit in that freedom which is modeled on Christ. Such freedom transcends both antinomian libertinism as well as repressive legalism. The freedom to forego, to submit, to respect everyone, demands a lifestyle in which love interacts with the realities of the world. The author still hoped that such a lifestyle would "put to silence the ignorance of the foolish" (2:15, 12).

Another feature of the NT domestic codes is the direct address, for example, "slaves" (2:18). This too is a novelty, for slaves were not directly addressed in contemporary Hellenistic models. To be addressed means to be recognized as a person. The NT bypassed the Aristotelian tradition according to which a slave owner could never do an injustice to a slave, since, as property, the slave was not a person. The NT aligned itself with more enlightened views of the first century. Although no one in the first century, not even manumitted slaves, advocated the abolition of slavery, it would be superficial to argue that 1 Peter sanctioned the social status quo.

> The rich man in his castle,
> The poor man at his gate,
> God made them high and lowly
> And ordered their estate.

This approach to the social problem in terms of a hierarchial divine social order is exactly what is not found in 1 Peter. Nowhere in the NT is slavery or poverty regarded as an ordinance of God. First Peter gave new dignity to slaves, however, by connecting their fate with that of their Lord and Redeemer (2:20-25). They, not their masters, are cited as models of Christian conduct when in freedom they bear unjust suffering and follow in Christ's footsteps. Thereby they exhibit the evil of an unjust society that tolerates and encourages unfair treatment. Christian conduct is not to be determined by the whims and ill will of pagans and slave masters, but by the Lord as model of the Christian lifestyle. This lifestyle includes the bearing of unjust suffering that exposes evil and seeks to overcome it by doing good. First Peter calls for not a passive attitude of infinite resignation but an active demonstration of love (3:9; 2:12) that seeks to change evil-doing neighbors into brothers and sisters, because they are also God's creatures (2:13). The reciprocal love among Christians (1:22; 3:8; 4:7-9) is the goal of love toward the enemy in 1 Peter (3:9), but the latter is the criterion of whether the former is "unhypocritical" (1:22; 2:1).

In distinction from the domestic codes of Colossians and Ephesians, 1 Peter does not contain admonitions to the owners of slaves. Perhaps the author believed that slave owners cannot be true Christians who express reciprocal love and are required to do so (1:22; 3:8). It is improbable, however, that the church membership of the regions mentioned in 1:1 had no slave owners (cf. Eph. 6:9; Philemon).

A most interesting discussion on the domestic code in 1 Peter between John H. Elliott and David Balch is available in print in Talbert, ed., *(Perspectives on First Peter)*. For Balch, the domestic code is "one aspect of early Christian acculturation in the Hellenistic society over against the Jesus tradition itself" (98). With apparent approval, he quotes E. Schweizer, who argued that the domestic code in 1 Peter represents "the paganization of Christianity." One should note, however, in the first place, that the author and the recipients of his letter did not have the choice of deciding in which societal structures they wished to live, nor did they have the opportunity of living in a theocracy where the law of God is the law of the land. Their sole choice was whether they "do that which is good" within the societal structures in which they found themselves or lose their identity by assimilation.

Second, to compare the casuistic OT laws on slavery (Exod. 21:1-6) with the exhortations of 1 Peter is to compare two different forms. Balch's concluding statement (97) is at least partly the result of form-critical confusion at this point: "whereas the commands in the Torah *protect* slaves, the NT exhortations are *repressive*" (emphasis mine). In the light of this sweeping statement, one should read Exod. 21:5-6, which is part of the section he cites: "If his master gives him [the male slave] a wife and she bears him sons and daughters, the wife and her children shall be the master's and he [the male slave] shall go out alone" when he is set free. The only alternative to this brutal disruption of a slave family is for the slave father to reject his freedom and submit to permanent slavery in order to remain with his family. What is protective about that? Note that the wife of the slave is not even asked. Yet, Balch continues: "the OT does not emphasize the subordination of wives." Is that so?

Balch surmised that the author of 1 Peter "certainly owned slaves" (95). For this there is no evidence. But assuming for the moment that he did own slaves, would it then not be obvious that all exhortations in his letter applied also to him (e.g., 1:22; 2:1, 13a, 17; 3:8; 4:7-11)? On the one hand, if he treated his slaves cruelly (2:18), would not he and his actions then stand condemned—by his own words? On the other hand, if he treated his slaves in accordance with his own exhortations, what is "repressive" about such treatment within the context of the first century? The absence of exhortations to slave owners in 1 Peter can be interpreted in more than one way. It is generally recognized that the domestic code in this letter deals only with the most problematic situations, namely, of slaves and wives living in pagan households; hence, the absence of exhortations to Christian slave owners. But even they would be indirectly addressed in all exhortations cited above. The author may have believed that the idea of Christian slave owners constitutes a contradiction in terms and therefore he did not address them. Finally, the absence of admonitions to Christian slave owners may be due to the literary development of 1 Peter. Though the hypothesis is generally rejected, it still seems probable to me that 1:3— 4:11 was originally an address to newly baptized Christians, and if there were no slave owners among them, there would have been no reason to address them. Be that as it may, Christian slave owners are not excluded from the imperatives of this letter.

Third, the author was quite aware that Christians live in two houses. By God's gracious election, through rebirth and faith, they are members of God's household; by birth and fate they may have to live as slaves in their owners' houses, or in the houses of unbelieving husbands. All had to live within the house of a more or less hostile culture. Therefore, they experience suffering, are tempted to assimilate (1:14; 2:11, 15; 4:3) in order to avoid suffering, and they are challenged in this letter to express their distinctive identity (1:3—2:10) and their distinct ethos (e.g., 2:20; 3:8-12, etc.) in spite of the hostility encountered in their cultural house.

The culture in which Christians lived obscured the distinction between fear reserved for God alone and respect (honor) for the emperor (2:17) by practicing emperor worship. The culture tolerated retribution, which, for the people of God, was a denial of their nonretaliating Lord (2:24). The culture engaged in activities that were outside the parameter within which their new identity was to be expressed (e.g., 4:3-4). First Peter does not advocate assimilation to the prevailing Hellenistic culture. This letter is an exhortation to maintain Christian identity and to express it in everyday life within a hostile context. Therefore nonconformity (1:14; 2:11; 4:2-4) and resistance (5:8-9) are the other side of doing good and living according to the will of God (1:14-17, 22; 2:1, 12, 14, 15, 19; 3:6, 10-12, 13-17; 4:7-11, 19).

In conclusion, the ethics of 1 Peter does not reflect the popular ethos of much of life in mainline Protestant churches of today. When freedom turns into license to do what feels good, when divorce rates among laity and clergy skyrocket, when promiscuity is celebrated as an alternative life-style, when submission to one another becomes irreconcilable with the quest for self-fulfillment, then the ethics of 1 Peter either functions as a warning against cultural assimilation, or else it is set aside as being irrelevant. First Peter's idea of freedom, grounded in being slaves of God (2:16), and the Christology that undergirds both submission to everyone (2:13) and bearing unjust suffering (2:20-25) can be turned into a gilded frame of rhetoric around our petty thoughts of liberation as we denigrate the exhortations of this magnificent letter.

Exhortations cannot be "applied" casuistically to different situations. A girl subject to incest by a sick father dare not be admonished: "submit." Workers who are exploited by management may not be told: "bear innocent suffering quietly." But both may be comforted by him who grants a new identity, an unfailing hope, and a new purpose, "so that we may live to righteousness" (2:24b). What this requires in specific situations demands the imaginative reflection of the community of faith, hope, and love, First Peter is not a letter of casuistry—it is a letter of exhortation, encouragement, and consolation. As a letter of exhortation it functions in a way similar to Israel's apodictic law. It sets parameters or boundaries for the conduct of the elect exiles and indicates what they may not do under any circumstances (e.g., 1:14a; 2:11; 4:3). Within those boundaries the community will have to express ever anew what "unity of spirit, sympathy, love of brothers and sisters" (3:8-9; 4:7-11) require in particular instances.

The Elect Exiles

The references to the pagan background of the people addressed indicated clearly that they are gentile, not Jewish, Christians (1:14, 18; 2:9-10; 4:3-4.). It may seem surprising that the author would refer to gentile Christians as "aliens and exiles" 2:11; 1:17) of the "Dispersion" (1:1) when they are in fact living among their own kin and in their own land. Yet they are foreigners in their own country because of (1) their election, (2) their worship of God, (3) their origin, (4) their lifestyle, (5) their innocent suffering.

1. *Election* signifies God's gracious design prior to a person's obedient response. In contrast to Romans 9–11 the election of Gentiles in 1 Peter meant that they inherited all titles of honor that had formerly applied to Israel (2:9).

The ultimate ground of the election of Gentiles to be God's holy and elect people lies in God's foreknowledge (1:2), which designated Christ to be God's elect foundation stone (2:4-6). It is possible that 1:1-2 incorporated a baptismal blessing: "Chosen according to the foreknowledge of God the Father through the sanctification by the Spirit unto obedience and sprinkling with the blood of Jesus Christ." Election is mediated through the sanctifying activity of the Spirit, who operates through the word of God (1:23) and baptism (3:21). "Sanctification by the Spirit" is identical with conversion or rebirth (1:3). The goal of election is "obedience" to God (1:14) and his word (2:2). The next phrase is difficult: "and sprinkling with the blood of Jesus." Its background is not the blood of the Passover lamb (1:19), but the blood of the covenant of Exod. 24:5-8 (cf. Heb. 9:20), half of which Moses threw against the altar. The other half he threw upon the people, who pledged, "We will be obedient." The election of Gentiles should result in their obedience within the covenant ratified by Christ's blood and accepted by them at their baptism. Sprinkling with Jesus' blood also implies that their sins are forgiven.

Once they were not God's "holy nation" but "conforming" to their pagan environment and "the futile ways inherited from your ancestors" (1:14, 18; 4:3-4). But now in God's great mercy they have been elected to be his people (2:10). Formerly they were "no people," aliens with respect to God (2:10), but at home in the world. Now they are "God's own people" (2:9), but live like exiles and aliens in their own land (2:11).

2. They are also aliens because they do not *worship* the gods of the land. The importance of this point becomes obvious when one recalls that polytheism and politics were inseparable in the Hellenistic Roman culture. By abstaining from idolatry, which functioned as the ideological foundation of the empire, the Christians were automatically an "out-group" like the Jews. But in distinction from Jews, they had not received official privileges from the Caesars. As aliens in an idolatrous world (4:3), Christians owe their ultimate allegiance to the one true God about whom the author of 1 Peter cannot speak adequately until he has said Father (1:2, 3, 17), Spirit (1:2, 11-12; 2:5; 3:18; 4:6, 14), Christ (1:2, 3, 19-21; 2:21-25; 3:18-22). It is precisely "for the name of Christ" that proceedings were taken against them (4:14-15), which prompted the writing of this letter.

3. Also their different *origin* indicates why the metaphors "aliens" and "exiles" are appropriate for them. They have been reborn (1:3, 23; 2:2), not "through corruptible seed" but "through the living word" and sacrament (1:23; 3:21). This means that one cannot understand faith exclusively in terms of existential decision. Baptism and faith are interpreted by the author in terms of the miracle of rebirth. This concept is borrowed from Hellenism, but in distinction to the rebirth offered in Hellenistic mystery religions, 1 Peter does not think in terms of an ontological transformation resulting in the deification of the person initiated. For this author, rebirth is the miracle of a new beginning within a new relationship established by God resulting in a new obedience and lifestyle. This life is no longer under the domination of sin (4:1; 2:1, 24). The reborn shall live by faith (1:8; 2:6), hope (1:21), and love (1:22), and they must fight within themselves the invisible struggle against "the desires of the flesh" (2:11) during the time of their sojourn "in the flesh" (4:2). Their new birth stands under the same apocalyptic reservation (1:5, 7; 4:7; 5:6) that applies to Christ's victory over the demonic spirits. Even though 1 Peter announced their defeat (3:19, 22), the struggle continues and the devil must still be resisted (5:8).

4. God's people are foreigners in their own land also on account of their *lifestyle* (4:4). In a time like ours when antinomianism parades in our churches under the disguise of liberation, we would do well to listen to 1 Peter's exhortations, for example, "Live as free men, but don't use your freedom as a pretext for doing evil" (2:16). The people of God must be distinguishable from the surrounding society also by their lifestyle. It is not extraordinary feats that are expected of them, but the profession of faith and a faithful practice of that profession in word and deed. First Peter expected Christian conduct to have evangelistic power (2:12, 15; 3:1, 16). It is also significant that elders are to be "examples to their flock" in their conduct (5:3).

5. The existence of God's holy and elect people as aliens and exiles in the world is accentuated by *unjust suffering*. The author still hoped that through good conduct Christians might be able to avoid taunts, jeers, and other forms of verbal abuse (2:12; 3:13, 16), but he also knew that in spite of doing what is good, they still face suffering. He made use of several perspectives in interpreting innocent suffering. First, such suffering constitutes "various trials" (plural!) in accordance with "God's will," which they must undergo "for a little while" so that the genuineness of their faith can be tested (1:6-7; 3:17). His interpretation in terms of "testing" should be distinguished from the idea that suffering "purifies" the sufferer, an idea absent in 1 Peter. Second, unjust suffering leads to future eschatological "praise, glory, and honor" (1:7), and constitutes already now "grace before

God" (2:20), which results in the beatitude of 3:14. Third, innocent suffering is the manifestation of discipleship, of following in the footsteps of the suffering Christ (2:21-22; 3:18).

Still, the "fiery ordeal" may strike Christians as "something strange" (4:12). The author interpreted the final test (singular, 4:12) by taking up the apocalyptic idea of messianic woes. Before the end, the powers of evil will make one final assault against God's elect. The nearer the end, the more terrible the ordeal. But the reverse is also true—the more terrible the suffering of the righteous, the nearer is the end (cf. Dan. 12:1; *As. Mos.* 8:1; 4 Ezra 13:16-19, etc.; Mark 13:8; Revelation 4–21). Christians of Asia Minor participate in the messianic woes (1 Peter 4:13), which are also the beginning of God's final judgment (4:17) and at the same time the manifestation of the devil prowling like a roaring lion (5:8-9).

The participation in the messianic woes paradoxically is cause for rejoicing because it guarantees participation in Christ's glory (4:13). Moreover, it becomes the occasion when the Spirit of God's glory comes to rest upon the persecuted (4:14; cf. Luke 12:11-12) so that they endure "firm in the faith" until God "in his time" exalts them "to his eternal glory in Christ" (1 Peter 5:10). "Therefore . . . set your hope fully upon the grace that is coming to you at the revelation of Jesus Christ" (1:13).

FREDERICK W. DANKER

2 PETER

That the Second Epistle of Peter is a relatively late document (end of the first century to early second century) and certainly not from the pen of Peter, the apostle, is almost universally recognized. This writing is therefore to be classified as pseudepigraphic. Pseudepigraphy is a device whereby a writer adopts the persona of a deceased and revered authority figure for communication with contemporaries. In most cases there was no attempt to deceive the public, but to say, "If N. N. were living, this is what N. N. would say to us." Besides using a letter form, the writer casts some of his thoughts in a manner that suggests the common literary genre known as the farewell speech or testament, of which *Testaments of the Twelve Patriarchs* is a pseudepigraphic example and Acts 20:17-35 an instance of application within a larger work.

Of special interest is the question of the rhetorical unity of the document and its contemporary proclamatory value. The opening paragraph (1:3-11), following the formal greeting (vv. 1-2), is of key significance. Its syntax has long perplexed copyists, challenged textual critics, and puzzled commentators. In the interest of smooth translation, contemporary versions such as NRSV, REB, the Jerusalem Bible, and Today's English Version obscure what is at first sight merely rugged syntax in the original, but in the process obliterate the contours of the fundamental solution: adaptation of the literary form known as civic decree, which would be familiar to the readers of this thoroughly Hellenistic document.

A decree from the third century B.C.E., issued at Iasus, a city on the west coast of Caria in Asia Minor, displays the form in its most economic expression. After details of date it reads:

> Whereas Theocles, the son of Thersites, of Meliboea, has proved himself a perfect gentleman in his relations with Iasus and has rendered exceptional service to our citizens who visit Meliboea, be it *resolved* that Theocles, son of Thersites, be our public friend and representative; that he be granted exemption from whatever imposts our city has authority to exact, and that he be free to come and go both in war and in peace, without formality of treaty; and, finally, that he enjoy the privilege of a front seat at the games.

(No. 463 in Charles Michel, *Recueil d'Inscriptions grecques,* [Paris: Leroux 1900]. Details on the variations within the decreetal form and related diction in 2 Peter are discussed in Frederick Danker, *Benefactor,* 453–67.)

Basic to the pattern is the interplay of benefactor and recipient, of the former's largesse and the latter's grateful response. But our writer's unique contribution to the history of letters (supported by awareness of his formal departure from Jude's scheme) is his combination of the reciprocity pattern: Party B (benefactor) acknowledged by Party R (recipient) with a sequence in which the recipient is urged to be a benefactor, while at the same time anticipating a benefaction. The distribution of verses 3-11 would then be as follows: Party B (vv. 3-4a) confers the benefit on Party R (v. 4b). Party R (vv. 5-7), recipient of the benefit described in verse 4b, acts as a benefactor to his own community and reproduces characteristics of Hellenistic benefactors, as depicted in decreetal inscriptions. Party R continues to be viewed as a Party B in verses 8a and 11, but now Party B of verses 3-4a functions both in the spirit of a Hellenistic recipient of benefactions and as a benefactor (vv. 8b, 9b, 11).

In keeping with the decreetal pattern is the epistolary greeting (1:1-2), whose diction is not only Hellenistic (with *pistis,* ordinarily rendered "faith," equaling "commitment to responsibility," and *dikaiosyne,* "righteousness," equaling "fairness"), but follows patterns found in decrees of epistolary form.

Awareness of the fundamental structure of 1:1-11 goes far to account for the writer's emphasis on the use of the tradition of the transfiguration. Jesus, the Great Benefactor, has his credentials assured on the holy mount (1:17-18). But of chief interest is the question of the relevance of 1:1-18, with its climactic affirmation of the Great Benefactor's credentials, to the writer's preoccupation with the opposition described in the lurid tones of chapter 2.

Authority Crisis

Pervading this document is alarm over a basic threat to the unity of the fellowship. This threat stems from an attempt to discount prophetic utterance in the past on the basis of disappointed experience, and to pit one apostolic word, such as Paul's on liberation, against another. This epistle therefore emphasizes the importance of Jesus' transfiguration.

From one perspective, the Lord's transfiguration is proleptic and guarantees the apocalyptic windup. At the same time, the source of the affirmation in verse 17 ("*conveyed* to him by the Majestic Glory") not only confirms the identiity of Jesus but is presented as the primary factor in every authoritative utterance made to God's people. This is the point of the conclusion expressed in verse 19: "So we have the prophetic message more fully confirmed." That prophetic Scriptures are meant (and not necessarily excluding a pseudepigraphical writing such as *1 Enoch*, which was held in high esteem in some early Christian circles) is clear from verse 20. At the transfiguration, none other than God, Supreme Benefactor, confirmed that the prophetic Scriptures found fulfillment in God's climactic action in connection with Jesus Christ as Great Benefactor of humanity. In practical terms for 2 Peter's community, this means that "the day of the Lord" (see 3:10) will come, and its arrival is assured by the fact that its definitive character, "the power and presence of Jesus Christ" (1:16), had been observed in advance and confirmed personally by God.

To come up with a different interpretation, specifically one that would deny the fulfillment of the promise of the parousia—and with it the termination of the world as it is now known (3:4)—means to pit self-interested, or privately motivated, interpretation against the divine intention. But, as the writer states emphatically, it is a primary datum that no prophecy is to be subject to the vagaries of one's own hermeneutical viewpoint (1:20). This conclusion is rooted in the fact that "no prophecy ever was *conveyed* through human initiative"; on the contrary, "human beings received their message from God and uttered it, being themselves *conveyed* by the Holy Spirit" (v. 21). Like English "convey" or "bear," the Greek word *pherō* is used to express numerous ideas and is therefore well adapted to wordplay. Both it and the preposition *hypo* ("by") in the last phrase of verse 21 echo usage in verse 17. The affirmation heard by the apostles derived from "the Majestic Glory," and the words of prophecy similarly derive from a divine resource, the Holy Spirit. Written prophetic word and God's action in connection with Jesus Christ thus form a unity to which the writer appeals in 3:2: "to be mindful of the words previously uttered by the holy prophets, and also of your apostles' command, which is derived from the Lord and Savior." The rendering of this verse by the NRSV ("remember the words spoken in the past by the holy prophets, and the commandment of the Lord and Savior spoken through your apostles") comes close to the point: God's climactic revelation is Jesus Christ, and the apostolic command itself is therefore backed by the majestic authority of Jesus as "Lord and Savior" (see 1:1), the Great Benefactor. This authority finds confirmation in the divine voice (v. 17), which has consistently expressed itself in the prophetic word.

The divine word underlying the prophetic and apostolic word can speak with authority about the termination of all things, for the same divine word was responsible for the origin of heaven and earth "out of water" and for the destruction of the world through the instrumentality of water (3:5-6). The writer parallels the fact of creation and of the flood with the fact of the world's present existence and its certain destruction. Between creation and the flood there was a considerable interval, and there is an interval between prophetic word about the end and the realization thereof. In his peroration (3:14-18) the writer warns his readers against misinterpretation of Paul's writings. Through the expression "wisdom given him" (3:15), 2 Peter puts the apostle Paul in the class of the prophets who were *"conveyed"* or "moved" by the Holy Spirit (1:21). The writer then goes on to strengthen this estimate of the apostle's authority by classifying his writings with "the other scriptures" (3:16). At the same time he suggests that the "twisting" (3:16) of Paul's writings is of the same order as the idiosyncratic interpretation denounced in 1:20.

The writer's emphasis on authoritative guidance for the church is of a piece with his interest in the "godly" life, as expressed in his decreetal terminology (1:3, 7). Unified doctrinal formulation with a view to organizational consensus is therefore foreign to the thought that finds expression in this document, for this writer himself indulges in neologisms, even with respect to his authoritative source, Jude. Nor is there any suggestion of an ecclesiastical teaching office as clearinghouse for correct interpretation. Rather, this writer is interested in the kind of instruction that maintains the proper relation between avowed allegiance to Jesus Christ and performance in the arena of everyday decision. Orthodoxy for this writer means to instruct the Christian community in such a way that present activity increasingly develops correspondence with expectation levels for the future (3:13-14). Out of such concern the writer's attack on false teachers develops.

In effect, 2 Peter's discussion of the prophetic word (1:19-21) constitutes a rhetorical bridge to the periodic bravura piece in chapter 2. Meeting the tacit objection that not all prophecy is necessarily of divine origin, the writer acknowledges that "there were false prophets among the people" (2:1). Thus the stage is set for confrontation with the "false teachers" (v. 1). "False" teachers are people whose instruction lacks divine endorsement. Their utterances are not to be trusted. Such teachers should constitute no more of a surprise to the community than did false prophets among God's people of old. As the future tenses in 2:1-12 indicate, they have in fact been anticipated and are now current hazards (2:13ff.). In contrast to these "false teachers" are the "holy prophets" and "your apostles" (3:2). For this writer, then, orthodoxy means maintenance of purity in eschatological motif. Such concern is in keeping with the apostolic instruction, to which he himself submits by adopting the pseudonym of Peter rather than introducing himself as a new authority for Christian communities.

Christology, Soteriology, and Ethical Response

In view of the writer's emphasis on authoritative tradition, it is evident that he could presume the acquaintance of his readers with the principal contours of that tradition, including especially Paul's letters. From a methodological point of view one is therefore ill-advised to expect 2 Peter to spell out in detail what is already familiar to his readers. His aim is not to recall for them the details of their apostolic instruction, but to recall *them* to the importance of adhering to the instruction they already know (see 2:15, 21; 3:1-2). Much of Jack T. Sander's negative verdict on ethical content in the NT *(Ethics in the New Testament* [Philadelphia, Fortress Press, 1975], passim), and especially in 2 Peter, stems from lack of recognition of such a presumptive approach by NT writers.

Examination of the writer's decreetal terminology lends precision to our understanding of his description of Jesus as "our God and Savior" (1:1). This is no metaphysical assertion, and it is not to be isolated from the writer's self-understanding. He stands in relation to Jesus Christ as subjects throughout the Roman Empire stood in relation to their emperor and his viceroys. For them the emperor was *divus* ("divine"), and he could expect unreserved submission and loyalty. It is this dynamic aspect of anticipated obedience that the author of 2 Peter aims to stress by his high Christology, and he reinforces it by defining himself under the pseudonym of Simon Peter as a slave. "Slave" is the antonym of "master," and for the latter 2 Peter uses two Greek words: *kyrios* (1:2 and passim) and *despotēs* (2:1). Jesus Christ is the ultimate authority over every human being, and he possesses that authority by virtue of his claim through purchase (2:1). Salvation, the supreme benefaction, has a dynamic quality: purification from sins has already taken place (1:9), and escape from the defilements of the world is an accomplished reality (2:20).

Precisely in connection with this endorsement of Pauline "objective justification," more properly, "objective reconciliation," 2 Peter senses the point of origin of "gnostic" libertinism. Instead of recognizing that allegiance to Jesus Christ as Lord means the renunciation ("repentance"; 3:9) of their former master, defined as "corruption" in 2:19-20, the false teachers construe the objective deed of Jesus Christ as an invitation to self-indulgence. Hence the "false teachers" and those who are capitivated by them live in contradiction to their avowed commitment *(pistis,* 1:1), which can have no meaning apart from the divine character exhibited in the "fairness" (righteousness) of "our God and Savior Jesus Christ." Such is the twist Paul's theology suffers at their hands.

Nor are the slaves of Jesus expected to function out of their own resources. Second Peter shares with Paul the view that the Spirit is active in Christians, but this activity is described in terms of "his [Jesus'] divine power, which has given us everything that pertains to life and piety" (1:3; cp. Rom. 8:3-4 and 29-30), as opposed to lust of the flesh (2 Peter 2:18; cp. v. 10). Both terms, "life" and "piety," are thematically and structurally significant.

Life is opposed to impiety and lust, which are subject to corruption and destruction (1:4; 3:7; cp. 2:12, 19), that is, they have no future. Piety is the opposite of lust and unrighteousness (2:8-9) and the kind of life perpetrated at Sodom and Gomorrah (2:5-6). To escape from "destructive lust" means to enjoy anticipation of a share in the Lord's divine nature (1:4), to be prepared for the judgment (1:8), and to be equipped for the kingdom that is eternal (1:11).

In the rhetorical "climax" or stepladder figure (1:5-7), 2 Peter conveys both the substance of Christian response to God's action in Jesus Christ and, by implication, its negatives. Faith (*pistis,* v. 5) is, as noted earlier in connection with the usage in verse 1, commitment or acceptance of responsibility. The Hellenistic benefactor effects a commitment through actions that win the classification of "excellence" or "nobility" *(aretē)* through such discharge of commitment. Since the verdict of excellence is not won without unselfish expenditure, its opposite is self-interest and greed *(pleonexia,* 2:3, 14; cp. vv. 13, 15). Nobility in turn requires knowledge *(gnōsis,* 1:5); for, according to this writer, without knowledge one cannot avoid the path of self-indulgence. Hence he sets forth as primary his understanding that prophecy is not subject to the whims of an interpreter (1:20), and that in the last days scoffers will arise who live in accordance with their own interests (3:3). By contrast, the false teachers revel in matters of which they are ignorant (2:12). Since their ignorance is equated by this writer with self-indulgence (see esp. 2:10-14) and is cited in connection with all manner of sensuality (vv. 7-22 passim), he emphasizes self-control *(enkrateia),* which has as its upshot faultlessness and blamelessness (3:14), in contrast to the blemishes of the false teachers (2:13). Self-control requires endurance *(hypomonē,* 1:6) in the face of a delayed parousia; in contrast, the false teachers selfishly capitalize on apparent nonfulfillment of the promise and bolster their position with an arrogant display of independence (2:10-12; cf. verses 5-6). The antidote to self-indulgence is piety *(eusebeia,* 1:6; cp. v. 3), which expresses itself in awe before God's activity in history (3:11-12) and in submission to God's lawful expectations (2:9). Such piety recognizes the value of community concern (*philadelphia,* 1:7, the writer's substitute for the more usual *philanthrōpia*) and its concomitant, peace (1:2; 3:14), both of which are antithetical to "destructive partisan views" (2:1; NRSV: "destructive opinions"). Strengthening this sense of community is "esteem" *(agapē,* 1:7; NRSV: "love"), which recognizes neither social nor intellectual conferment to the disadvantage or demotion of others; love is fundamentally respectful of personhood. The false teachers, with their ill-conceived sense of community, use their prestige to develop their own little fiefdoms (cf. 2:13-19) in opposition to the comprehensive reign of God (1:11), and direct emotions of affection into illicit channels (2:14,

18). Far from themselves having affection for people, they are, like Balaam, strictly in love with personal advantage (2:15). In contrast, true apostolic teachers do not seek their own advantage but the improvement of their fellow Christians, the "loved ones" (3:1, 14, 17), even as the Lord is merciful to sinners (3:9). Paul, now deceased, remains *"our* beloved Paul" (3:15). In a related vein, God acknowledges the Son as the "loved one" (1:17).

In the concluding exhortation (see esp. 3:8-14) 2 Peter closely associates a plea for moral stability with traditional cosmological diction. For modern proclaimers and their audiences, whose knowledge bank includes information about planets in existence for millions of years, and which now are even viewed at close range, such juxtaposition might seem to imperil the ethical imperative. But our increased knowledge of the universe suggests a new cosmological context for the conveyance of the writer's ethical earnestness.

Dominating the writer's thought is a view of humanity under divine judgment. History has at intervals provided exhibits of this truth (2:1-8). One of the most serious catastrophes, the flood, marked a change from one type of world to another (3:5-7), from the *kosmos* of that time to the present heavens and earth (v. 7). The very waters that were suspended in the heavens and confined in the earth (cf. Gen. 7:11) became the instruments (this is the point of the plural in the phrase *di' hōn,* "through which," 2 Peter 3:6) of the earth's destruction. Humanity in rebellion is set forth against a universe that has seen radical changes in its structure. History itself gives the lie to the idea that the universe is stable. Contemporary probes of the heavens indicate that planets other than our own have experienced striking changes, some of which involve systems that can support life. The one possibility for stability lies in the ethical sphere, in commitment to benefaction of humanity through the power of the Supreme Benefactor. Along such a route *(hodos,* "way," one of the writer's favorite terms) people can realize their distinctive identity. Hence the writer contrasts the stability of Christians with the behavior of the division makers (2:15, 18; 3:17): "errant" as a planet. The Greek verb *planaō* ("go astray") and its nominal cognate *planē* ("error") would suggest a planet's *(planētēs)* motion, which to the ancients appeared to be irregular (see, e.g., Plato *Timaeus* 40b-d). Within the great cosmos the false teachers are microcosms, woefully adrift, whereas the true believers are on course.

Such stability in ethical decision, within the framework of the rubrics expressed in 1:5-7, is of a piece with the ultimate divine purpose, the triumph of righteousness (3:13). This triumph is independent of any cosmological metathesis defined in specific apocalyptic rhetoric, including that of the writer. God will have the last word, and the Christian is committed to eventual newness, the ultimate realization of humanity. Such newness spells the elimination of self-aggrandizing exploitation of one's fellow human beings; of the promotion of personality cults, which destroy the ethical identity of their adherents; and of the cynicism that extols individualism at the expense of the common good. To feel a sense of hospitality for any of these dehumanizing strategies is unthinkable. No rhetoric is too severe to express horror at their emergence, especially among Christians. Hence the writer borrows from Jude, along with much of his content, the type of diction best suited for expression of such indignation. Similar moral outrage found expression in the popular philosophy of the time, of which the best known are the discourses of Epictetus.

That 2 Peter borrowed from Jude, not vice versa, is, like the pseudonymous authorship, generally recognized. But the function of his variations from Jude's presentation deserves more than passing attention by proclaimers of 2 Peter's points of view.

Jude's sequence is presented in two sets, each with three examples. Set A (2:5-9) displays examples of groups subject to judgment; set B (v. 11), examples of corrupt people, who are mentioned by name. In his adaptation of this material 2 Peter drops Jude's reference to "the people" who had been rescued out of Egypt (Jude 5), having mentioned a few verses earlier that there were "'false prophets among the people" (2 Peter 2:1). This alteration gave him the opportunity to introduce the principal cause of the conduct that elicits God's judgment.

In keeping with the strong apocalyptic motif found in his source (Jude 6), 2 Peter begins with the angels who, according to Jude, sinned in the manner described in Gen. 6:1-4 and *1 Enoch* 6. Their example is crucial to 2 Peter's argument, being introduced with a monitory condition (2:4), whose apodosis is left to the imagination of the reader, who would correctly conclude, "If angels who transgress are not spared, how will mere human beings who engage in arrogant practices fare?" (see 2:10-12).

Jude does not mention the generation living at the time of the flood, but 2 Peter finds the exhibit important because of the contrast between the rebels who were destroyed and Noah, a "proclaimer of righteousness" (2:5) and therefore a model for 2 Peter's own generation of true teachers. Similarly he secures a confirmatory contrast between the residents of Sodom and Gomorrah and "righteous Lot" (2:6-8), whose credentials are drawn not from Genesis but from a tradition that found expression in another part of the Bible, Sir. 16:8. The letter expatiates on Peter's character in order to exemplify the virtue of *hypomonē*, a strong theme in his document and closely associated with righteousness (cf. 1:6).

In place of Jude's reference to a single angel, Michael, 2 Peter heightens the rhetorical effect by generalizing with the plural "angels" and highlights the arrogance of the false teachers with the description of these respectful angels as "greater in might and power" (2:11).

By eliminating the names of Cain and Korah from the triad in Jude 11, the writer focuses his public's attention on the moral deficiencies of Balaam, who becomes the whipping boy in the writer's expanded execration of false teachers (2:15-16).

Comparison of 2 Peter's list of notorious criminals with that of Jude discloses a functional unity within the longer document. The first three (the sinful angels, the generation at the time of the flood, and the residents of the Cities of the Plain) project the certainty of divine judgment, with ultimate retribution for rebellious scoffers and with affirmation of the moral loyalists. The fourth, Balaam, is cited between two excoriations (2:12-14 and 17-22) of the type of persons who are disrupting the Christian community and whose behavior is in sharp contrast with that which is described in the authoritative words of "the *holy* prophets and also of *your* apostles' command, which is derived from the Lord and Savior" (3:2).

Special Problems

The history of interpretation reveals that interpreters have encountered special difficulty at a minimum of four points in the text of 2 Peter. The first of these includes the syntactical relationship of 1:3-5 to the verses that precede and follow. I have suggested that the civic-decree form and its associated diction largely account for the syntactical peculiarity. The second is at 1:19, but it is probable that the understanding of Jesus as Supreme Benefactor, and endorsed by the heavenly voice, leads to the affirmation of verse 19, that the prophetic word is now even more firmly established. The third is at 3:6, in which the phrase *di' hōn* ("through which") must certainly refer to the waters above and those beneath the level of the earth. The fourth, and the most notorious, is found at 3:10, where the tradition of manuscripts and versions is so fluid that several emendations have been offered for the last part of verse 10. Translations therefore vary considerably, some of them ambiguous or at variance with one another. For example, the RSV rendered: "and the earth and the works that are upon it will be burned up." The "works" here appear to be understood as the visible productions of humankind. The NEB reads: "and the earth with all that is in it will be laid bare." The question is whether, with NEB, the word *heurethēsetai* is to be read or, with RSV, some word meaning "burned up" or "destroyed." A simple emendation, however, will account for the apparently more difficult verb *heuriskomai* and yet assign it a more probable syntactical usage.

One should note, first of all, that the conjunction *kai* after the word *gē* is suspect and may well have been written very early by mistake in place of the original writer's probable *kata*. Codex Alexandrinus actually contains such a mistake, reading *kai* instead of *kata* in 3:13 just before the phrase *to epangelma autou* ("his [God's] promise"). If *kata* is to be read also in verse 10, one should note that *gē* written in uncial script could be either dative or nominative case. Since the *iota* subscript to indicate the dative for the noun *gē* would not be expected in the uncial script, a copyist in the very earliest stages of transmission of 2 Peter might have thought that both the nouns *gē* ("earth") and *erga* ("works") were nominatives and naturally to be joined by *kai*, instead of *kata*, with *ta* in *kata* easily bypassed because of the following article *ta*. Therefore in place of *kai gē* (nominative) *kai ta en autē erga heurethēsetai*, I propose *kai gē* (dative) *kata ta en autē erga heurethēsetai*. By making this simple mistake, understanding *gē* to be nominative and writing *kai ta* instead of *kata ta*, the copyist obscured the natural use of *heurethēsetai* with the dative in the legal sense "it will be found to so and so" (meaning "so and so will be judged"), and he opened the door for other variants. In *Ps. Sol.* 17:8 [ed. Rahlfs], a pseud-epigraphical work emanating from Pharisaic circles around the first century, the judicial denotation of *heuriskesthai* occurs with both a dative and the preposition *kata: heurethēnai autois kata ta erga autōn*, meaning "they will be judged according to their works." The proposal here made does not depend on this passage for its validity, for it is based on textual-critical grounds pertinent to the Petrine wording. At the same time, the intertestamental text parallels the main lines of the grammar in the reconstructed text of 2 Peter 3:10 (*kai gē kata ta en autē erga heurethēsetai*), rendered literally: "And it will be found to the earth according to the works in it," that is, "And the earth will be judged according to the works in it." The term "earth" is here applied to its inhabitants, as in Matt. 5:13; 10:34; Luke 12:49, 51, and the word "works" denotes moral performance. The NRSV endeavors to do justice to both the findings of textual criticism and the thematic content of 2 Peter with its rendering: "and the earth and everything done on it will be disclosed." But REB is even clearer: "the earth with all that is in it will be brought to judgement."

JUDE

The Scripture readings appointed for Sundays in Episcopal, Lutheran, Methodist, Presbyterian, and Roman Catholic churches do not contain one lesson from Jude, not even for the day commemorating Saint Simon and Saint Jude. This letter is indeed a liturgical stepchild. In 1974, D. J. Rowston called Jude "the most neglected book in the New Testament." This situation has certainly changed. Today we have a thorough commentary on Jude by Richard J. Bauckham in addition to his detailed research report in *ANRW*. While Bauckham's commentary uses literary and tradition-historical analysis, a second, equally exciting study by Duane Frederick Watson uses rhetorical criticism for his interpretation of Jude. Both depend on E. Earle Ellis's seminal study on Jude, "Prophecy and Hermeneutic in Jude."

Form and Structure

Like other letters, Jude has an epistolary prescript (vv. 1-2), followed by an opening to the body of the letter (vv. 3-4) that states the occasion and the theme of his message. But the "body" of the letter reads "more like a homily" in two parts (Bauckham, *Jude,* 3). Part 1 (vv. 5-19) is a "midrash" on diverse references from the OT, the Pseudepigrapha, and the "apostolic" tradition. Part 2 (vv. 20-23) consists of exhortations, followed by a doxology (vv. 24-25). E. Earle Ellis's investigation of Jude 5-19 had already reached a similar conclusion that this section consists of "a carefully worked out commentary," a midrash, to which Jude adds verses 1-4 and the concluding exhortations and doxology (vv. 20-25; Ellis, 225). Both Ellis and Bauckham are aware that Jude's midrash differs significantly from rabbinic midrashim as well as from the *pesher* exegesis of Qumran. Jude employs typology (vv. 5-7, 11), quotes from apocryphal books (vv. 9, 14-15) and from apostolic prophecy (17-18), and instead of presenting scriptural citations from the OT he summarizes scriptural passages (vv. 5-7, 11). None of these features occurs in the commentaries of Qumran. But Jude and the exegetes of Qumran have one feature in common. Both are convinced that biblical texts are eschatological prophecy that "were written down for our instruction, upon whom the ends of the ages have come" (1 Cor. 10:11). As eschatological prophecy and as typology, biblical texts, according to Jude, speak directly to the present, without denying that the events and persons referred to in these texts took place, or existed, in the past (e.g., vv. 5-8).

The address in the prescript (vv. 1-2) is rather vague. The letter is sent to those who "are called, who are beloved in God the Father and kept (safe) for Jesus Christ." In short, it seems to be a catholic letter, addressed to the church at large, rather than to a specific congregation. Frederick Wisse notes that there is also a lack of specificity with respect to the heretics in this letter. He concludes that the author has no concrete heresy in mind but uses stereotyped phrases from the descriptions of the eschatological false prophets in Jewish and early Christian literature. According to Wisse, the purpose of Jude's letter is to inform Christians that the eschatological enemies of the last day have appeared. His purpose is *not* to rid the church of these heretics. It seems to me that, in spite of many good insights in Wisse's article, his conclusion concerning the purpose of the letter constitutes a false alternative. Without specific opponents in mind, Jude's letter would have no purpose. He is, in fact, trying to prove that the interlopers in their midst are ungodly persons and the false prophets of the last days. Jude calls his troops to battle, to fight for the faith (v. 3) and therefore to struggle against heretical teachers who have made inroads into churches he knew (v. 4). These heretics were even participating in the sacred community meals (v. 12) and Jude does not like it. His lack of specificity about the particular heresy of the false teachers is to be connected with the general address of verse 1. Since the letter is a "catholic letter" (contra Bauckham) addressed to all Christians, its author does not wish to be more specific concerning the false teachers.

It also seems to me that instead of postulating a prior "homily" (vv. 5-23; Bauckham) or "commentary" (vv. 5-19; Ellis) to which Jude gives an epistolary frame, one should note the unity of this letter. The unity finds expression in the catchword connections that appear not just within the section of verses 5-19, but between verses 1-4 and the rest of the letter. First, the catchword "keep" connects the prescript with the body of the letter and the doxology. Christians are "kept" safe for Jesus Christ (v. 1) when he comes in judgment with his myriads of angels (vv. 14-15), and they are exhorted to "keep" themselves in the love of God (v. 21), who is able to "keep" (Greek: "guard") them from falling (v. 24). In stark contrast to the elect, who are "kept" for salvation, the angels of Gen. 6:1-4 and *1 Enoch* 10:4-6 "did not keep" their assigned position and therefore they are "kept" in nether gloom for the judgment to come (v. 6). The same fate will befall the false teachers, who will be "kept" in the nether gloom of darkness forever (v. 13; NRSV: "reserved").

Moreover "faith," "love," and "mercy" connect the prescript (v. 2) with the body of the letter. For the "beloved in God" the salutation wishes that "love" be theirs in "abundance" (v. 2), even as they are exhorted at the end of the letter to keep themselves "in the love of God" (v. 21). The "mercy" of the salutation receives an eschatological thrust as the believers are exhorted to "wait for the mercy of our Lord Jesus Christ unto eternal life" (v. 21). His advent will either grant "mercy," or result in "condemnation" (vv. 14-15). Finally the "peace" that the salutation wishes to be in abundance among the recipients (v. 2) should overcome the "divisions" within their communities (v. 19a). The "faith" for which they are exhorted to "contend," to fight for (v. 3), is the "most holy faith" (v. 20) which the heretics seek to pervert (vv. 4-19), a faith that had been delivered to "the saints," to God's holy ones on earth (v. 3). These heretics are "ungodly" people (vv. 4, 15, 18), destined for "condemnation" (vv. 4, 10, 11, 13-15). In short, because Jude 1-4 is closely connected to the rest of the letter by means of catchwords, we should affirm the unity of this brief letter addressed to Christians anywhere.

Turning to the structure of Jude, we note that Bauckham holds that verses 5-19 are important "only as necessary background to the appeal." The appeal itself (vv. 20-23) is "the climax of the letter" (*Jude*, 4). This view can hardly be right for three reasons. First, the appeal of verses 20-23 is so general that it does not need verses 5-19 for support or as background. Second, the ratio between background (vv. 5-19) and appeal would be rather lopsided—fifteen verses for the background and four verses for the main point. Third, the appeal, as stated in the body opening (vv. 3-4), also calls for opposing the false teachers, and in so doing, contending for the faith. To defend "the faith" includes exposing the false teachers and their fate (v. 4). Hence verses 5-19 are not merely the "background" to the main point, but they are the chief part of the body of the letter.

Using rhetorical criticism, Watson proposes a rather different rhetorical outline (77-78). (For an introduction to rhetorical criticism, see the important study by George A. Kennedy.) Greco-Roman rhetorical handbooks distinguished among three kinds of rhetoric. *Judicial* rhetoric persuaded courts concerning right or wrong actions committed in the past. *Deliberative* rhetoric seeks to persuade, advise, or dissuade an audience concerning actions that would affect their future for good or ill. *Epideictic* rhetoric assigns praise or blame to persons in the present on the basis of their honorable or dishonorable actions. Watson classifies Jude as "deliberative rhetoric which relies heavily upon epideictic [in vv. 5-19] in its effort to advise and dissuade" (33). Watson's outline in its main headings is as follows. (Within the parentheses are my comments on the nomenclature.)

1. Epistolary prescript (Quasi-*Exordium*)—vv. 1-2
2. *Exordium*—v. 3 (functions as introduction, seeks to gain the audience's goodwill, and prepares them for what follows)
3. *Narratio*—v. 4 (states the facts of the case)
4. *Probatio*—vv. 5-16 (the proof, or proofs, seek to persuade the audience about the legitimacy of the case as presented)
5. *Peroratio*—vv. 17-23 (summation of the main points of the probatio and appeal to the audience)
6. Doxology (Quasi-*Peroratio*)—vv. 24-25

In Watson's rhetorical outline the polemics of verses 5-19 are not subordinated to the appeal in verses 20-23. It is the polemical situation, caused by the infiltration of false teachers into the church (as stated in the *narratio*, v. 4), that was of central concern to Jude. The difficulty I have with this outline is twofold. First, verses 17-18 appear not to be a recapitulation or summation of the previous *probatio*, but rather its climactic conclusion. Second, the caveat of Stanley K. Stowers should not be ignored: "The classification of letter types according to the three species of rhetoric only partially works. This is because the letter-writing tradition was essentially independent of rhetoric" (52). It seems to me that Jude does not have a *peroratio*. Instead it has concluding exhortations and a doxology (vv. 20-25), like other letters.

Content

1. Epistolary Prescript (vv. 1-2)

The letter claims to be written by Jude, a "slave [servant] of Jesus Christ and brother of James." "Slave" is not an indication of his social status, but a title of honor. Even kings called themselves slaves of a god or gods. This self-designation, found also in Rom. 1:1; Phil. 1:1; James 1:1; 2 Peter 1:1, probably indicates the position of honor and leadership that Jude held. "James," whose "brother" Jude is, refers to the leader of the Jerusalem church (e.g., Acts 15:13-21). Thus, the author would also be a brother of Jesus (Mark 6:3). Ellis thinks that "brother" in Acts means primarily "co-worker" (227–29), and hence our Jude could be Judas Barsabbas of Acts 15:22-34, a "co-worker" of James rather than his blood brother. But it seems improbable that "brother" in Acts meant anything but fellow believer. In Jude 1, however, "brother of James" would be understood by the recipients as referring to his natural kinship with James. The addressees are identified in general terms as those "called . . . beloved . . . and kept" safe, terms that also were applied to Israel, as well as to the church. Jude will repeat them in his following message and transpose them in his grand finale, his doxology (vv. 24-25). The salutation is a wish prayer that God would bless the recipients with abundant "mercy, peace, and love," themes that also will be taken up later on.

2. Body Opening (vv. 3-4)

The opening introduces the circumstances and the subject of the letter and seeks to establish common ground. Jude had wanted to write about "our common salvation," but his plan to do so was thwarted by a new development. He now finds it necessary to write an appeal, better, an exhortation, to "contend" or fight for "the faith that was once for all delivered to the saints" (v. 3). This faith is the tradition that together with "our common salvation" constitutes the common ground between author and recipients. (For faith as tradition see 1 Tim. 3:9; 4:1, 6; 2 Tim. 4:7.) What this faith includes is never stated, and need not be stated, because it is the common ground; its knowledge is therefore presupposed since it has been delivered once and for all, transmitted with fidelity. Hence, new traditions or new teachings cannot be true, and what is true doctrine and practice is not something new.

Since "the faith" has been "delivered" and since "delivered" is the technical term for the transmission of traditions, we conclude that "the faith" is presented by Jude as a body of doctrine *and* moral instruction, transmitted "once for all." Such "faith tradition" functions as a boundary around the community of believers and distinguishes the community from the world outside. One should not label this view as "early catholicism," because the confession that "Jesus is Lord" (1 Cor. 12:3) is already a doctrinal confession that also functions as a boundary.

The urgent need to fight for the faith is stated in verse 4, introduced by the Greek conjunction *gar*. Itinerant teachers, or prophets, have gained access to, have sneaked into, communities. The following is said about them. First, the condemnation of these people had been prophesied "long ago," in the OT (cf. vv. 5-7, 11-12), in *1 Enoch* (cf. vv. 14-15), and by the apostles (cf. v. 17). Second, these people are "ungodly" persons (cf. vv. 15, 18). Third, they "pervert the grace of our God into licentiousness," that is, into immorality, including sexual promiscuity. In short they are antinomians (cf. vv. 8a, 13a, 16b). Fourth, they deny "our only Master and Lord, Jesus Christ." They reject his authority. It is not clear whether "Master" refers to God, in which case the opponents might have held a gnostic doctrine of a demiurge who created the material world. Since the rest of the letter does not polemicize against such views it is better to see also in "Master" a reference to Jesus Christ. The opponents' denial of

Christ consists in their misconduct. Their disregard of the ethical norms of the tradition is a denial of Christ as Lord over their lives (cf. Titus 1:16). In this introduction the author establishes the need to fight for the faith. This means that the recipients must agree with the author about the prophesied fate as well as the nature and destructive work of the opponents. The opening of the letter places the recipients on notice that they have to make a decision regarding these false teachers, and Jude hopes to persuade them to make the right decision.

3. Middle of the Body of the Letter; Part I (vv. 5-19)

In this section, Jude presents "texts" followed by applications. The texts consist of prophecies (vv. 14-15, 17-18), of OT types (vv. 5-7, 11), or of summaries of OT narratives. The sources for the texts are three: the OT, pseudepigraphal writings, and apostolic prophetic tradition. The texts and their applications to the present are intended to enlighten the recipients concerning the opponents in their midst, so that they will struggle on behalf of the faith. One could entitle this section: Know your enemies, their nature and destiny.

The texts of this section are verses 5-7, 9, 11, 14-15, 17-18. The five corresponding applications of the texts to the present are verses 8, 10, 12-13, 16, 19. In the texts the verb tenses are past or, as in verse 18, future. However, the applications of the texts have only present verb tenses. Moreover, they have the same introductory formula, which is more obvious in Greek than in the NRSV. The formula, repeated five times, is: "these are the people who" referring to the false teachers present in the communities (Ellis, 222–23).

In the first text (three types, vv. 5-7), Jude now develops the statements made in the opening that the false teachers are ungodly and headed for destruction. His first text consists of summaries of three examples from the OT that his readers know quite well, because they "have been fully informed." His first example is: to be saved once does not mean to be saved for all times. The Lord (probably Jesus, or else God) saved Israel from Egypt in the exodus, but he afterward destroyed those who did not believe (v. 5; cf. Num. 14:35). Thus these unbelieving Israelites are a "type" for Christians, heretics and recipients of this letter alike. If they misuse the grace of God for indulging in immorality, and erode "the faith," they become subject to divine punishment, just like the wilderness generation. His second example is: the angels of Gen. 6:1-4, according to Jewish tradition, "did not keep" their assigned positions but descended to earth in order to marry women (cf. *1 Enoch* 10:4-6). Their punishment for rejecting God's lordship is that they are "kept in eternal chains" in the nether gloom until judgment day. His third example is: the Sodomites and their company of Gen. 19:4-25, according to Jude 7, desired to have sexual relations with angels (who appeared as "men," Gen. 18:16-22). Thereby the Sodomites transgressed the order of creation. They are the counterpart to the sexual lust of the fallen angels of Genesis 6. Their condemnation consists of punishment by "eternal fire."

Verse 8 brings Jude's application of these three "types," who serve as "an example" (v. 7). "In the same way" the false teachers "defile the flesh," just as the fallen angels and the Sodomites had done. Jude accuses the interlopers of sexual promiscuity. They also reject divine "authority," and hence erode "the faith," as all three examples had done; and finally, like the Sodomites, "they revile the glorious ones," literally, "they commit blasphemy" against those angels that represent God's moral order (cf. Acts 7:53; Heb. 2:2, in distinction from Gal. 3:19; 4:3). Their sins of sexual immorality, of rejection of divine authority, and of blasphemy against the angels are committed on the basis of their dreams. This statement cannot be deduced from the three OT types. It represents Jude's own description of the interlopers and of their claims. Their dreams (NRSV: "these dreamers") are the means by which they receive new revelations that are contrary to "the faith delivered to the saints." For dreams of false prophets see Jer. 23:25, 27, 32; 27:9; 29:8. In conclusion, Jude suggests that the false teachers base their teaching and antinomian practice on dreams resulting in the rejection of Christ's authority and of the moral order represented by the angels, "the glorious ones."

The second text (v. 9) summarizes a story from the *Testament of Moses*, a pseudepigraphal work that is lost but has been partially reconstructed. For additional information one should consult Bauckham's exhaustive study on the background and source of Jude 9 (*Jude*, 65–76). This second text is meant to support and amplify Jude's accusation that the false teachers "blaspheme" the angels, an accusation made in the previous verse (v. 8). The catchwords "blasphemy" and "blaspheme" occur in verses 8 and 9, and in the application of verse 10 (NRSV: "slander"). This second text contrasts their blasphemy against angels with the behavior of the archangel Michael. In this pseudepigraphal story the devil apparently accused Moses of murder (Exod. 2:12; Acts 7:28) and therefore the devil claimed the body of (the dead) Moses. The archangel Michael, functioning as Moses' advocate, "disputed" with the devil "about the body of Moses." Even though Michael knew that the devil's accusation was "blasphemy," slander, and lies, Michael did not presume to condemn the devil for slander. Instead he left the judgment of the devil up to the ultimate judge, saying: "The Lord rebuke you" (cf. Zech. 3:2).

Verse 10 provides the application: in contrast to Michael's example, "these men" in their lack of understanding "blaspheme." They slander not just the devil but angels who represent God's law and order and who as representatives of the law accuse them. Thus they place themselves above any moral authority and their conduct demonstrates it. "By those things that they do know (and practice) by instinct, like irrational animals, they are destroyed."

In the third text (three OT types, v. 11) three notorious individuals from the OT appear as types of the false teachers. Jude does not need to recount the stories of Cain (Gen. 4:8-11), of Balaam (Numbers 22–24; Deut. 23:4), or of Korah (Num. 16:1-48; 26:9-11), because he presumes that his readers are fully informed (v. 5). Moreover, he assumes that they are also aware of the postbiblical traditions about these three rogues. Jude introduces these types by pronouncing a prophetic oracle of judgment, a "woe" against the false teachers, "for" their behavior is like the behavior of the three OT types. The false teachers "walked in the way of Cain." Postbiblical traditions regard Cain "as the first heretic" (Bauckham, *Jude*, 79–81; Josephus *Antiquities* 1.52–66). They "abandoned themselves to Balaam's error for the sake of gain." In contrast to the biblical account of Num. 22:18 and so on, postbiblical traditions regard him as acting against Israel out of greed and leading Israel into apostasy by enticing the Israelites to fornicate with Midianite women (cf. Num. 25:1-3; Josephus *Antiquities* 4.126–30; see M. S. Moore; cf. Rev. 2:14). As Balaam's "error" (Greek *planē*) led Israel into sin, just so the false teachers are leading, or trying to lead, believers astray (cf. "the wandering stars," Greek *planētai,* of v. 13). Finally, "they perished in Korah's rebellion." In postbiblical traditions Korah became "the classic example of the antinomian heretic" (Bauckham, *Jude*, 83). Note that the three types are not in chronological order, probably because Korah's judgment was the most vivid. The earth swallowed up him and his companions. Thus he entered "the nether gloom of darkness" (v. 13; cf. v. 6). Also note the intensification of the verbs: walk, abandon themselves, perish. (The NRSV has present tenses in v. 11; the Greek text has three aorists, which in the light of the prophetc "woe" have a perfect-tense meaning.)

I translate the application in verses 12-13: "These are the people, reefs they are, (inviting shipwreck), who celebrate with you at your agape (meals), without reverent fear (toward God)." In the light of 2 Peter 2:13 the NRSV and others have "blemishes" in the text and "reefs" in the footnote. For the metaphor of shipwreck see 1 Tim. 1:19. The agape was still a regular meal in conjunction with which the Lord's Supper was celebrated in the evening (cf. 1 Cor. 11:17-34; Acts 2:46). The false teachers treat the agape as merely another meal, without reverence and fear toward God. The metaphor of reefs highlights the danger of being in their company. Just as the company around Korah experienced common disaster together with their leader, so believers who affiliate with the false teachers will experience shipwreck. Moreover, the intruders are people who "shepherd themselves." Like Balaam they are greedy, pursuing their own advantages and ignoring the welfare of others (cf. Ezek. 34:2-4). Then follow four metaphors from nature (from the sky, the land, the sea, and the heavens) with which Jude denounces the leadership of his opponents. The background of these metaphors is twofold. On one hand, *1 Enoch* 2:1—5:4 and other texts in this letter contrast nature, which obeys God's laws, with the wicked, who transgress his laws. On the other hand, *1 Enoch* 80:2-8 predicts that in the last days not even nature will obey God's law. The false teachers are like "waterless clouds" (cf. Prov. 25:14), manifestations of unfulfilled promises, "fruitless trees," which are good for nothing.

They are "twice dead," which refers to the second, eternal death after the final judgment (Rev. 20:6, 14; 21:8). Though the judgment lies in the future, their fate is already certain. They are like "wild waves of the sea casting up the foam of their own shame," which may refer to Isa. 57:20. There "the wicked are like the tossing sea . . . its waters toss up mire and mud." They are like the "wandering stars" of *1 Enoch* 80:6, to which Jude may be alluding. In *1 Enoch*, during the last days, stars make "errors" and "change their courses." The "wandering star" metaphor also links the interlopers to Balaam's "error" and to the destruction that resulted from Korah's rebellion (v. 11), because the "nether gloom of darkness will keep them forever" (v. 13). With these rhetorical blasts against the heretics, Jude hopes to persuade his people from associating with them, lest they share their fate.

The fourth text is verses 14-15 (cf. *1 Enoch* 1:9): "It was also about these (heretics) that Enoch, in the seventh generation from Adam, prophesied." Clearly for Jude, *1 Enoch* is a book of prophecy inspired by God. Tertullian therefore wanted to include it in the canon, while others in the third century wanted to exclude Jude. Second Peter, which used Jude as a source, omitted the quotations from *1 Enoch* and the reference to the *Testament of Moses* (Jude 9, 14-15). Jude substituted "Lord" (Jesus) for God (thus *1 Enoch* 1:9) in agreement with other NT writers (e.g., 1 Thess. 3:13; 2 Thess. 1:7). Instead of the coming of God, the church after Easter expected the coming of Jesus, who as God's representative will complete salvation and execute judgment. Note the fourfold "all" and the four occurrences of "ungodly/ungodliness" in the Greek text and the RSV of verse 15 (not the NRSV). All people whose speech and conduct is "ungodly," like the false teachers, are the ones who will be subject to judgment when the Lord comes at his glorious parousia, surrounded by myriads of holy angels. *1 Enoch*'s prophecy is delivered in prophetic aorists, even though the judgment on "all ungodly" for "all their deeds of ungodliness" lies in the future for both *1 Enoch* and Jude. The prophetic past tense either emphasizes the inevitability of the judgment to come, or else it narrates the prophet's past visions about future events, telling what he saw.

The application in verse 16 is: "These (heretics) are grumblers and malcontents" (literally, "murmurers"), like the wilderness generation (v. 5; cf. Exod. 15:34; 16:2; 1 Cor. 10:10) and like the people around Korah (Num. 16:2-30). "They indulge their own lusts [cf. vv. 7, 8a, 10b]; they are bombastic in their speech [cf. v. 8b and the example of Korah, v. 11; cf. also *1 Enoch* 5:4], flattering people (or 'showing partiality to certain people'] for their own advantage" (v. 12b). It is possible that Jude here alludes to *Testament of Moses* 5:5. At any rate Jude depicts the heretics as ingratiating themselves with "arrogant" language about freedom from moral restraint and freedom for indulgence in the lusts of the flesh.

The fifth text (prophecy of the apostles) occurs in verses 17-18. The opening direct address, "you beloved," marks an inclusion with the direct address of verse 3. Moreover, the reminder of verse 17 ("you should remember") links up with the reminder in verse 5. Both the direct address and the reminder indicate that the apostolic prophecy and its application are the climactic conclusion of this section. Jude now complements the ancient prophecy of *1 Enoch* with a recent prophecy by "the apostles" (plural): "But you, beloved, must remember the predictions of the apostles of our Lord Jesus Christ; for they said to you: 'In the last time there will be scoffers [cf. vv. 4, 8, 10, 11, 15], indulging in their own ungodly lusts' " (cf. vv. 4, 8a, 16). Predictions about the appearance of false prophets/teachers in the final time before the end are frequent in the NT (e.g., Mark 13:22; Matt. 7:15; 24:11, 24; Acts 20:29-30; 1 Tim. 4:1-3; 2 Tim. 2:16-18; 4:3-4; 1 John 2:18; 4:1-6; 2 Peter 3:2-4), though the exact form of the prediction in Jude 18 occurs only here.

The application comes in verse 19. With three short phrases Jude gives his final characterization of the heretics, whose appearance had been predicted by the apostles for the time before the end. These people, first of all, "create divisions" in Christian communities (see below for an alternate translation). Second, they are "psychics" (Greek *psychikoi*, "worldly people") and as such they cannot but follow their own passions, like animals (cf. v. 10b), because, third, "they do not possess the Spirit," as they claim they do (cf. v. 8a). It is possible that instead of causing "divisions" within communities, we should translate and interpret: these people "make distinctions" among church members, namely, between themselves on one hand, who possess the Spirit, enabling them to promulgate new revelations, received in Spirit-inspired dreams (cf. v. 8a), and on the other hand the ordinary church folk, who are mere "psychics" without the Spirit. Jude with some irony would turn their claim on its head in verse 19, denouncing the heretics as mere psychics, devoid of the Spirit (so Kelly, 284).

In favor of the alternate interpretation is the fact that the heretics still participate in the agape (v. 12a), which means that "the divisions" (of the first translation) are not absolute. Moreover, those interpreters who favor the authenticity of Jude, and therefore an early date, would have some difficulties with a gnostic or protognostic interpretation of verse 18. Yet in favor of the first interpretation, one could argue that just as Korah formed his own group within Israel (cf. v. 11), so likewise the heretics gathered their own clique within the community. At any rate, according to Jude "these people" are devoid of the Holy Spirit (cf. Rom. 8:9b).

4. Middle of the Body of the Letter; Part II (vv. 20-23)

Just as part I closes with a direct address (v. 17), so part II opens with one, "beloved" (v. 20). Thus far Jude has pointed out the theological identity of the enemy (they are ungodly, etc.) and their fate (judgment will fall upon them). He also has made it clear that association with them is a dangerous matter. In order to carry on the fight for the faith the believers must know their opponent. But they themselves must be equipped spiritually in order to contend for the faith, and they need to receive some directives on how to deal with heretics in their midst. In this second part of the middle of the body of the letter, Jude addresses these two concerns.

Verses 20-21 are exhortation and encouragement. Jude's central exhortation has the form of an imperative: "keep yourselves in the love of God." This imperative is supported and explicated by three present-tense Greek participles that are subordinate to the imperative and further explain it. To keep oneself in God's love (cf. vv. 1-2) means first of all to build oneself up on the foundation of "the most holy faith," which has been "delivered once for all to the saints" (v. 3). This faith is the immutable tradition that has been transmitted to the church. The tradition is holy, because its ultimate origin lies in God. Entrusted to God's holy ones on earth, the faith tradition disagrees totally with the message of the false teachers. The Greek participle *epoikodomountes* ("building yourselves up") alludes to the church as household and temple of God (cf. Eph. 2:19-22; 1 Peter 2:4-10; 1 Cor. 3:9-11, 16; 2 Cor. 6:16). By building themselves up on the foundation of the holy tradition the believers grow into God's eschatological household and temple. Thus they keep themselves in God's love.

Second, to keep oneself in God's love requires prayer "in the Holy Spirit" (cf. Rom. 8:26-27; Eph. 6:18). Perhaps the false teachers rejected prayer altogether. In the *Gospel of Thomas* we read: "If you pray, you will be condemned" (log. 14; cf. log. 16). At any rate, for Jude the false teachers cannot pray in the Holy Spirit because they "do not have the

Spirit" (v. 19). Prayer is the believer's response to the love of God, who grants the Holy Spirit to his "beloved." Whether Jude includes glossolalia (cf. 1 Cor. 14:6-19) in his reference to prayer in the Spirit cannot be decided one way or the other. But we can agree that the Holy Spirit is active not just in glossolalia (cf. 1 Cor. 14:19).

Third, to keep oneself in God's love means to "wait for the mercy of our Lord Jesus Christ that leads to eternal life" at his parousia. Then when his judgment falls upon the ungodly, those who remained faithful in their struggle for the faith will be saved by "the mercy" of Jesus Christ. Salvation is by his mercy, not by our faithful struggle, even though without faithful struggle there is no salvation. This tension may not be dissolved. Before the ultimate judge, I, as an antinomian, cannot presume on his mercy, just as I, as a faithful Christian, cannot invite the ultimate judge to listen to a recital of my virtuous deeds. Salvation will be ours only by the Lord's mercy. Condemnation will be ours through our own antinomianism. We may also take note of the triads God, Christ, and the Holy Spirit; and faith, love, and hope in terms of waiting for the Lord.

Verses 22-23 contain directives for dealing with the false teachers and their followers. Thus far, Jude has drawn clear boundaries that are needed in order to preserve the integrity of the community. The remaking of boundaries had become necessary because they had been violated through the secretly gained admission of false teachers (v. 4). How to deal with them and with those influenced by them is the subject of this final subsection. Except for the last clause in verse 23, the Greek text is no longer clear and neither is the meaning of some words. Every translation is therefore rather uncertain. The different texts, as represented in Greek manuscripts, are conveniently laid out by Metzger (727–29) and by Bauckham (*Jude*, 108–11). According to Metzger a majority of the committee "was disposed to prefer as original the triple arrangement of the passage," which would refer to three groups of people (728), while according to Bauckham the text of p^{72}, which refers to two groups of people, seems preferable. Following Metzger's majority opinion, the NRSV reads:

Have mercy on some who are wavering; save others by snatching them out of the fire; and have mercy on still others with fear, hating even the tunic defiled by their bodies.

Bauckham's translation, based on the shorter text, is as follows:

Snatch some from the fire, but on those who dispute have mercy with fear, hating even the clothing that has been soiled by the flesh.

Bauckham's shorter text seems preferable to me, at least for now, and surely the last line in the NRSV is poorly translated. Instead of "tunic," an outer garment, the text refers to the clothing worn next to the skin; and instead of "bodies," the text speaks of "flesh," meaning "corrupted flesh" (thus NIV). In his final exhortation Jude advises his readers to care for the false teachers and the people influenced by them and to try to change them. If they are successful they will "snatch them from the fire" of hell (v. 7) by bringing them back to the faith. (For admonitions of erring believers see Matt. 18:15-17; Luke 17:3; Gal. 6:1; 2 Thess. 3:15; James 5:19-20.) On those "who dispute" (cf. v. 9) and argue against the faith, have "mercy with reverent fear" toward God, knowing that their persistent abandonment of the faith will lead to their condemnation. The final clause, which is without variant readings, may allude to Zech. 3:1-5, where the high priest is clothed with filthy garments. The picture in Jude is of undergarments, soiled by excrement, and drives home a point in hyperbolic fashion, that exposure to contamination by sins of the flesh is to be abhorred (vv. 6-7, 8a, 10, etc.). Soiled garments are contrasted to the white garments of the conquerors in Rev. 3:4-5. There, an exhortation precedes the metaphor: "*remember* what you *received* and heard; *keep* that and *repent*" (Rev. 3:3). If so, they too "shall walk" with Christ "in white" (Rev. 3:4). In Jude, showing "mercy" toward those who have strayed reflects the mercy they have received and hope for (vv. 1, 23). Simultaneously showing mercy toward the straying is coupled with abhorence of their sins (cf. 1 Cor. 5:11). Jude hopes that through his readers "some" will be saved.

5. *Concluding Doxology (vv. 24-25)*

> Now to him who is able to keep you from falling,
> > and to present you without blemish in the presence of his glory with rejoicing,
> > to the only God our Savior, through Jesus Christ our Lord,
> > belong glory, majesty, power, and authority,
> > before all time, now and forevermore. Amen.

In place of the customary epistolary postscript Jude concludes his letter with a triumphant doxology which simultaneously encloses his prayer for his people that God through Christ would keep them from falling (into heresy and sins) so that at the end God himself can present them without blemish, in faultless integrity (Exod. 29:1; Eph. 1:4; Phil. 2:15; Rev. 14:5), before his radiant glory in his heavenly temple, where they will join in exultation with the whole redeemed people of God and the company of heaven (1 Peter 1:6; 4:13b; Rev. 19:1-8). For similar doxologies, see Rom. 16:25-27; Eph. 3:20-21; 1 Tim. 1:17; *Mart. Pol.* 20:2. All theology and all exhortations find their ultimate conclusion in prayer, praise, adoration, and doxology to the one whose majesty spans the ages, past, present, and future.

The Opponents

What can one learn about the opponents from this letter? Since Jude refers to them as shepherds (who care only for themselves; v. 12), we can safely infer that they regard themselves as teachers. Since they come from outside the communities (v. 4), one can identify them as itinerant teachers. Jude accuses them of greed (vv. 11, 12) and of flattering people (v. 12). While these are traditional topics of Jewish and early Christian polemics, there is no reason to think that they do not apply to them. From Jude's point of view they are guilty of sexual misconduct, "perverting the grace of God" into freedom for immorality (v. 4). Since Paul also had to guard against antinomian conclusions that might be drawn from his preaching (cf. Rom. 6:1, 15; Gal. 5:13), some interpreters connect the opponents of Jude to antinomian Paulinists. Moreover, Paul's teaching might have had some influence on Jude's opponents. According to Paul, the law was given "by angels" (Gal. 3:19-20), but believers, led by the Spirit, are "not under the law" (Gal. 5:18), nor are they any longer under "the elemental spirits of the universe" (Gal. 4:3, 8-9; cf. Col. 2:8, 15-23), which also enslave, just like the law. Whether aspects of Paul's teaching influenced Jude's opponents cannot be established beyond doubt, though the possibility remains that it might have. Jude's opponents reject the authority of angels, who for Jude are the representatives of the moral order; their rejection of angels in blasphemous words results in immoral deeds (vv. 8-10). Jude reverses the self-understanding of the heretics, who think of themselves as Spirit-endowed individuals, when he writes that they are devoid of the Spirit (v. 19) and live by the instinct of animals (v. 10). They surely claim to possess the Spirit while other Christians in their opinion are mere worldly ("psychic") people (v. 19). Through dreams they receive new spiritual insights or revelations that are the basis of their heresy (v. 8). Their denial of the Lord Jesus Christ consists in their antinomianism in thought, word, and deed. The letter does not indicate that they hold a docetic Christology, or deny his resurrection or parousia. For Jude antinomian libertinism under the disguise of new insights mediated by the Spirit and dreams constitutes denial of Christ.

The Author

The authenticity of this letter by Jude, brother of James, both of whom are brothers of Jesus, is most eloquently upheld by Bauckham. But in spite of his arguments it seems to me that the letter is pseudonymous for the following reasons. First, why would Jude not only allude to but cite from *1 Enoch,* when his brother Jesus, to the best of our knowledge, had not paid the slightest attention to that or similar books? Note, however, that *1 Enoch* had become popular in some Christian circles during the second century.

Second, the vocabulary, the rhetoric, and even the style of this letter would be rather remarkable for a Palestinian Christian. Bauckham surmises that Jude "was probably still a very young man when he became a Christian missionary" (*Jude,* 15), and he learned Greek during his missionary work. But this suggestion does not hold. Jude's letter is addressed to Christians among whom he did not work as a missionary. Had he done so, he would not have had to take recourse to "the predictions of the apostles" (vv. 17-18), but could have reminded them of what he had told them when he was with them. The pseudonymous author of 2 Thessalonians used this device (2 Thess. 2:5, 15; 3:10), but he could use it only because Paul had been a missionary-apostle and everyone knew that. To assume that Jude acquired his linguistic skills while doing missionary work but wrote to Christians among whom he did not work requires too much of our imagination.

Third, one would expect that the brother of James, writing before James's death to Christians who also included Jews, would have to deal not only with the issue of the law of Moses but also with the Apostles' Decree. According to Acts 15 the Apostles' Decree was the "judgment" first spoken by James (Acts 15:19-21, 28-29; 21:25-26). Had Jude written the letter after James's martyrdom in 62 C.E. one would expect some reference to it in verse 1. If it had been written during the 50s to Jewish and gentile Christians, then the absence of at least a brief reference to the Torah and to the Apostles' Decree becomes incomprehensible, since the letter claims to be written by the brother of James (cf. Acts 21:17-24). By contrast, the letter reflects a period when the issue of the validity of Torah is a dead issue. The place of the law of Moses and of the Apostles' Decree is taken over by traditions about moral conduct, which for the author of this letter are part of the faith delivered to the saints (v. 3).

Fourth, Jude tells us that the apostles (plural) predicted the appearance of scoffers and antinomians before the end time (v. 17). Luther already felt that our author "speaks of the apostles like a pupil from a time long afterward" (WA, Bibel VII, 384). We may ask, did the apostles make such a prediction? There is no basis for it in Paul's undisputed letters. But such predictions appear with ever-greater frequency toward the end of the first century, when apocalyptic fervor gripped parts of the church and of Judaism. In short, it seems that this letter is pseudonymous.

But why choose the pseudonym Jude? Apparently the fairly educated Jewish Christian author had high regard for Jude, the brother of James.

Toward the end of the first century a "dynastic Christianity" (Rowston) developed in Jerusalem where Jude's descendants functioned as leaders "of churches" (Eusebius *Ecclesiastical History* 2.20.1). Since Jesus' brother Jude was esteemed in Jewish Christian circles, it seems probable that a Greek-speaking Jewish Christian who may have known Jude (Reike, 191) wrote this letter in his name and for his honor, calling believers to fight for the faith, including moral conduct.

The time of writing is prior to 2 Peter, because 2 Peter used Jude. A date around 90–100 C.E. may be more probable than a later date. The place of writing is unknown. A proximity to the place of the book of Revelation might be suggested, because apocalyptic fervor and an imminent-end expectation permeate both writings and because the threat of antinomianism is present in both (cf. Rev. 2:14-15, 20-23). Moreover, if the opponents of Jude misused some aspects of Paul's teaching concerning the law, as found in Galatians, then Asia Minor would be a probable place for Jude to have been written.

The author does not address his letter to the leaders of churches but to Christians at large, because he, like Paul and others before him, believes that all true Christians are endowed with the Holy Spirit in prayer (v. 20) and in their fight for "the faith." His weapon in the struggle against heresy is not the ministerial office as such but "the faith once for all delivered unto the saints" (v. 3). For Jude the gospel never existed without doctrine and moral obligations. Paul would agree with him. The confession "Jesus is Lord" (1 Cor. 12:3) is also a doctrinal statement confessed in opposition to the many gods and many lords of the Hellenistic landscape (1 Cor. 8:5). For Jude "the faith," like the *parathēkē* of the Pastoral Epistles, draws the boundary line between truth and heresy in word and deed.

The author has frequently been denigrated by interpreters because of his polemics. One should not try to absolve him by arguing that verses 5-19 are merely the "background" to his real message of verses 20-23. Rather we should realize that from Genesis 1 to Revelation 22 the Bible is also a polemical book. Polemics is necessary because of our inclination to sin and idolatry. Therefore, Moses and the prophets, Jesus and the apostles, the evangelists and the pseudonymous NT authors also engaged in polemics. The modern preacher who can no longer say that this or that particular belief or conduct is wrong ought to ask the government for job retraining. Polemics is implicit in every Christian confession of faith. The situation may arise where polemics, as practiced by Jude, is the most effective way of recalling those who doubt or waver (v. 22). Finally, Jude may help us to realize anew that the real enemies of the church are not just the enemies outside (like hostile pagan neighbors) but the compromisers and synthesizers within the church, who mouth slogans of liberation but in fact "pervert the grace of our God" into immorality and thereby "deny" the Lordship of Christ.

1-2-3 JOHN

Choice of language, historical assumptions, and slippery terms often exercise a determinative role in the way we read NT documents, especially "the Johannine Epistles." Even this conventional designation masks assumptions and difficulties. In what sense are these writings *Johannine*? It is generally acknowledged that they were not written by the apostle John but stand in some relation to the Johannine tradition. Here again the documents allow for various interpretations. Are they early reflections of the life and thought of the Johannine community, prior to its mature expression in the Gospel, or are they later efforts to correct misinterpretations of the Gospel? One's view of the historical setting of the Johannine Epistles affects one's understanding of the significance of the schism they reflect, the teachings of the opponents, and the relation of each faction to the community and its tradition. Neither is the term *epistles* without difficulty. While 2 and 3 John are among the best NT examples of Hellenistic epistles, 1 John lacks the distinguishing features of an epistle.

The following pages briefly survey the issues posed by these documents and various interpretations that have emerged in recent commentaries and monographs. The issues are so interrelated that they can hardly be considered separately. One's decisions in one area have implications for the others. Because of the dominance of historical reconstructions, however, we consider the historical context first, then the literary contours, canonical context, and theological distinctives of these writings.

Historical Context

Earlier works (e.g., C. H. Dodd) set the epistles in the broad cultural and intellectual milieu of early Christianity. Following the impetus of efforts in the late 1960s and 1970s to reconstruct the history of the Johannine community and to interpret the Gospel of John in relation to that history, Raymond E. Brown published his massive commentary on the Johannine Epistles (1982), which interprets every reference in the epistles in the context of the history of the Johannine community. Because all subsequent interpretations stand in dialogue with Brown's work, we will take it as a baseline and note ways in which publications during the past decade have adopted or challenged its conclusions.

Schism in the Johannine Community

Each of the epistles affords glimpses of their life setting. The tendency has generally been to read the three letters together, as coming from approximately the same period in the history of the Johannine community and reflecting aspects of the same setting. Each deals with conflicts. First John refers to antichrists (2:18), those who have gone out from the community (2:19), the children of the devil (3:10), and false prophets (4:1). Similarly, 2 John warns of deceivers, "those who do not confess that Jesus Christ has come in the flesh" (v. 7; cf. 1 John 4:2). Third John does not mention theological issues directly but deals with the problems caused by Diotrephes' refusal to receive emissaries such as Demetrius who were sent by the elder. The elder, therefore, writes to Gaius, appealing for his help. Are the various groups or individuals referred to in the letters related, and if so how? Because of its brevity and the similarities between it and 1 John, 2 John is usually interpreted as a letter warning a sister church about the problems troubling the Johannine community that are described in 1 John. This assumption still leaves unresolved the question of whether 1 John refers to one, two, or several groups of opponents.

Brown takes the conflict between the elder and the opponents or secessionists as the life setting of the epistles and the key to understanding them. Moreover, he maintains that the elder stood in opposition to one well-defined group. This group, which represents a significant but indeterminate portion of the community, has broken relations with the elder and his group, and the elder now writes to those who remain loyal to him to encourage them not to be misled by the views of the secessionists.

Other features of Brown's work are dealt with below. Influential as his work has been, not all interpreters have been convinced. Some have differed on major issues, such as whether the epistles precede or follow the composition of the Gospel (or better, whether they were written early or late in its composition history), whether there was a schism in the community, whether it was the central factor in the life setting of the epistles, and whether there was one or more groups of opponents. Since the identity of the opponents is crucial to one's reading of the epistles, we will deal with that issue before considering other interpretations of their rhetoric of hostility.

Profiles of the Opponents

One's grasp of the elder's theology is shaped and limited by his concern to respond to the errors of the opponents. First John does not give the elder's systematic presentation of his theology but his response to the theological and ethical differences at issue between him and the opponents. Foremost among the theological issues are implied christological errors. The opponents apparently denied that Jesus is the Christ (2:22), and that Jesus Christ had come in the flesh (4:2). Related to the christological issues are allusions that suggest that the opponents questioned the atoning significance of Jesus' death (2:1; 4:10; 5:6) and believed that they had already "passed from death to life" (3:14), that they were without sin (1:6, 8, 10), and that they would not be judged but were already abiding in Christ (2:4, 6, 9). The Spirit was the guarantee of their sinlessness and the authority for their teaching (2:27). Compounding the difficulties between the opponents and the elder were their moral or ethical errors. At least from the perspective of the elder, the opponents failed to practice the commandment to love one another (2:7-11; 3:14-17; 4:7-21).

Brown concludes that the opponents cannot be identified with any other known group. They were Christians who held an exaggeratedly high Christology. Hence, they were not Jews, Jewish Christians, Ebionites, or libertines. Neither can they be identified with any other group in the NT or in the second century: they were not the docetic opponents of Ignatius of Antioch, second-century Gnostics, or followers of Cerinthus. The issues in dispute are drawn from implications of the Johannine tradition itself. They represent differences that emerged within the community during the decade following the composition of the main body of the Gospel of John. Both the elder and the opponents appealed to that Gospel. Indeed, Brown attempts to show that "every idea of the secessionists (as reconstructed from the polemic in I and II John) can be plausibly explained as derivative from the Johannine tradition as preserved for us in the Gospel of John" (72).

The Christology of the Gospel of John is arguably the highest in the NT, affirming as it does the preexistence of the Word and Jesus' oneness with the Father. Deriving their views from this tradition, the secessionists placed such emphasis on the Son's origin and identity with the Father that they negated the importance of the ministry of Jesus (4:3). They also denied that Jesus had come in the flesh (4:2), not because they denied that Jesus was the Christ (John 20:30-31), but because they held such a high view of the Christ that they denied that he could have been truly human. As Brown points out, these views could have emerged as interpretations of the Johannine tradition, in which Jesus is identified with the preexistent Logos: his signs exemplify his continued sovereignty over the created order, and he is one with the Father and does not ask for information from others or pray for a change in the Father's will. John does not narrate the birth of Jesus. The secessionists may have read the coming of the Spirit upon Jesus at his baptism as the moment of incarnation. Similarly, taking their cue from John's interpretation of the cross as Jesus' "lifting up" and his return to the Father, with little emphasis on vicarious suffering, the opponents deemphasized the salvific significance of the cross in favor of the revelatory role of the Christ who revealed the Father (John 1:18).

If the secessionists were deficient in emphasis on moral behavior, it may well have been because there is a marked lack of moral teachings in the Gospel of John. It contains nothing like the Sermon on the Mount but reduces ethical instruction to the command to love one another. No specific sins are mentioned in the Gospel. Rather, sin consists primarily in unbelief (16:8) or rejection of the revelation (3:19; 15:22). Because they believed that they had received the revelation of the Christ and knew God, the secessionists could well have believed that they were without sin, that they knew God, and that they already had eternal life (John 5:24; 17:3). Similarly, the secessionists' emphasis on the Spirit and a realized eschatology could be explained by appeal to relevant aspects of the Johannine tradition as reflected in the Gospel.

In Brown's view, therefore, the debate between the elder and the opponents is an intra-Johannine debate only tangentially related to other developments in early Christianity. Both the elder and the opponents were influenced by the earlier stages of the Johannine tradition, so both the issues and the avenues of response open to the elder were conditioned by this shared tradition. On the one hand, the opponents were not Gnostics but represented a step toward Gnosticism; Gnostics may have taken up their way of reading the Gospel. On the other hand, the interpretation of the Gospel of John by the elder opened the way for an orthodox reading of the Gospel and prepared the way for its acceptance by Irenaeus and the church.

Other interpreters assess the life setting of the epistles differently. Rudolf Schnackenburg, whose commentary was originally published in 1975, treats 1 John as essentially independent of the Gospel. The question of their relationship cannot be settled since both similarities and differences are evident. Like Brown, Schnackenburg finds the elder in debate with one group of opponents, one which cannot be identified with any known group, but Schnackenburg contends that the opponents held gnostic views and were not greatly different from those against whom Ignatius contended. The christological differences are focused on the differences between the elder and the opponents regarding whether one is saved through the death of Christ or through coming to a special knowledge of God.

Pheme Perkins (1979) appeals to the conventions of oral cultures as a caution against assuming that the community was ripped apart by controversy. Calling for a "less polemicized reading of 1-3 John" (xxiii), she contends that the opponents remained in close contact with the rest of the community, so their teachings continued to be a threat to it.

Kenneth Grayston (1984) takes a divergent line of thought. The key to his understanding of the epistles is his conclusion that the epistles were written before, not after, the Gospel. Rejecting arguments that the opponents bear strong resemblances to the views of Cerinthus or those opposed by Ignatius, and working from references in 1 John itself, Grayston describes the opponents as a group that has withdrawn from the community because they could not accept the elder's separation from the world (2:15-17—contrast Perkins, who finds that the opponents charged that the Johannine Christians were not ascetic enough). They exercised prophetic gifts and claimed to be guided by the Spirit and born of God. They therefore regarded themselves as without sin. It was inappropriate for them to call Jesus *the* Anointed One since they all possessed the Spirit. Here the elder and the opponents differed most sharply—the elder claiming that those who reject the Son reject the Father, and opponents relying on inspiration by the Spirit with little regard for formulaic christological confessions. The Gospel later gave a more creative theological response to the difficulties from within and from outside the community, affirming the centrality of Christ while recognizing the experience of the Spirit.

Like Brown, Stephen Smalley (1984) places the epistles after the Gospel and views the setting of the epistles as an outgrowth of tendencies already at work in the Johannine community at the time the Gospel was written. Diverging from Brown, however, Smalley describes two tendencies at work in the community. On the one hand, Jewish Christians held a low view of Jesus and a high view of the law; on the other hand, Hellenistic (gnostic) Christians held a high view of Jesus and a low view of righteousness or the law. Both the evangelist and the elder offered balanced positions regarding Christology and ethics. By the time 1 John was written, however, a group comprised primarily of Hellenistic, gnostic Christians had withdrawn from the community. In response to this development, the elder wrote to encourage those who remained within the community and to respond to the heretical tendencies of both Jewish and Hellenistic Christians within the community.

In a series of articles and monographs, Judith Lieu has focused fresh attention both on the two shorter epistles and on the problems of interpreting the Johannine materials more generally. While recognizing the references to schism in the community, she cautions that 1 John, as indeed each of the Johannine writings, must be taken on its own terms. First John should not be read as a polemical document in which the elder's views are posed in response to those of the secessionists. Lieu questions whether the secessionists claimed to be spirit-filled or maintained a docetic Christology.

The epistle hardly offers data for reconstructing their views. Therefore, neither can one say that they derived their views from the Gospel (*Second and Third Epistles of John*, 209). The epistle stands as an independent expression of the Johannine faith. Its contacts with the Gospel do not indicate that it reflects a later stage in the community's history. Rather, its points of contact may be due to the fact that the Gospel and epistles draw on common elements of the community's tradition. If there is dependence, the clearest evidence for it is 2 John's dependence on 1 John (ibid., 76). In contrast to the majority of interpreters, therefore, Lieu does not interpret 1 John in the context of polemic against heretical views. Rather, the epistle confirms Johannine Christians in their faith while warning about those aspects of their faith that could lead to heretical views.

After surveying the history of interpretations, François Vouga (1990) notes that although there is evidence of a schism, the form of the antithetical statements indicates that the so-called opponents remained within the community also. One must exercise caution to avoid anachronistically reading the views of later groups into the meager evidence supplied by the epistles. The common ties of both the elder and the opponents to the Johannine tradition have influenced the nature of the elder's argument. He reminds the community of the traditions it has held from "the beginning" (1 John 1:1). His eschatological self-consciousness is rooted in his Christology, but the christological formulas assert not the incarnation of the Christ but his role as the Revealer. The epistle, therefore, does not oppose heresy but apostasy, such as would have resulted from the persecution of Christians in the Roman world. The elder—rather than the opponents—can be seen as representing a step in the development of Gnosticism (Vouga, 46–48).

While not differing sharply from Brown's reconstruction of the views of the opponents, John Painter (1991) analytically reviews the evidence for their position and diverges from Brown at several points. Painter sorts the evidence, which he notes is expressed in 1 John in highly stylized forms, into five strands: (1) seven "boasts"—three in 1 John 1, three in 1 John 2, and one in 1 John 4:20; (2) the evidence of what the opponents denied (in 1 John 4:1-6); (3) the opponents' view of and emphasis on the Spirit; (4) the so-called antitheses, where the phrase "everyone who" is followed by a participle and a statement that opposes the elder's views to those of the opponents; and (5) the lack of appeal to the OT. Taken together, these strands of evidence reveal that the opponents differed from the elder primarily on their view of God and the role of the Spirit. They claimed to possess the Spirit and to participate in the "light nature" of God. Christological differences were secondary. What they denied, however, was the identity of Jesus and the Christ. The opponents probably came from a gentile background. One can draw parallels between them and the *pneu-matikoi* against whom Paul polemicizes in 1 Cor. 12:3. For the opponents, Jesus received the "anointing from the holy one" at his baptism. Like Jesus, they had received the anointing, they had God's seed, and therefore there was no need to find any saving significance in Jesus' death.

Authorship and Sequence

The dominant view is that the Johannine Epistles were written by one author, who was neither the apostle nor the evangelist. Judgments regarding the authorship and date of the epistles vary just as much as reconstructions of their historical setting.

In a famous series of articles, C. H. Dodd (1937), W. F. Howard (1947), W. G. Wilson (1948), and A. P. Salom (1955) reviewed the grammatical and stylistic evidence, reaching different conclusions regarding whether the Gospel and epistles were written by the same author. It is scarcely debatable that the Gospel and epistles are as similar in style as any other documents in the NT, including Luke and Acts and the various Pauline epistles. Nevertheless, disparities are evident in the use and frequency of particles, compound verbs, and other idioms. Dodd also argued that the epistles diverge strikingly from the Gospel in their eschatology, the significance of the death of Christ, and the doctrine of the Holy Spirit. He concluded, therefore, that the epistles were written by a disciple of the Fourth Evangelist.

Responses to Dodd put a different spin on the same evidence by noting that the Gospel was the result of a long process of composition, while the epistles responded to a particular situation. The Gospel covers a wider range of subject matter, and the evangelist drew on oral and written sources, which probably contained the Aramaisms found in the Gospel. Such considerations may blunt the force of the stylistic and theological differences between the Gospel and the epistles, but they have not settled the matter.

In a vigorous challenge to prevailing views on the Johannine writings, Martin Hengel (1989) has argued that they are all the work of one man, not the apostle John but John the elder who is mentioned in the Papias fragments. This John was the head of the Johannine school in Asia Minor. The epistles reflect his personal authority and teaching but do not presuppose the Gospel, the final editing of which followed the writing of the epistles. Because of the specific theological issues posed by the crisis in the community, one would not expect the epistles simply to repeat the christological formulations of the Gospel. Second and 3 John do not reflect the final disintegration of the Johannine school but the sovereignty of the elder as he addresses problems threatening a vigorous network of Johannine house churches. The elder does not argue or cajole; he instructs and decrees.

Hengel's assessment of the situation differs from Brown's in several significant respects. He finds no evidence that the opponents appealed to the Gospel, and he cautions against reading the dispute as solely an intra-Johannine controversy. In Hengel's view the Johannine school was quite open. It was not cut off from developments among Christians in Asia Minor generally, and there is no reason to suppose that the opponents were an organized group or had a fixed doctrinal system. Under the influence of philosophical and religious teachings not greatly different from those (later) of Cerinthus, they emphasized the immutability of God: God might enter a human being, but God could not become truly human and suffer and die.

For Hengel, therefore, the Johannine Epistles are the work of the aging head of the Johannine school, John the elder, late in the first century but prior to the final redaction of the Gospel. The view that the epistles precede rather than follow the Gospel has also gained ground recently through the work of Georg Strecker (1986) and Charles Talbert (1992).

Strecker traces the beginnings of the Johannine school in the two shorter epistles. The essential characteristic of a school, he maintains, is that it traced its origin to a founder. The importance of setting the Johannine writings in a school context is that the Gospel and first letter do not need to be explained on the basis of earlier sources—they grew out of the nonliterary, oral tradition of the school. The tensions and differences in the writings are the result of debates within the school.

Second and 3 John are now in the canon because of the authority of the elder, who was the founder of the Johannine school. Moreover, the two shorter epistles are the oldest Johannine writings.

Second John 7-11 is a key to understanding the two letters. Second John 7 is distinguished in form and content from 1 John 4:2 through the use of the present participle. It is not to be read in the light of 1 John 4:2, but has instead a future meaning: Jesus Christ "will come in the flesh." The elder was a chiliast who looked forward to a thousand-year messianic reign. Debates over chiliasm persisted around Ephesus into the second century.

Third John 9 is a reference to 2 John. Strecker maintains (following Käsemann) that the presbyter was an outsider—from the perspective of orthodox teaching—because of his chiliastic views.

Papias knew a tradition of elders in Asia Minor, and Polycarp of Smyrna is the first to cite 1 John. Irenaeus later traced the Gospel to the son of Zebedee in Ephesus. John the elder is the author of 2 and 3 John. His significance lies not in the formation of the great church but in the founding of the Johannine school, which had a marginal existence. His theology preserved an apocalyptic orientation: (1) preaching means mediation of communion with God; (2) truth is a key concept; and (3) Christ's teaching is recognized primarily through *agapē*. The dualism that characterizes the

Gospel and 1 John is not yet recognizable. These later writings are independent and written by different members of the Johannine school. In 1 John chiliasm can no longer be detected; Docetism is combated. Still, the apocalyptic worldview is retained (2:28; 3:2). First John 2:14 refers to 2 John. A realized eschatology emerges more clearly (2:18), and there is a stronger movement toward ecclesiastical institutions. The "anointing" (2:20, 27) refers to baptism. The future-eschatological emphases that remain in the Gospel are not ecclesiastical redaction but the remains of the older tradition from the elder.

Like Strecker, Talbert regards 2 John as the first of the epistles. The schism evident in 1 John had not yet occurred when 2 John was written because the opponents could still be found within the church in 2 John. The order of the letters, therefore, is 2, 3, and then 1 John, and the letters were composed either before or alongside the Gospel. They reflect issues and concerns that are also evident in the Gospel: correct Christology and ethical behavior. Second John 7 has a linear sense: "the Word became flesh and remained flesh even after the resurrection" (Talbert, 10). Parallels with Ignatius's letter to the Smyrnaeans show that the concerns of the epistles are at home in the struggles of the churches in Asia Minor early in the second century. Third John reflects a move toward the situation of 1 John in that steps are already being taken to exclude from the fellowship those who proclaim a different teaching. One church group may have met in the house of Gaius and another in the house of Diotrephes.

First John begins with a piece of eyewitness tradition (vv. 1-5). The author was not an eyewitness and did not write in this way simply to identify with the line of tradition-bearers reaching back to the eyewitnesses. Rather, the author cites this tradition, which was known to the readers, and then interprets it in the body of the letter (1:6—5:12). The opponents held that one who possessed the Spirit knows God and therefore does not sin. Consequently, neither the death of Jesus nor participation in the Christian community has any soteriological significance. In response to the opponents, the elder maintained that the Christ had come in the flesh, that knowledge of God came through the incarnation, that pneumatology was subordinate to Christology, that love of God was manifest in love and koinōnia within the Christian community, and that Christians needed cleansing from postbaptismal sin also.

The variety of theories regarding the identity of the elder, the life setting of the epistles, the nature of the teachings they oppose, and the sequence in which they were written spread a range of options before the interpreter. If these issues cannot be settled, at least they alert the reader to interpretive options. From their historical setting, therefore, we turn to the literary contours of the epistles themselves.

Literary Contours

The three Johannine Epistles represent three different types of written communication. First John follows no established pattern, conforms to no known genre, and is not easily reduced to an orderly, linear outline. Second and 3 John follow the conventions of the Hellenistic letter form, though they are quite different. Second John is addressed to a sister church, while 3 John is a personal letter to Gaius. By becoming familiar with the literary form of the epistles, the interpreter can read them in the light of their constituent elements.

The Genre of 2 and 3 John

The conventions of a letter, while subject to variations, were well established in the first century. The circumstances of scattered Christian communities and traveling apostles, evangelists, elders, and their emissaries made letter writing common for introduction of one's self and one's message (e.g., Romans), encouragement and exhortations for fellow Christians (Ephesians and 1 Peter), pastoral direction (1 and 2 Corinthians), or intercession for a third party (Philemon).

Duane F. Watson has analyzed the structure of both 2 and 3 John, showing how effectively they employ the conventions of Greco-Roman rhetoric. Second John is a "deliberative parenetic-advisory letter" that presumes that the elder is on friendly terms with his audience. The *exordium* (v. 4) elicits attention and goodwill, but the *praescriptio* (vv. 1-3) also functions like an *exordium*. The elder cites his position and relationship to the church, invokes a familial metaphor, and repeatedly invokes the truth. In the *narratio* (v. 5) the elder relates the facts so that he can use every detail to his advantage. The *probatio* (vv. 6-11) seeks to persuade the church to "love one another according to the commandment." It employs definitions and reduplications and provides rationales and motivations for accepting the proposition. A *peroratio* is not often used in deliberative rhetoric, so verse 12 merely offers a conventional statement of the elder's hope to visit the church. The epistolary closing also functions as a *peroratio* (Watson, "2 John").

The same rhetorical units can be found in 3 John, though the rhetoric of the letter is different because the setting and purpose of the letter are different from 2 John. The elder is writing to encourage Gaius to continue to offer hospitality to Johannine Christians. His hospitality is all the more necessary now since Diotrephes has refused to receive the emissaries from the Johannine school. Third John is a mixed letter whose rhetoric is best classified as epideictic. Gaius does not have to be persuaded to offer hospitality; the letter is intended "to increase Gaius' adherence to an honorable value he already holds" (Watson, "3 John," 484). The *exordium*

(vv. 2-4) introduces the concerns and *topoi* of the *probatio*. The *praescriptio* (v. 1) serves many of the same functions as the *exordium*. Major sections of the letter are introduced by the address "Beloved" (*agapēte*; vv. 2, 5, 11). The *narratio* (vv. 5-6) recounts an act that is relevant to the subject of hospitality, again in such a manner that the elder can use the details to his advantage. The *probatio* (vv. 7-12) introduces the key issue—the need for Gaius to continue to extend hospitality to those sent by the elder. It consists of a variety of types of amplification and the negative example of Diotrephes. Demetrius provides an example of one doing good (v. 12). The conclusion of the letter serves as a *peroratio* (vv. 13-14). Epideictic rhetoric does not require a *peroratio*, and in 3 John it does not use either recapitulation or emotional appeal. The postscript (v. 15) also serves as *peroratio* (Watson, "3 John").

Although the elements of the letters are similar, 2 and 3 John have their own peculiar structure, especially in the body of each letter (see Funk). Second John opens with a typical epistolary introduction or prescript (vv. 1-3) that identifies the sender and the receiver: "The elder to the elect lady and her children." The elder is sufficiently well known that no other identification is needed. He uses tact and commendation to secure goodwill, but he expects that his authority will be respected. The "elect lady" is apparently a reference to a sister church rather than to a particular individual. "Her children," then, are the members of the community. Benedictory greetings follow. The appeal to love and truth establishes the credentials of the author and the authority of the gospel vested in him. The elder loves "in truth," the faithful "know the truth," the truth abides in them, and it will continue forever. Verse 3 combines common early Christian concepts with those that are typically Johannine. Grace, mercy, and peace (which also appear together in 1 Tim. 1:2 and 2 Tim. 1:2) are experienced in truth and love. The end of verse 3, therefore, forms an *inclusio* with the reference to love and truth in verse 1 and reconfirms the context in which the letter is written.

The body of the letter is composed of two distinct but related parts: a request that the sister church love those who walk in truth (vv. 4-6), and a warning not to receive those who spread deception (vv. 7-11).

An expression of joy or thanksgiving often followed the greeting. Second John 4 follows this convention and again sounds the themes of truth and familial kinship: "I was overjoyed to find some of your children walking in the truth, just as we have been commanded by the Father." The occasion for joy is not the receipt of a letter but the faithfulness of those he addresses. A petition normally contained three elements: a statement of the background, a verb of petition, and a description of the desired action. The background statement was introduced by the formula "I was overjoyed" (*echarēn lian*) in verse 4, and the petition itself follows in verse 5: "I ask you . . . let us love one another." On the basis of reports of the faithfulness of these fellow believers, Johannine Christians in a sister community, the elder extends a further request. The effect of the request is softened by including himself and his community in it: "let us love one another." Just what did the elder want from this sister community? The command to love was not a new one. Indeed, it was the center of the Johannine ethic. In effect, it summed up the request for hospitality, cooperation, faithfulness, and assistance in the struggle against those who would deceive the community. Verse 6 describes the desired action, again in traditional and stylized language. Fulfilling the command to love one another meant living according to the commandments of Christ that they had received through their community tradition, and the command was that they should love one another. Undergirding this petition are appeals to commandments, the leitmotif of truth and love introduced in the prescript, and an appeal to the tradition they had heard "from the beginning."

A warning comes next in verses 7-11. It too follows the pattern of a petition: statement of the background (v. 7), a verb of warning (v. 8), and then a description of the desired action (v. 10). Verses 9 and 11 explain the rationale for the warning and the specific response that is sought.

The warning is linked to the petition by a causal conjunction, "for" or "because" at the beginning of verse 7. The other side of the elder's concern for truth and love in the community is the warning to take necessary precautions against those who would distort their teachings and destroy their love for one another. The allusion to "many deceivers" reminds one of the many disciples who turned away from Jesus in Galilee (John 6:60, 66) and the many false prophets who had gone out from the community (1 John 2:18; 4:1). The mark of their deception (cf. 1 John 1:8; 2:26; 3:7) is their denial of "Jesus Christ come in the flesh." In spite of the allusion to the parousia in 1 John 3:2, the problem in the community was not that some denied the parousia but that they denied the incarnation. The use of the present participle, "come" or "coming," here rather than the aorist or perfect participle may be due to the influence of the use of the present participle in reference to Jesus in the Gospel, a desire to emphasize the timelessness of Christ's coming, or attraction to the present participle, "confess," earlier in the sentence. The reward they might forfeit is probably their salvation, or "life" in the Johannine sense.

The elder charges that the deceivers and antichrists do not abide in the "teaching of Christ," which can be read as either "Christ's teaching" or "the teaching about Christ." Either way, the deceivers are charged with not abiding in the teachings received by the community. What they viewed as progress or a higher Christology the elder regarded as departure from the truth. Specifically, the elder counsels the church not to receive any who do not affirm this teaching. Do not receive them into the church; do not even extend a greeting to them. One who does so shares in their evil works.

The problem in view here is the same as that which the elder deals with at greater length in 1 John, and phrases in the shorter letter seem to be echoes of the longer. Nevertheless, there is no evidence that the recipients had received or heard 1 John. As in 3 John, the situation involves scattered communities and traveling emissaries. Just as the elder sends this letter to the church, conveyed no doubt by a loyal associate, he fears that the opponents will be sending their own representatives to the sister community.

In the letter's closing (vv. 12-13), the elder expresses his hope to come to the church himself. He has much to say to them, but hopes to be able to do so face-to-face rather than in writing. The spoken word is regarded as more effective, powerful, or trustworthy than the written. Greetings from the church are sent, invoking once again the language of kinship; they are "the children of your elect sister."

The form of 2 John, conforming as it does to the form of Hellenistic letters especially in its prescript, falls into three main parts:

    I. Prescript (vv. 1-3)
        A. Address (vv. 1-2)
        B. Greetings (v. 3)
   II. Body (vv. 4-11)
        A. Petition (vv. 4-6)
        B. Warning (vv. 7-11)
  III. Closing (vv. 12-13)
        A. Desire for personal visit (v. 12)
        B. Greetings (v. 13)

The elements of 3 John are similar but more complicated. The address is nearly the same: A to B, "whom I love in truth." As in many Hellenistic letters, a thanksgiving or a health wish follows. Third John is distinctive, but not unique, in that it contains both. As in 2 John, a formulaic expression of joy follows the address. The elder is overjoyed at the reports from the brethren that Gaius is "walking in truth." The parallels between 2 John 4 and 3 John 3 are striking. The petition that follows is again based on reports from others regarding Gaius's faithfulness.

The body of the letter contains three sections of alternating praise and reproof: (1) praise of Gaius for his hospitality (vv. 5-8); (2) criticism of Diotrephes for his defiance (vv. 9-10); and (3) praise of Demetrius for his truthfulness (vv. 11-12).

The body of the letter is introduced by a vocative, which precedes a petition (as in 2 John 5). The petition that follows is implicit rather than explicit, and the statement of the background is divided between the praise of Gaius that precedes the petition and the criticism of Diotrephes that follows it. The elder is requesting that Gaius continue to offer hospitality and support to those whom he sends to the church, and specifically that he would receive Demetrius, who was probably the bearer of the letter, and treat him "in a manner worthy of God" (v. 6). The petition is tacitly presented in three admonitions spread over the four verses of this section of the letter (vv. 5-8):

1. "you do faithfully whatever you do for the friends";
2. "you will do well to send them on in a manner worthy of God";
3. "we ought to support such people, so that we may become co-workers with the truth."

The virtues of the traveling Johannine Christians are also extolled. They are worthy of Gaius's hospitality "even though they are strangers to you" (v. 5) because "they began their journey for the sake of Christ" (v. 7). A further virtue also confirms their need: they do not accept support from nonbelievers (v. 7). Finally, the petition also includes a promise of reward. When Gaius has extended hospitality to the Johannine Christians in the past they have praised his faithfulness before the church, so he may assume that he will again be honored for his faithfulness if he receives Demetrius.

The elder's criticism of Diotrephes for refusing to offer the sort of hospitality he was requesting from Gaius serves subtly to add further incentive for Gaius to grant the petition. If he refuses to do so, he will expose himself to similar criticism. The conventions of honor and shame in Mediterranean societies are clearly evident in this letter.

The elder's complaints regarding Diotrephes are detailed in verses 9-10:

1. Diotrephes "likes to put himself first";
2. he does not acknowledge the elder's authority;
3. he is spreading false charges against the elder and those loyal to him;
4. he refuses to welcome "the friends"; and
5. he prevents others from doing so and expels them from the church.

Just as the elder had expressed the prospect of reward to Gaius, he threatens rebuke for Diotrephes. One will be honored, the other shamed. Public shame is the only threat at the elder's disposal, however. He apparently has no power or authority to stop Diotrephes or to coerce his cooperation.

He has written to the church (v. 9)—a lost letter, probably not either 1 or 2 John—and he will deliver a public rebuke when he comes (v. 10).

In addition to the incentive of a negative example, the elder's criticism of Diotrephes also implicitly warns Gaius that he may expect opposition from Diotrephes. Here our lack of knowledge of the positions of the respective persons prevents us from understanding the situation more clearly. Was Gaius a member of the same house church as Diotrephes, or a member of a sister church? He was presumably not an unbeliever (v. 7). The role of Diotrephes has drawn sharply divergent interpretations. For purposes of discussion one can distinguish the theological and ecclesiastical elements of Diotrephes' position. *Theologically*, was Diotrephes an adherent of the false teachings the elder opposes in 1 and 2 John, were theological issues not a factor, or was Diotrephes actually following a practice similar to that advocated by the elder in 2 John ("do not receive them") in an effort to shield his church from the theological controversy that had damaged the sister churches? *Ecclesiastically*, was Diotrephes a member of a house church who had usurped the power of leadership, a prophet or church leader whose offense consisted in defying the elder, or a church leader ordained by bishops in the emerging church hierarchy in Asia Minor? The possible combinations of these elements have resulted in six theories (which Brown, 732–36, discusses in detail): (1) Diotrephes is an early example of the presbyter-bishop (like Ignatius a few years later); (2) Diotrephes represents a charismatic form of church leadership; (3) Diotrephes offers hospitality to Johannine Christians but has begun to use his role as host to control the church and its teachings; (4) Diotrephes is one of those whom the elder opposes in 1 and 2 John; (5) in doctrine and authority Diotrephes is a representative of the emerging, orthodox church; and (6) both Diotrephes and the elder oppose the secessionists. Brown himself favors a combination of 3 and 6—Diotrephes has no official position; he agrees theologically with the elder but excludes all outsiders in an effort to block the false teachings because he cannot be sure of the views of the itinerants.

The third section of the body of 3 John (vv. 11-12) commends Demetrius. Letters of commendation or parts of letters that praised a third party were common. This section also begins with a vocative, "Beloved" (cf. vv. 2, 5, 11) and continues the petition: do not imitate the evil (Diotrephes) but the good (as Gaius has in the past). Others have testified regarding Demetrius, and the elder adds his own testimony to theirs. The encouragement that Gaius knows that the elder's testimony is true echoes not only references to truth earlier in the letter (vv. 1, 3, 4, 8, 12) but also the community's affirmation of the witness of the Beloved Disciple (John 19:35; 21:24).

The body of the letter and the petition to Gaius are completed by the commendation of Demetrius. The petition has been tacitly and subtly presented (vv. 5-8), the background in Gaius's own faithfulness and Diotrephes' failure has been described, the virtues of the desired action have been described, the prospect of reward has been given, at least implicitly, as has an implicit threat of rebuke if Gaius fails to grant the petition. The virtues of the traveling Johannine Christians have been noted, and the faithfulness of Demetrius has been warranted by the elder. The elder's appeal to Gaius for his hospitality in this difficult situation has therefore been made with subtlety and rhetorical skill.

The closing parallels the closing verses of 2 John. Verses 13-14 express the desire to visit Gaius personally so that they can speak face-to-face. The elder still has much to say to him. The final verse extends greetings from the church, described here not in relation to the elder ("children") but in their relationship to Gaius ("friends"). "Friends" had become a technical term for fellow Johannine Christians (see John 3:29; 11:11; 15:13-15).

Although it does not treat theological issues directly, 3 John offers the church a glimpse into a significant period of its beginnings and an appeal for unity that has enduring value. In form, it follows much the same pattern as 2 John.

I. Prescript (vv. 1-4)
   A. Address (v. 1)
   B. Greetings (vv. 2-4)
II. Body (vv. 5-12)
   A. Petition (vv. 5-8)—praising Gaius for his hospitality
   B. Warning (vv. 9-11)—criticism of Diotrephes for his lack of hospitality
   C. Commendation (vv. 11-12)—of Demetrius for his faithfulness
III. Closing (vv. 13-15)
   A. Desire for personal visit (vv. 13-14)
   B. Greetings (v. 15)

The Genre and Structure of 1 John

Both the elements of a Hellenistic letter and the clear structural markers one finds in the two shorter letters are missing from 1 John. Brown notes that of the twenty-one books of the NT classified as epistles, "I John is the least letterlike in format" (87), and quotes Westcott (*Epistles*, xxix): "No address, no subscription, no name is contained in it of person or place; there is no direct trace of the author, no indication of any special destination." The result is that interpreters have suggested a variety of different theories as to the character of the letter and its structure. Following numerous earlier commentators, Kümmel considered 1 John to be "a tractate intended for the whole of Christianity, a kind of manifesto," which was not intended for any specific readers (*Introduction*, 437). C. H. Dodd judged it to be "a somewhat informal tract or homily" written for a particular circle well known to the author, "a circular letter like 1 Peter and (probably) Ephesians, addressed to the churches of a whole region" (*Epistles*, xxi). A circular letter would carry an appropriate address and identification of its author. A tractate would focus more clearly on a specific topic, and a homily would deal with scriptural texts. Such designations, therefore, fail to render the *form* of 1 John more intelligible. More recent commentaries situate the letter in relation to specific problems within the Johannine community itself. Smalley suggests that "1 John approximates to what might be termed today (and not in academic circles alone!) a 'paper,' " written as teaching and further discussion of christological and ethical issues within the Johannine church (Smalley, xxxiii). Schnackenburg commends the work of W. Nauck, noting that 1 John appears to be "an official missive" written to strengthen a group of readers who have survived the danger of apostasy (6). Similarly, Grayston prefers the term *enchiridion*: "an instruction booklet for applying the tradition in disturbing circumstances" (4). Brown declines to offer any classification of the genre of 1 John—"they do little to clarify the nature of 1 John"—preferring instead to describe its function (90).

In contrast to 2 and 3 John, therefore, the interpreter cannot rely on the genre of 1 John to provide clues to its structure. Generally, the same paragraphs or small units recur in most analyses of 1 John. On the issue of whether the progression of these units reveals an overall design or structure, commentators are divided. Those who find such a structure appeal alternatively to recurring statements of theme, structural transitions, chiastic patterns, differences in the material or argument, and/or similarities to the structure of the Gospel. Analyses of the structure of 1 John in recent commentaries bring to light interesting perspectives on the epistle and the problem of determining its structure.

In a departure from previous interpretations, but one endorsed by Moody Smith (1991, pp. 23–24), Brown regards 1 John as being patterned after the plan of the Gospel and therefore having a prologue, a conclusion, and two major parts:

Prologue (1:1-4)
    I. The obligation of walking in light in response to the gospel of God as light (1:5—3:10)
        A. "*This is the gospel*: God is light and in him there is no darkness at all" (1:5)
        B. Three boasts and three opposite hypotheses (1:6—2:2)

    C. Three claims of intimate knowledge of God (2:3-11)
    D. Admonitions to believers to resist the world (2:12-17)
    E. Warning against the secessionist antichrists (2:18-27)
    F. The contrast between God's children and the devil's children (2:28—3:10)
 II. The obligation of loving deeds in response to the gospel that we should love one another according to the example of Jesus as the Christ come in the flesh (3:11—5:12)
    A. *"This is the gospel*: We should love one another" (3:11)
    B. Admonitions to believers to show love in deeds (3:12-24)
    C. The spirits of truth and deceit (4:1-6)
    D. The absolute necessity of loving one another in order to love God (4:7—5:4a)
    E. Faith as the conqueror of the world (5:4b-12)
Conclusion (5:13-21)

The structure Brown proposes is clearly related to his thesis that 1 John reflects a debate with opponents whose views were drawn from the gospel traditions. The repetition of the assertion "This is the gospel" in 1:5 and 3:11 serves to mark off two major sections approximating the division of the Gospel into a prologue (1:1-18), the Book of Signs (chaps. 2–12), the Book of Glory (chaps. 13–20), and the epilogue (chap. 21). In response, one may question whether the assertion in 1:5 and 3:11 is sufficiently prominent to serve as a key to the structure of the document and whether such a twofold structure makes sense when there is no correspondence between the content of each major part and the corresponding section of the Gospel. The clearest evidence for such parallels is found in the prologues of the two writings.

Smalley also finds two major sections in the body of 1 John, but without any parallel to the structure of the Gospel:

   I. Preface: The Word of Life (1:1-4)
  II. Live in the light (1:5—2:29)
    A. God is light (1:5-7)
    B. First condition for living in the light: renounce sin (1:8—2:2)
    C. Second condition: be obedient (2:3-11)
    D. Third condition: reject worldliness (2:12-17)
    E. Fourth condition: keep the faith (2:18-29)
 III. Live as children of God (3:1—5:13)
    A. God is Father (3:1-3)
    B. First condition for living as God's children: renounce sin (3:4-9)
    C. Second condition: be obedient (3:10-24)
    D. Third condition: reject worldliness (4:1-6)

    E. Fourth condition: be loving (4:7—5:4)
    F. Fifth condition: keep the faith (5:5-13)
IV. Conclusion: Christian confidence (5:14-21)

The strength of this analysis is its appealing balance and symmetry and
the way it finds a repetition of the themes of the first half of the letter in
the second half. Like other structures surveyed below, it takes as key
elements statements about God's nature, but it passes over the statement
that God is love (4:8).

Several different proposals find three major sections. Edward Malatesta
(1978) follows the major divisions identified by R. Law, adding an epilogue:

Prologue (1:1-4)
    I. First exposition of criteria of new covenant communion with God
        (1:5—2:28)
        A. Walking in the light and freedom from sin (1:5—2:2)
        B. Knowledge of communion with God and observance of the
            new commandment of love (2:3-11)
        C. Believers contrasted with the world and with antichrists (2:12-28)
    II. Second exposition of criteria of new covenant communion with God
        (2:29—4:6)
        A. Doing right and avoiding sin (2:29—3:10)
        B. Love: its nature, exigencies, and signs (3:11-24)
        C. Discernment of spirits (4:1-6)
    III. Third exposition of criteria of new covenant communion with God
        (4:7—5:13)
        A. (missing)
        B. Love comes from God and is rooted in faith (4:7-21)
        C. Faith in the Son of God is the root of love (5:1-13)
Epilogue (5:14-21)

This scheme is structured around the three statements of God's nature:
"God is light" (1:5), "he is just" (2:29), and "God is love" (4:8). Attractive
as this carefully wrought analysis is, it has its weaknesses: (1) the second
statement (in 2:29) is stated offhandedly in a conditional sentence, (2) it
lacks the solemnity of the other two both by its syntax and by its use of
the pronoun, (3) the "he" may well be a reference to Jesus rather than
God, (4) the attributes are not limited to their respective sections but are
spread through other sections of the epistle (just: 1:9; 2:1; love: 2:5, 15;
3:1, 16, 17), and (5) the "A" member of the first two parts is missing from
the third.

A similar structure was proposed by T. Häring (1892) and followed (with variations) by A. E. Brooke (1912) and more recently by Charles H. Talbert:

Introduction (1:1-4)
  I. First presentation of the two tests of fellowship with God (1:5—2:27)
    A. Ethical thesis—walking in the light as the true sign of fellowship with God (1:5—2:17)
    B. Christological thesis—faith in Jesus as the Christ as the test of fellowship with God (2:18-27)
  II. Second presentation (2:28—4:6)
    A. Ethical thesis—doing of righteousness as the sign that we are born of God (2:28—3:24)
    B. Christological thesis—the Spirit which is of God confesses Jesus Christ come in the flesh (4:1-6)
  III. Third presentation: combination of the two theses (4:7—5:12)
    A. Love as the basis of faith (4:7-21)
    B. Faith as the basis of love (5:1-12)
Conclusion (5:13-21)

The strength of this analysis is that it recognizes that the two dominant motifs of 1 John are christological and ethical. The outline discloses which of the two motifs is dominant in each section and shows how the two are interrelated in the third major section of the epistle. The weakness of this proposal has seemed to many to be its artificiality and the change in the dominant motifs in the third section.

Talbert follows this same basic approach but with three significant differences: (1) he takes 1 John 1:1-5 to be a piece of eyewitness tradition and the remainder of the body of the epistle as an exposition of that tradition; (2) he divides the body into four sections rather than three; and (3) he identifies 5:13 as a statement of purpose.

The proclamation (1:1-5)
The exposition (1:6—5:13)
A Ethical exposition (1:6—2:17)
B Christological exposition (2:18-28)
A' Ethical exposition (2:29—3:24a)
  B' Christological exposition (3:24b—4:6)
A" Ethical exposition (4:7-12)
  B" Christological exposition (4:13-16a)
A''' Ethical exposition (4:16b—5:4a)
  B''' Christological exposition (5:4b-12)
The statement of purpose (5:13)
The postscript (5:14-21)

This proposal has the same merits as the previous one: it highlights the twin concerns of christological and ethical error. It is innovative, however, in dividing the body into four major sections and in splitting verses where the two themes occur together (3:24; 4:16; 5:4). It has long been recognized, however, that 1 John uses such transitional verses to mark a shift from one topic to another.

Others have placed more emphasis on the identification of the basic units of the text than on the symmetry or design in their composition. Schnackenburg found major divisions following 2:17 and 3:24 (which would yield three major sections) but cautioned that the overarching structure was not as significant as the identification of the individual units. J. L. Houlden divided the body into seven parts. I. Howard Marshall defines fourteen major paragraph divisions (counting the prologue and conclusion).

Close study of the structures summarized in the foregoing discussion reveals that while some units or divisions are widely recognized, there are differences of interpretation with regard to both the epistle's major divisions and its various paragraph units. For example, a recurring dilemma is whether 2:18-27 and 4:1-6 belong with what precedes them or what follows. So frustrating is the effort to find some order to the content of the epistle that Lieu's contention that there is none seems justified: "This 'distinctive' structure is in reality an absence of any clear structure, for the author keeps taking new directions or returning to old themes without constructing any obvious system" (*Theology*, 4).

In the light of the absence of anything approaching consensus regarding the structure of the text, one must ask what the various proposals reveal about 1 John and what functions they serve. First, it is obvious that the text is sufficiently open, ambivalent, obscure, or complex to allow for various constructions or readings. Each reading or interpretation of the text constructs its structure by emphasizing certain "keys," perspectives, or themes. Häring (1892), Brooke (1912), Law (1914), Malatesta, and Talbert all emphasize 1 John's statement of criteria or tests for fellowship with God. These structures sensitize the reader to the twin themes of the letter: christological and ethical. Malatesta and, in a different way, Smalley highlight 1 John's descriptions of God's nature: light, just, Father, and love. Brown has called attention to the relationship between 1 John and the Gospel both in the basis for the schism it reflects and in the structure of the two documents. Each structure, therefore, represents a "reading strategy," a means of approaching the text and constructing meaning from its openness and ambiguity.

Meaning is related not only to the historical or social setting of the text and its internal structure, however. It also derives from 1 John's intertextual relationships, including its place in the biblical canon.

Canonical Context

The significance of the Johannine Epistles becomes more readily apparent when they are situated in their canonical context. Some of their themes are deeply rooted in the biblical tradition, and their particular contribution to the canon is set in relief by taking note of their canonical context.

The Gospel of John

Like moons orbiting a planet, the epistles are tied to the Gospel of John. The epistles share with the Gospel the same Christian tradition. From the similarity of the prologue of 1 John to the technical use of the term "friends" for fellow Johannine Christians in the conclusion of 3 John, the epistles move the reader into the same thought world as the Gospel. Both deal with christological and ethical concerns, the centrality of christological confession and observing the love command, and obtaining "life," understood in a distinctively Johannine sense. The ethic of the community in both the Gospel and the epistles is limited to separation from the world, living "just as" Jesus did, keeping the love command, and abiding in Christ.

Differences between the Gospel and the epistles are readily explained as the result of differences in genre and character, different authors within the school of writers that had developed around the Beloved Disciple, and deliberate efforts to clarify or qualify traditional Johannine teachings.

Christology dominates both the Gospel and the epistles. The Gospel portrays Jesus as the revealer of the Father, the Son, the Word become flesh. As we have seen, the epistles reflect debate that has resulted in schism over this issue. The distinctive references to Father and Son that characterize the Gospel (in contrast to the Synoptics) are also typical of 1 and 2 John, though the epistles never use the term "Son of Man."

The use of the term "flesh" in the Gospel is instructive. Aside from passages that have often been judged to be rather late additions to the Gospel (1:13-14; 6:51-58), the term "flesh" appears in the Gospel only three times:

> What is born of flesh is flesh, and what is born of spirit is spirit (3:6)
> It is the spirit that gives life; the flesh is useless (6:63)
> since you have given him authority over all flesh (17:2).

In none of these is "flesh" used to describe Christ's nature. Indeed, in each reference "flesh" is subordinated to the spirit or to the authority of Christ. One can readily understand how some Johannine Christians might have invested such authority in the Spirit and taken such a low view of flesh as to deny that the Christ could have come in the flesh.

The epistles also share the dualistic thought world of the Gospel. The following antithetical pairs appear in both: God—the devil, light—darkness, truth—falsehood, spirit—flesh, from the Father—from the world. In other places, dualistic terms that appear in one do not occur in the other. For example, the term *antichrists* does not occur in the Gospel. The contrast above—below does not feature in the epistles; the Gospel refers to the Spirit as the Spirit of truth, while 1 John adds a contrast to the spirit of deception. Such differences hardly move one into a different thought world.

Other differences between the Gospel and the epistles are noteworthy. The epistles have no overt reference to the sacraments, though one should note the use of water in 1 John 5:6-8 as an allusion to the baptism of Jesus. In contrast to the Gospel, the epistles do not refer to bread or to "living water" or to eating flesh. Other similarities and differences in the theological perspectives of the Johannine writings will be discussed in the section on theological distinctives below. Here it is sufficient to note that the epistles must be read in conjunction with the Gospel so that their use of distinctively Johannine idioms and concepts can be understood and set in context.

The relationship between the epistles and late strata of the Gospel, especially the prologue (John 1:1-18), and John 6:51-58, and also the later sections of the farewell discourse require special attention. In the farewell discourse, parallels with 1 John's use of the love command, attention to the role of the Spirit, keeping the commands of Jesus, separation from the world, and abiding in him reflect similar concerns and the same general period in the history of the Johannine community. Whether the similarities are sufficient to establish that the author of the epistles was also the redactor of the Gospel is debatable. At this point the issue remains unsettled.

The Hebrew Scriptures

On the one hand, whereas the Gospel quotes and alludes to the Scriptures so frequently that the interpreter is constantly searching out biblical references in order to cast light on the texture and intertextual relations of the Gospel text, scriptural allusions are sparse in the epistles. The two shorter letters do not refer to the Scriptures—due in large measure no doubt to their brevity and subject matter. More surprising is the lack of appeal to the Scriptures in the debate with the opponents in 1 John. Just as 1 John does not refer to "the Jews" (*hoi Ioudaioi*), it also does not quote from the Hebrew Scriptures. The debate concerns division in the community and christological formulations, so the appeal is to community tradition, "what you heard from the beginning," rather than to scriptural authority. The only biblical reference is to "Cain who was from the evil one and murdered his brother" (3:12).

On the other hand, the epistles breathe the same atmosphere as the Hebrew Scriptures. Jeremiah's description of the new covenant (Jer. 31:33-34) forms an essential literary and theological context for 1 John 2:3-11 and much of the rest of 1 John (see esp. Malatesta). Moreover, 1 John elevates keeping commandments as a requirement for abiding in fellowship with God. The essential nature of God is described in terms drawn from the Scriptures: light, righteousness, and love. The concept of truth that is so carefully defined in 1 John and the role that is ascribed to the Spirit are again an extension of the treatment they receive in the Hebrew Scriptures. Therefore, while the Johannine Epistles do not quote the Scriptures, one must be careful not to give too much weight to this silence.

The Pastoral Epistles

Parallels between the Johannine Epistles and the Pastoral Epistles should also be noted. Each collection is attached to the name of an apostle (John and Paul) though in all probability neither collection was written by that apostle. Instead, these are writings that perpetuate the traditions of the apostle (or in the case of the Johannine Epistles, the Beloved Disciple) within communities established by them, writings that were written by their close associates.

In both cases the epistles stand in close relation to other writings in the same tradition and were composed to offer guidance in the interpretation of those earlier traditions. Noticeably different, however, is the role of the apostle or founder of the tradition in the two collections. The Pastoral Epistles claim apostolic authorship and appeal overtly to the authority of the apostle (e.g., 1 Tim. 1:12-17), whereas the Johannine Epistles make no reference to the Beloved Disciple and no appeal to his authority.

Both collections of epistles prescribe a posture for the community both in relation to its tradition and in relation to society. The Pastoral Epistles warn against teaching "any different doctrine" (1 Tim. 1:3) and warn those who desire to be teachers of the law (1:7). Timothy is repeatedly instructed to hold to the tradition he has received: "The saying is sure and worthy of full acceptance . . ." (1:15; cf. 3:1; 4:6). He is to "keep the commandment" (6:16). In the context of other (false) teachings, the Pastorals counsel orthopraxy in addition to orthodoxy: avoid dissension and disputes (6:4), guard against sins (5:24) and the pursuit of riches (6:17), and establish the authority of the elders (5:17-22). Deceitful spirits are contrasted to the Spirit (4:1), and God is described as dwelling in "unapproachable light" (6:16). Keeping "the faith" (1:19; 4:6; 6:12) leads to "eternal life" (6:12), "the life that really is life" (6:19). The author claims he is speaking "in faith and truth" (2:7) and writes the letter in the hope that he can soon come in person (3:14).

The parallels in the Johannine Epistles are clear. They warn against those who proffer a different teaching, who are branded deceivers, false prophets, and antichrists (1 John 2:18, 26; 4:1). In response, the elder appeals to the authority of the tradition they have received: "Let what you heard from the beginning abide in you" (1 John 2:24; cf. 3:11; 2 John 9). He stresses keeping the commandments (1 John 2:3-4; 3:24; 5:2). First John's instructions on orthopraxy include avoiding sin, purifying oneself, and asking for forgiveness (1:9; 3:3, 6-9). The love of the Father is not found in those who pursue wealth (2:15-17). To maintain orthodoxy and orthopraxy in the community the elder maintains his authority, implicitly in 1 and 2 John and explicitly in 3 John. His opponents are guided by "the spirit of the antichrist" (4:3) and "the spirit of error" (4:6) rather than the Spirit who has anointed the faithful (2:20, 27). God is light (1:5), but the deceivers walk in darkness (2:11). Whereas "the faith" never appears as a noun in the Gospel, 1 John 5:4 announces, "And this is the victory that conquers the world, our faith." The reward promised for the faithful is "eternal life" (5:11, 20). Finally, in 2 and 3 John, the elder claims to be writing "in truth" and declares his hope of coming so that he can speak to the recipients personally.

Apart from the Gospel of John, the Johannine Epistles have more in common with the Pastoral Epistles than any other writings. With these they are similar in character, purpose, and date. In contrast to the Pastoral Epistles, which counsel maintaining good relations with society (1 Tim. 2:1-2), however, the Johannine Epistles maintain a more sectarian vision for the church. In what sense then are they "general epistles"?

The General Epistles

Each of the General Epistles makes its own distinctive contribution to the NT canon. Hebrews is the only book of the NT to develop the confession of Jesus as priest. Affirming the superiority of the new covenant in Christ's death, the author of Hebrews picks up where the Gospels end, describing the role of the heavenly Christ. He is seated at the right hand of Majesty (Ps. 110:1), officiates at a heavenly altar, and makes intercession for the faithful. He is a high priest after the order of Melchizedek, being superior to the Levitical priesthood, making one sacrifice for all, and offering himself as the sacrifice.

James carves its niche by exploring the relationship between faith and good works. Safeguarding against misinterpretations of the Pauline vision of justification by faith, James insists that true faith will be expressed in good works; therefore one is saved by works, not by faith alone.

First Peter offers encouragement for Christians experiencing persecution or hardship. It offers a theological interpretation of the nature of the church.

Christians are "exiles of the Dispersion . . . chosen . . . destined . . . sanctified" (1:1-2). The church is a spiritual house, a holy priesthood (2:5), "a chosen race, a royal priesthood, a holy nation, God's own people" (2:9).

Second Peter affirms the authority of the apostolic tradition and warns against false teachings and those who deny the expected parousia of Christ. Jude, likewise, issues a stern warning to the church to guard against false teachings.

In the context of the General Epistles, the Johannine Letters offer their own distinctive contributions to the NT canon. First John is the only book of the NT to define God's nature as love, and its observation that we are able to love because we have experienced God's love (4:7-21) ranks with 1 Corinthians 13 as one of the NT's most profound treatments of the theme. There is no substitute elsewhere in the biblical literature for this exposition of John 3:16 and the new command to love one another. First John repeatedly guides the church and offers assurance with the formula "By this we know. . . ." First John links together faith in Christ and love for others. It offers a high view of the role of the Spirit in Christian experience while maintaining the need for obedience.

The concerns of 2 John are similar, if more briefly stated. Its words on love and truth as the spheres of Christian life call for further reflection. Third John does not enter into these theological areas. Instead, it highlights the need for cooperation and those who will offer hospitality in the life and mission of the church. When there is controversy and dissension, the church needs harmony and goodwill, not theological uniformity.

Like the other General Epistles, therefore, each Johannine Letter makes its distinctive contribution to the NT canon, and each offers instruction that transcends its original historical setting in application. Their concerns are relevant to the experience and needs of the church in every generation. In essence, their theological distinctives are the heart of their enduring significance.

Theological Distinctives

The theological content of the Johannine Epistles is so entwined with their historical setting and epistolary form that efforts to distill or abstract the theology of the letters is likely to produce only a formless and ahistorical caricature. Theology is worked out in historical context, and its form and meaning are inseparable. The following survey of the thought of the epistles should therefore form an extension of one's consideration of these topics, not a separate enterprise.

The distinctiveness of the epistles' theology could be assessed in two ways. One could treat the distinctive theological idiom of the epistles— for example: the word of life, anointing, abiding, walking in life/darkness, born of God—or one could hold the epistles up to the common categories of theological reflection to highlight areas of agreement with other NT writers and features peculiar to these epistles. The former would serve as a guide to reading the epistles and grasping their language more fully, the latter facilitates comparison with other NT documents and assessment of the value of the epistles for Christian theology. The following paragraphs follow the second approach, while treating the subject matter of the epistles in their own idiom.

God

It has often been noted that whereas the Gospel is Christocentric, the epistles are theocentric. At least, the epistles give more attention to God's nature and functions than the Gospel. Perhaps as a corrective to the christological speculation of the opponents, the elder frequently writes of God's relationship to the world and to the believer. Where the masculine pronoun is used, it is often difficult to determine whether the reference is to God or Jesus, but the term *God* appears nearly as often in the epistles as in the Gospel of John: 83 times in the Gospel and 67 times in the epistles.

The various facets of the concept of God in 1 John can be gathered under the following rubrics: God's nature, God's work, God and Jesus, God and the world, and God and the believer.

As we have seen, 1 John is notable for its brief declarations of God's nature. The assertion "God is light" and there is no darkness in him (1:5) is made in the context of refuting the opponents' claims to sinlessness while failing to live rightly. Light and darkness therefore have ethical rather than cosmological overtones. To say that God is light and to exhort others to "walk in the light as he himself is in the light" (1:7) affirms the holiness and righteousness of God. There is no evil in him. The life of the believer, therefore, ought to reflect the believer's fellowship with God.

The second declaration of God's nature is stated obliquely: "If you know that he is righteous" (2:29). The pronoun may refer to Jesus, since the preceding verse speaks of "him at his coming," but the remainder of verse 29 speaks of being "born of him," where the pronoun must refer to God. If light is interpreted ethically, then there is little difference between righteousness and light in the idiom of 1 John. Again, the character of God is taken as a guide for the life of those who claim to know God or have fellowship with God.

The third declaration, "God is love" (4:8, 16), gives specific direction to the first two. God's nature as light and righteous is seen in his love. Indeed, this section of the epistle (4:7-21) appears to be a commentary or midrash on John 3:16, which was no doubt a well-known Johannine maxim regarding God's love. As in the previous contexts, the discussion of this aspect of God's nature is tied to admonitions that the faithful ought to love one another (2:7-11; 3:17). The genius of this treatment of Christian ethics in the light of the community tradition regarding the doctrine of God, however, is that it recognizes that our ability to love is based on our experience of God's love. Furthermore, God's love is "perfected" or completed only when it finds expression in our love for one another (2:5; 4:17-18). The doctrine of God in 1 John, therefore, is never without application to the ethics of the community that claims to have fellowship with God. He is "faithful and just" (1:9), the "true one" (5:20; cf. John 17:3) before whom all others are idols (5:21).

Given the ethical application of affirmations of God's nature, it is not surprising that the statements about God's work concern God's relationship to the believing community. God sent his only son (4:9, 10, 14). If we confess our sins, "he will forgive us our sins and cleanse us from all unrighteousness" (1:9). In one of the most beautiful passages in the epistle, the elder marvels over "what love the Father has given us" (3:1; cf. 4:10-11, 16). God gave us eternal life (5:11), and he will give life to those whose sins are forgiven (5:16).

God is known through his relationships—with Jesus, the world, and the believer. That God is confessed as Father is due primarily to the confession that Jesus is the Son of God, a confession that appears frequently in 1 John and in various forms: "the Son of God" (7 times), "his son" (9 times), and "the son" (6 times). Typically, the verbs that appear in conjunction with the terms have to do with confessing and denying, being manifest or known, sending or being sent, having or knowing, and bearing witness.

In a negative sense, the world represents all that is opposed to God (2:15-17; 5:4-5). The world lies under the power of the evil one (5:19), but God sent his only Son into the world "so that we might live through him" (5:9).

A significant number of the statements about God in 1 John concern God's relationship to the believer, which fits the linkage between declarations of God's nature and ethical guidance for the community that we observed earlier. Those who confess that Jesus is the Son of God "have" the Father and the Son (2:23), which seems to be equivalent to saying that they "know" God (2:14; 4:6, 7) or "have fellowship with God" (1:3, 6), rather than with the world. They are therefore "children of God" (3:1, 2; 5:2, 19), "born of God" (4:7; 5:1, 18); they have "God's seed" (3:9-10). They are therefore "from God" (3:10; 4:2-3, 4, 6). Likewise, love is from God (4:7), and spirits may be "from God" (4:1). This relationship, however, is based on both christological confession (4:15) and doing "God's will" (2:17; 5:14) or keeping God's commandments, which are not burdensome (5:2-3). Love of God, loving one another, and keeping God's commands are all interrelated (5:2-3). In this relationship, there is a mutual abiding of God in the believer and the believer in God (2:14; 4:12-13, 15-16). When the faithful ask, they receive from God (3:22; 5:14-15), but no one has ever seen God (4:12; cf. John 1:18; 5:37; 6:46).

Another cluster of sayings about God offers assurance to the community. When he is revealed we will be like him (3:2). God is greater than our hearts and knows everything (3:20), and whatever is born of God conquers the world (5:4). The testimony of God (5:9-10) is greater than human testimony, and that testimony is eternal life (5:9-11).

Christ

For all the references to God, the rhetoric of 1 John does not attempt to change the readers' perspective on God except as it relates to the role of Jesus in bringing knowledge of God and fellowship with God. As with the Gospel, the heart of 1 John is christological. As we have seen, its Christology is directly related on the one hand to the tradition of the Johannine community and on the other to the teachings of the opponents. In this mix, 1 John defines an alternative interpretation of their shared tradition and a corrective to the opponents' Christology.

The prologue of the epistle holds the key to understanding its relationship to the Gospel. It has been interpreted alternatively as a piece of community tradition, an early version of the Gospel's prologue, or commentary on the Gospel prologue. Just as the Gospel begins with confession of the Word that became flesh, "and we have beheld his glory," so 1 John begins with a declaration of "the word of life," which was from the beginning, and which "we" have heard, seen, and touched. This one was "the eternal life that was with the Father" (1:2). Central to the concern of 1 John is the confession that Jesus is the Christ, the Son of God, who has come in the flesh. Each of these terms appears repeatedly and in different combinations. This concern is evident from the opening affirmation that "our fellowship is with the Father and with his Son Jesus Christ" (1:3) to the closing and in a sense climactic confession of "his Son Jesus Christ. He is the true God and eternal life" (5:20).

The christological concerns of 1 John focus on specific issues: that Jesus is the Christ (2:22; 5:1), the Son of God (5:5, 10), that he has come in the flesh (4:2), and that his death is the atonement for sin (1:7; 2:2; 4:10). Surprisingly there is no reference to the resurrection of Jesus. That point was evidently not under dispute. First John does affirm that we have "an advocate with the Father, Jesus Christ the righteous" (2:1).

One of the characteristically Johannine formulations is the confession that the Father sent his only Son. He was "the one who was born of God"

(5:18). The purpose of the incarnation is defined in a series of different assertions:

> he was revealed to take away sins, and in him there is no sin (3:5)
> The Son of God was revealed for this purpose, to destroy the works of the devil (3:8)
> God sent his only Son into the world so that we might live through him (4:9)
> the Father has sent his Son as the Savior of the world (4:14).

The principal purpose for the incarnation, therefore, was salvific, and specifically to effect atonement for sin. The revelatory aspect of his work (see John 1:18) is subordinated to the work of atonement (cf. John 1:29, 36). Therefore, the confession of one who came through "water and the blood" (1 John 5:6-8) is required for salvation. He laid down his life for us (3:16).

The consequence of this confession is that "no one who denies the Son has the Father; everyone who confesses the Son has the Father" (2:23). Saving knowledge or fellowship with God is achieved only by confessing that the Son is the atonement for sin. The believer then abides in him, and he in us (2:6; 3:24; 4:15). One who "has" the Son has life (5:11-12). Jesus is therefore the source and foundation for the life of the believer. He gave the command that we love one another (3:23), and in the absence of more specific ethical instruction, it is sufficient to say that the believer ought "to walk just as he walked" (2:6).

The Spirit and Authority

The references to the Holy Spirit in 1 John are surprising, especially when read in the context of the Gospel. First John has no references to "the Holy Spirit"; the "Paraclete" is identified as "Jesus Christ, the righteous," rather than the Spirit; "the Spirit of truth" is used only in opposition to "the spirit of deception"; and the term "the anointing," which does not appear in the Gospel, is used three times. The "Spirit of God," another term that does not appear in the Gospel, occurs in 1 John 4:2 (cf. "his Spirit," 4:13). The elder is concerned to distinguish "the Spirit of God" or the Spirit of truth from other spirits (4:1-6). The test is christological: the Spirit that confesses Jesus has "come in the flesh" is from God. By the way in which this test is stated, it appears that the real concern is to expose those who claim to have the Spirit but who do not affirm the incarnation.

This impression is strengthened when we take note of the other references. The elder assures the faithful that they have been anointed by "the Holy One," and that therefore they do not need anyone to teach them

(2:20, 27). These assurances echo the words of Jesus in the farewell discourse in John that the Paraclete would teach the disciples "everything" (John 14:26). First John 5:6-8 ties the Spirit to the incarnation and death of Jesus, "the water and the blood." The three bear witness together, and by implication the Spirit is conveyed only through Jesus' incarnation and death.

Although the references to the Spirit in 1 John often depart from the terms used in the Gospel, its teachings on the Spirit are consistent with the Gospel's. As in the Gospel, the Spirit is closely linked to Jesus. One might have expected the elder to recall the promise that the Spirit would "remind you of all that I have said to you" (John 14:26), but instead he urges the community to abide in what they had heard from the beginning. Nevertheless, as in the Gospel, a chief function of the Spirit is to teach. The anointing of the Spirit, moreover, is not a special gift to a chosen few; they have all received the anointing (2:20). Therefore, they should not be misled by those who claim to be prophets (2:27), for they are false prophets (4:1). The Spirit is the proof that they abide in God (4:13), but both the experience of the Spirit and the experience of fellowship with God are given only to those who believe in the Son of God (5:6-10).

Soteriology, Sin, and Perfectionism

The differences between the elder and the opponents regarding the incarnation and death of the Son of God are linked to sharp differences in their respective views of sin and salvation.

The opponents apparently believe that through the Spirit they have received knowledge of God. In the Gospel, sin consists primarily in unbelief (John 16:8) and rejection of the revelation that came through Jesus (John 15:22). The dualism of the Johannine tradition divides humanity and human experience into two antithetical spheres, one characterized by truth, light, and righteousness, the other by deception, darkness, and sin. It is unthinkable that those who walk in the light of the knowledge of God should sin. The opponents may reason that since they have received the revelation of God, since they believe and have received the Spirit, therefore they have no sin. They may even think that they have never sinned (1:10). The realized eschatology of the Johannine tradition fuels the opponents' distorted views of sin and perfectionism. The devil and his lawlessness have been defeated by Christ, the judgment lay in one's present choice of light or darkness (John 3:19-21), and the believers have already crossed from death into life (1 John 3:14; John 5:24).

The elder shares the ideal of perfectionism and much of his tradition's emphasis that the hopes for the future have already been realized in Jesus, but his understanding of sin and salvation differ sharply from that of the opponents. Sin is not just unbelief but wrongdoing (5:17). The means of forgiveness is not just the revelation in Jesus but his atoning death: "the blood of Jesus, his Son, cleanses us from all sin" (1:7). Forgiveness requires confession of wrongdoing (1:9).

The elder also has a more realistic view of postbaptismal sin. Believers too continue to sin, but therein lies the problem. On the one hand, like the opponents, the elder affirms the ideal of perfectionism. Sin cannot continue to mark the lives of those who are children of God (3:6-9). They cannot sin. On the other hand, Christians do sin (5:16-17). They need to pray for each other and to ask for forgiveness for one another. The elder distinguishes mortal sin from that which is not mortal. He does not even counsel that one should pray for those whose sin is mortal. In the context of the epistle, the mortal sin must be the refusal to confess Jesus as the Christ, the Son of God who came in the flesh. Since forgiveness is received through christological confession, those who refuse to confess have no hope of forgiveness or life. In the embattled situation of the epistle, the elder says one should not even pray for such persons, or at least he does not say that one should pray for them (5:16).

The problem that has always plagued interpreters is how to hold together what the elder says in his denial of the opponents' slogans in 1 John 1:6-10 and what he says in 3:6-9. Some have dealt with the problem by appealing to the difference in tenses: aorist in chapter 1 and present in chapter 3— the believer cannot *continue* in sin. But that solution seems facile. Judith Lieu (*Theology*, 65) situates the problem in the elder's adoption of a dualistic framework that is not his own, but other connections with the Gospel of John make it difficult to suppose that the dualism of the Gospel is not assumed here also. Whatever the explanation, the elder's pastoral concern for sin within the community clashes with his adherence to the ideal of perfection. What ought to be does not prevail in the community. The opponents' wrongdoing and lack of obedience to the love command are clear evidence that they are walking in darkness while claiming sinlessness, and the elder does not want the faithful to be drawn away by such deception. The remedy for sin is confession, intercessory prayer, and the intercession of the Paraclete, Jesus Christ the righteous (2:1). By correct christological confession, obedience to the commands, and abiding in what they have heard from the beginning, the faithful can abide in the love of Jesus and in fellowship with God.

Ecclesiology

The search for ecclesiology in the Johannine Epistles requires that one construct patterns out of shreds of evidence. Only 3 John uses the term "church" (vv. 9-10), and none of the letters addresses the issue of the nature of the church directly.

The first observation that one may make is that those parts of the letters that touch on ecclesiology concern the boundaries or limits of church fellowship. Who is admitted to its fellowship and who is excluded from it? First John refers to those who have gone out from the church (2:19; 4:1). Second John advises that certain "deceivers" not be admitted to the church, and 3 John complains that Diotrephes has refused to receive emissaries the church has sent. The two shorter letters speak to the situation of traveling evangelists, prophets, teachers, or emissaries. Exclusion in this context means that they would not have been given hospitality and would not have been allowed to speak to a gathering of the church.

The departure or exclusion of the opponents in 1 John implies a more lasting schism. The situation is not irrelevant to the two shorter letters, however, for each seems to have been written in the same context and may be related to efforts to prevent the effects of the schism from reaching sister churches. The events that led to the schism are unknown. First John describes only the theological and ethical differences between the two groups. We do not know whether nontheological issues were also involved. We do not know the size of each group, the events that precipitated the rupture, or whether the opponents left of their own accord or were forced out.

The inferences we can make involve the concept of the church implied by the letters. The elder expects to be heard, but he appeals to community tradition and the authority of the Spirit rather than to his office. All have been anointed with the Spirit, so they have no need that anyone teach them. These references imply an egalitarian, democratic understanding of the church. They all have fellowship with God, and they are to love one another. The prime command has to do with showing God's love within the church. This view of the church accords well with the metaphors in the Gospel, which picture the church as a flock of sheep, or branches of the vine. The epistles do not command unity, but 1 John is written "so that you also may have fellowship with us," and so that "our joy may be complete" (1:3-4).

The spiritual locus of the church is defined more precisely than its organization. Its fellowship is with God (1 John 1:3), in the light, in truth, in righteousness, and in love—metaphors for God's nature. In Johannine dualism, there is no middle ground. The epistles therefore reflect a church fellowship with a high view of both the sinfulness of the world and their own sinlessness. Their pervasive dualism and high christology, led them to a high view of their nature as believers. They are sharply marked off from the world, so it is not surprising that significant attention is given to maintaining the boundaries of the church's fellowship.

One can draw both positive lessons and warnings from the experience of the Johannine church. On the one hand, where the church is in danger of losing its distinctive identity, the Johannine Epistles sketch a church that is sharply distinguished from the world. Its fellowship is with God; its doctrine is truth; its ethic is love; and its members are "brothers and sisters," "beloved," and "friends." They are "children of God." On the other hand, such a sharply defined community is susceptible to internal dissension and the arrogance that one has a monopoly on truth, or that one is untouched by the sin that afflicts others.

Eschatology

First John is marked by the realized eschatology of the Gospel but balances it with anticipation of what still lies in the future. The apparent renewal of emphasis on the future probably arose as a corrective to the inferences the opponents were drawing from the community's emphasis on present experience.

Believers already have fellowship with the Father (1:3). They are children of God (3:1), who have been "born of God" (3:9). They have "overcome the evil one" (2:14). They have already "crossed from death into life" (3:14), and they are already experiencing eternal life (5:11-13).

In the light of such realized eschatology, it is important that the elder also uses traditional eschatological terms: "It is the last hour" (2:18), and antichrists have come. The elder looks forward to "when he is revealed" (2:28), where the pronoun may refer either to God or to Christ. His hope is that "we may have confidence and not be put to shame before him at his coming" (2:28). At his coming, the true nature of the children of God will be revealed (3:2). They will see God as he is (3:2), and if they love one another, they may have "boldness on the day of judgment" (4:17).

These references to the future enter naturally into the flow of the epistle, but they are double-edged. On the one hand, they warn against an over-emphasis on the believer's present status, and they assure believers of the confidence they may have before God. If the opponents have ceased to be concerned about keeping the commandments, living righteously, or showing love for others, the elder warns that "all who have this hope in him will purify themselves, just as he is pure" (3:3). Celebration of the fulfillment of hopes for the messianic age in the coming of Christ cannot be an occasion for complacency or lack of faithfulness.

On the other hand, the elder could not allow anyone to charge that his gospel gave no basis for confidence before God or that he was upsetting the community with fears about the future. The elder therefore balances the proclamation of the fulfillment of future hopes in the coming of Christ by restating traditional hopes for the coming of Christ (or God) in victory and judgment at the end of time (cf. John 6:39, 40, 44, 54). Nonetheless, the attitude that characterizes his expectation of the end is "boldness" or confidence (2:28; 3:21; 4:17; 5:14). It is a confidence born of the believer's present experience of fellowship with God and obedience to God's commands.

Brief as these letters are, they make a significant contribution to the theology of the NT. As we have seen, however, that theology is couched in a distinctive Johannine idiom and cannot be interpreted without sensitivity to the historical setting of the Johannine churches at the time of their composition. When read in that context, however, the Johannine Epistles offer a glimpse of the life and theology of Johannine Christianity that can serve both as a guide and as a warning to the contemporary church.

SELECTED BIBLIOGRAPHIES

Hebrews

Commentaries:

Attridge, H. W. *The Epistle to the Hebrews*. Hermeneia. Philadelphia: Fortress Press, 1988. *This is the definitive commentary for this decade.*

Bourke, M. M. "The Epistle to the Hebrews." In *The New Jerome Biblical Commentary*. Englewood Cliffs, N.J.: Prentice-Hall, 1990. Pp. 920–41.

Bruce, F. F. *The Epistle to the Hebrews*. NICNT. Grand Rapids: Eerdmans, 1964

Buchanan, G. W. *To the Hebrews*. AB 36. Garden City, N.Y.: Doubleday, 1972.

Manson, W. *The Epistle to the Hebrews*. London: Hodder and Stoughton, 1951.

Montefiore, H. W. *A Commentary on the Epistle to the Hebrews*. HNTC. New York: Harper & Row, 1964.

Westcott, B. F. *The Epistle to the Hebrews: The Greek Text with Notes and Essays*. Reprint, Grand Rapids: Eerdmans, 1974.

Monographs and Articles:

Attridge, H. W. "Hebrews, Epistle to the," in *ABD* 3:97–105.

Käsemann, E. *The Wandering People of God: An Investigation of the Letter to the Hebrews*. Roy A. Harrisville and Irving L. Sandberg. Minneapolis: Augsburg, 1984.

Lindars, B. *The Theology in the Letter to the Hebrews*. Cambridge: Cambridge Univ. Press, 1991.

Manson, T. W. "The Problem of the Epistle to the Hebrews" in *Studies in the Gospels and Epistles*. Manchester: Manchester Univ. Press, 1962. Pp. 242–58.

Sowers, S. O. *The Hermeneutics of Philo and Hebrews*. Richmond, Va.: John Knox, 1965.

Williamson, R. *Philo and the Epistle to the Hebrews*. Leiden: Brill, 1970.

For *additional bibliography on Hebrews, see* Grässer, E. "Der Hebraer-brief, 1938–1963." *Theologische Rundschau* 30 (1964): 138–40.

James

Dibelius, M. *James: A Commentary on the Epistle of James.* Rev. H. Greeven. Ed. H. Koester. Trans. M. Williams. Hermeneia. Philadelphia: Fortress Press, 1976.

Hartin, Patrick J. *James and the Q Sayings of Jesus.* JSNTSup 47. Sheffield: Sheffield Academic Press, 1991.

Johnson, Luke T. "Friendship with the World/Friendship with God: A Study of Discipleship in James." In *Discipleship in the New Testament.* Ed. F. F. Segovia. Philadelphia: Fortress Press, 1985. Pp. 166–83.

Laws, Sophie. *A Commentary on the Epistle of James.* HNTC. San Francisco: Harper & Row, 1980.

————. "The Doctrinal Basis for the Ethics of James." In *SE* 7 (1982): 299–305.

Tamez, Elsa. *The Scandalous Message of James: Faith Without Works Is Dead.* New York: Crossroad, 1990.

1 Peter

Balch, David L. *Let Wives Be Submissive: The Domestic Code in 1 Peter.* SBLMS 26. Chico, Calif.: Scholars Press, 1981.

Beare, Francis W. *The First Epistle of Peter: The Greek Text with Introduction and Notes.* 2nd ed. Oxford: Blackwell, 1961.

Best, Ernest. *1 Peter.* NCBC. Reprinted Grand Rapids: Eerdmans, 1982.

Bigg, Charles. *A Critical and Exegetical Commentary on the Epistles of St. Peter and St. Jude.* ICC. Edinburgh: T. & T. Clark, reprint 1961.

Blass, F. and Debrunner, A. *A Greek Grammar of the New Testament and Other Early Christian Literature.* Chicago: Univ. of Chicago Press, 1961.

Brox, Norbert. *Der Erste Petrusbrief.* EKKNT. Zurich: Benziger, 1979.

Dalton, William J. *Christ's Proclamation to the Spirits: A Study of 1 Peter 3:18—4:6.* AnBib 23. 2d edition. Rome: Pontifical Institute Press, 1989.

Daube, David. "Participle and Imperative in 1 Peter," an appended note in *The First Epistle of St. Peter,* Selwyn, 467–88.

Davids, Peter H. *The First Epistle of Peter.* NICNT. Grand Rapids: Eerdmans, 1990.

Elliott, John H. *A Home for the Homeless: A Social-Scientific Criticism of 1 Peter, Its Situation and Strategy.* Paperback edition, with a new introduction. Minneapolis: Fortress Press, 1990.

Goppelt, L. *A Commentary of 1 Peter.* Trans. and augmented by John E. Alsup. Grand Rapids: Eerdmans, 1993. *This is the best commentary available at present.*

Hunzinger, Claus-Hunno. "Babylon als Deckname für Rom und die Datierung des 1. Petrusbriefes." In *Gottes Wort und Gottes Land*. Ed. H. Graf Reventlow, Göttingen: Vandenhoeck & Ruprecht, 1965. Pp. 67–77.

Kelly, J. N. D. *A Commentary on the Epistles of Peter and of Jude*. HNTC. New York: Harper & Row, 1969.

Krodel, Gerhard. "Persecution and Toleration of Christianity until Hadrian." In *The Catacombs and the Colosseum: The Roman Empire as the Setting of Primitive Christianity*. Ed. Stephen Benko and John J. O'Rourke, Valley Forge: Judson Press, 1971. Pp. 255–67.

Martin, Troy W. *Metaphor and Composition in 1 Peter*. SBLDS 131. Atlanta: Scholars Press, 1992.

Metzger, Bruce M. *A Textual Commentary on the Greek NT*. New York: United Bible Societies, 1971.

Michaels, J. Ramsey. *1 Peter*. WBC 49. Waco, Tex.: Word, 1988.

Moule, C. F. G. "The Nature and Purpose of 1 Peter." *NTS* 3 (1956–57): 1–11.

Moulton, James H. *A Grammar of NT Greek*, Vol. 1, *Prolegomena*. 3d edition. Edinburgh: T. & T. Clark, 1957.

Reike, Bo. *The Epistles of James, Peter, and Jude*. AB 37. Garden City, N.Y.: Doubleday, 1964.

Schutter, William L. *Hermeneutic and Composition in 1 Peter*. WUNT 2/30. Tübingen: Mohr (Siebeck), 1989.

Selwyn, Edward G. *The First Epistle of St. Peter*. London: Macmillan, 1964.

Stowers, Stanley K. *Letter Writing in Greco-Roman Antiquity*. LEC 5. Philadelphia: Westminster, 1986.

Talbert, Charles H., ed. *Perspectives on First Peter*. Macon, Ga: Mercer Univ. Press, 1986.

Thuren, Lauri. *The Rhetorical Strategy of 1 Peter: With Special Regard to Ambiguous Expressions*. Åbo (Finland): Åbo Akademis Förlag, 1990.

2 Peter

Commentaries:

Bauckham, Richard J. *Jude, 2 Peter*. WBC 50. Waco, Tex.: Word, 1983. *Surveys the gamut of scholarly opinion.*

Kelly, J. N. D. *A Commentary on the Epistles of Peter and of Jude*. HNTC. New York: Harper & Row, 1969. *The best treatment of all three letters available in English.*

Mayor, J. B. *The Epistle of St. Jude and the Second Epistle of St. Peter*. London: Macmillan, 1907, and reprints. *An old but very useful work.*

Monographs and Articles:

Boobyer, C. H. "The Indebtedness of 2 Peter to 1 Peter." In *New Testament Essays: Studies in Memory of T. W. Manson.* Ed. A. J. B. Higgins. Manchester: Manchester Univ. Press, 1959. Pp. 34–53.

Danker, F. W. *Benefactor: Epigraphic Study of a Graeco-Roman and New Testament Semantic Field.* St. Louis: Clayton, 1982. Pp. 453–67.

———. "2 Peter 3:10 and Psalm of Solomon 17:10 [ed. Swete]." *ZNW* 53 (1962): 82–86.

Fornberg, Tord. *An Early Church in a Pluralistic Society: A Study of 2 Peter.* Coniectanea biblica, NT 9. Lund: Gleerup, 1977.

Käsemann, E. "An Apologia for Primitive Christian Eschatology." In Käsemann, *Essays on New Testament Themes.* Trans. W. J. Montague. SBT 41. London: SCM, 1964. Pp. 169–95.

Jude

Bauckham, Richard, J. *Jude, 2 Peter.* WBC 50. Waco, Tex.: Word, 1983.

———. "Jude: An Account of Research." In *ANRW* II.25.4. Berlin: de Gruyter, 1986.

Ellis, E. Earle. *Prophecy and Hermeneutic.* Grand Rapids: Eerdmans, 1978.

Kelly, J. N. D. *A Commentary on the Epistles of Peter and of Jude.* HNTC. New York: Harper & Row, 1969.

Kennedy, George A. *NT Interpretation through Rhetorical Criticism.* Chapel Hill: Univ. of North Carolina Press, 1984.

Metzger, Bruce M. *A Textual Commentary on the Greek New Testament.* New York: United Bible Societies, 1971.

Moore, Michael S. *The Balaam Traditions: Their Character and Development.* SBLDS 113. Atlanta: Scholars Press, 1990.

Reike, Bo. *The Epistles of James, Peter, and Jude.* AB 37. Garden City, N.Y.: Doubleday, 1964.

Rowston, Douglas J. "The Most Neglected Book in the New Testament." *NTS* 21 (1975): 554–63.

Stowers, Stanley K. *Letter Writing in Greco-Roman Antiquity.* LEC 5. Philadelphia: Westminster, 1986.

Watson, Duane F. *Invention, Arrangement, and Style: Rhetorical Criticism of Jude and 2 Peter.* SBLDS 104. Atlanta: Scholars Press, 1988.

Wisse, Frederick. "The Epistle of Jude in the History of Heresiology." In *Essays in the Nag Hammadi Text in Honor of Alexander Böhlig.* Ed. M. Kause, Leiden: Brill, 1972. Pp. 133–43.

1–2–3 John

Commentaries

Brooke, A. E. *A Critical and Exegetical Commentary on the Johannine Epistles*. ICC. Edinburgh: T. & T. Clark, 1912.

Brown, Raymond E. *The Epistles of John*. AB 30. Garden City, N.Y.: Doubleday, 1982.

Culpepper, R. Alan. *1 John, 2 John, 3 John*. Knox Preaching Guides. Atlanta: John Knox, 1985.

Dodd, C. H. *The Johannine Epistles*. MNTC. London: Hodder and Stoughton, 1946.

Grayston, Kenneth. *The Johannine Epistles*. NCBC. New York: Harper & Row, 1973.

Houlden, J. L. *The Johannine Epistles*. HNTC. New York: Harper & Row, 1973.

Marshall, I. Howard. *The Epistles of John*. NICNT. Grand Rapids: Eerdmans, 1978.

Perkins, Pheme. *The Johannine Epistles*. New Testament Message. Wilmington, Del.: Glazier, 1979.

Schnackenburg, Rudolf. *The Johannine Epistles*. Trans. Reginald and Ilse Fuller. New York: Crossroad, 1992.

Smalley, Stephen. *1, 2, 3 John*. WBC 51. Waco, Tex.: Word, 1984.

Smith, D. Moody. *First, Second, and Third John*. Interpretation. Louisville: John Knox, 1991.

Talbert, Charles H. *Reading John: A Literary and Theological Commentary on the Fourth Gospel and the Johannine Epistles*. New York: Crossroad, 1992.

Vouga, François. *Die Johannesbriefe*. HNTC 15/III. Tübingen: Mohr (Siebeck), 1990.

Westcott, B. F. *The Epistles of St. John: The Greek Text with Notes*. Reprint, Grand Rapids: Eerdmans, 1976.

Monographs and Articles

Bogart, John. *Orthodox and Heretical Perfectionism*. SBLDS 33. Missoula, Mont.: Scholars Press, 1977.

Dodd, C. H. "The First Epistle of John and the Fourth Gospel." *BJRL* 21 (1937): 129–56.

Funk, Robert W. "The Apostolic Presence: John the Elder." In *Parables and Presence: Forms of the NT Tradition*. Philadelphia: Fortress Press, 1982. Pp. 103–10.

Häring, Theodor. "Gedankengang und Grundgedanke des ersten Johannesbriefs." In *Theologische Abhandlungen*. Carl von Weizsäcker Festschrift. Freiburg: Mohr (Siebeck), 1892. Pp. 171–200.

Hengel, Martin. *The Johannine Question*. Trans. John Bowden. Philadelphia: Trinity Press International, 1989.

Howard, W. F. "The Common Authorship of the Johannine Gospel and Epistles." *JTS* 48 (1947): 12–25.

Kümmel, W. G. *Introduction to the New Testament*. Revised edition. Trans. H. C. Kee. New York: Abingdon Press, 1975.

Law, Robert. *The Tests of Life: A Study of the First Epistle of St. John*. Edinburgh: T. & T. Clark, 1909.

Lieu, Judith. "Authority to Become Children of God: A Study of I John." *NovT* 23 (1981): 210–28.

———. *The Second and Third Epistles of John*. Studies of the New Testament and Its World. Edinburgh: T. & T. Clark, 1986.

———. *The Theology of the Johannine Epistles*. Cambridge: Cambridge Univ. Press, 1991.

Malatesta, Edward. *Interiority and Covenant*. AnBib 69. Rome: Biblical Institute Press, 1978.

Nauck, Wolfgang. *Die Tradition und Charakter des ersten Johannesbriefes: Zugleich ein Beitrag zur Taufe im Urchristentum und in der alten Kirche*. WUNT 3. Tübingen: Mohr (Siebeck), 1957.

Painter, John. "The 'Opponents' in 1 John." *NTS* 32 (1986): 48–71.

———. *The Quest for the Messiah: The History, Literature and Theology of the Johannine Community*. 2nd ed. Nashville: Abingdon Press, 1993.

Salom, A. P. "Some Aspects of the Grammatical Style of 1 John." *JBL* 74 (1955): 96–102.

Strecker, Georg. "Die Anfänge der Johanneischen Schule." *NTS* 32 (1986): 31–47.

Von Wahlde, Urban C. *The Johannine Commandments: 1 John and the Struggle for the Johannine Tradition*. New York: Paulist, 1990.

Watson, Duane F. "A Rhetorical Analysis of 2 John according to Greco-Roman Convention." *NTS* 35 (1989): 104–30.

———. "A Rhetorical Analysis of 3 John: A Study in Epistolary Rhetoric." *CBQ* 51 (1989): 479–501.

Wilson, W. G. "An Examination of the Linguistic Evidence Adduced against the Unity of Authorship of the First Epistle and the Fourth Gospel." *JTS* 49 (1948): 147–54.

INDEX

151